P9-CAO-503

The William Conner House, built in 1823

SONS OF THE WILDERNESS

JOHN AND WILLIAM CONNER

By

CHARLES N. THOMPSON

These sons of the wilderness still survive.
—PARKMAN, *Conspiracy of Pontiac*

PRESS

Published by Conner Prairie Press
Noblesville, Indiana
1988
Second Edition

Originally published by
Indiana Historical Society
1937

Copyright © 1988 by Conner Prairie

All rights reserved.

ISBN 0-9617367-6-3

Library of Congress
Catalog Card Number
88-070987

Second Printing, 1988
Third Printing, 2000

Cover art by R. Carol Skinner

*This commemorative edition
is dedicated to those
who built Indiana's frontier,
record its history,
and preserve its historic places .*

ILLUSTRATIONS

CONTENTS

INTRODUCTION TO THE 1988 EDITION

I t is highly appropriate as we celebrate the opening of the new Conner Prairie Museum Center to present a reprint edition of Charles N. Thompson's *Sons of the Wilderness: John and William Conner*, originally published by the Indiana Historical Society in 1937. The unavailability of this volume in past years has been a source of frustration to those seeking a richer understanding of early Indiana history. Now that the book has been restored to circulation, the story of the Conner family can be told once again, serving as an example of how one family contributed to the development of the American West.

*   *   *

Charles Nebeker Thompson was born in Covington, Indiana, on 7 July 1861. He received his bachelor and master of arts degrees at Indiana Asbury University (now DePauw University) in 1882 and 1885 respectively. During his college years, Thompson also studied law and was admitted to the Bar of Indiana in 1885, beginning his practice with John F. Carson in 1886. He quickly developed a specialty in building and loan associations and later in public utilities, for which he served as board member and legal counsel. Thompson assisted in the formation of the Marion Trust Company in 1896 which later merged with the German American Trust Company to form the Fletcher Trust Company, for which he served as director from 1896 to 1934. He also was involved in many educational and historical organizations. Thompson served on the Board of Trustees of DePauw University, as Treasurer of the Society of Indiana Pioneers, member and President of the Indiana Library and Historical Department, and as an appointee to represent the state of Indiana on the Cumberland Gap Memorial Commission.

Charles N. Thompson's association with the Conner family began on 7 October 1891 when he married Julia Alice Finch Conner, the daughter of John Cogswell Conner and Alice Finch Conner, the great-granddaughter of John Conner and great-grandniece of William Conner. In the early 1920s, Julia

(xi)

Thompson began to investigate the history of her Conner lineage, which culminated in the presentation of a paper at the Indiana History Conference in December 1925. Regarding the Conner family, Julia noted that "one can scarcely look into a book of early Indiana history that has no mention of them [the Conners]. But there are many errors and in no place is there anything like a full history of them; . . . It is my purpose to try to correct misstatements and to sketch a portrait a little truer than most I have seen in print. The picturesque fact that both brothers were Indian captives seems to have thrown out of focus the perspective of most writers." Before she could proceed further with her work, Julia Conner Thompson died on 26 December 1928.

Friends and associates of Charles N. Thompson noted the impact of his wife's death. Attorney Herman W. Kothe observed that Charles "considered that he owed it to the memory of his wife to write and publish the history of the Conner family." Likewise, attorney Henry M. Dowling described Thompson's research as "a labor of love on his part, and it was a labor to which he devoted himself with unstinted energy."

Thompson's project was advanced by the work of yet another dedicated devotee of Indiana history. In 1934 Eli Lilly, heir to the Lilly pharmaceutical company and president of the Indiana Historical Society, purchased the William Conner house and property along White River to restore the site "where the commissioners met to decide on the location of the new capital of Indiana." With Lilly's restoration project and Thompson's historical research, the story of the Conner family gradually unfolded.

Thompson's completed manuscript, *Sons of the Wilderness: John and William Conner*, was published by the Indiana Historical Society in 1937. He dedicated it as a memorial to his wife who had devoted years of her life in pursuit of the Conner family's history.

Charles Nebeker Thompson died at his summer home near Harbor Springs, Michigan, on 16 August 1949.

*   *   *

For generations, local history was considered to be a "poor relation" to the elite families and important issues of national political and economic history. Individuals writing on local subjects struggled desparately to legitimize their focus on what might be considered unimportant and irrelevant historical events and figures. Consequently, local historians felt compelled by the style of professional historians to concentrate on the "heroic" individuals of local history, dressing them in biographical garb resembling the cloaks of the nation's Founding Fathers. As a result, local figures assumed personas that were "larger than life," heroic in every detail, virtuous in every characteristic. They led an almost mythical and deified existence. These imitations of the Founding Fathers and "great men" of history may have provided another generation with important identifications for their age, but these interpretations have not necessarily withstood the tests of time or the rigors of historical revision. Rather than forcing local historical figures to adhere to a prescribed mold of greatness, it is essential to look at them as human beings, with warm flesh tones and human failings, participating in the course of history. No longer obligated to follow in the footsteps of the "great men" of history, our pioneers and founders will then settle into their proper places in local history, leaving a legacy of their deeds and thus enhancing our own understanding of history and the significance of their lives.

Before the compilation of the Conners' biography in the 1930s, the Conner family was shrouded in the mist of historical uncertainty. Their relations with the local native American people were the substance of romance and legends; the extent of their participation in the commercialization of the West was unknown. It was generally assumed that because the Conners were raised among Moravian missionaries and Delaware Indians and because they were "trusted" interpreters for Delaware chiefs, that they shared deep sympathies with the native American civilization. Oral traditions also suggested that the Conners, after crossing into the frontier of the Old Northwest and the Indiana Territory, continued to live a "backwoods" frontier existence, pursuing the life of trader, Indian scout, and frontiersman.

With the publication of *Sons of the Wilderness*, many of these issues were finally resolved. Thompson had presented a well-documented, very readable historical work that described and explained the Conners' involvement in the transformation of the

American West. He related accounts of the Conners' activities with the federal government and its official relations with the local tribes of native Americans; their affiliation with the military leaders of the young republic and their handling of local problems associated with the rapidly expanding nation; and their alliance with the politicians of the new state of Indiana. Clearly, Thompson had offered a new, revised look at the Conners, one which showed, as Thompson himself stated, that "they were typical of their age" and which clarified their participation in the foundation of the new state and the young nation.

It is not enough for us to rely solely upon a bare skeleton of historical facts from which to learn about the historical past. Rather, we must seek to *interpret* the historical story in order to learn about its particular contribution to the larger sweep of historical events. This is the point where the task becomes more difficult. How we interpret those facts depends greatly upon what we hope to accomplish and what questions we seek to resolve.

In the December 1984 issue of the *Indiana Magazine of History*, John Lauritz Larson and David G. Vanderstel presented a new analysis of the Conners. Their article, entitled "Agent of Empire: William Conner on the Indiana Frontier, 1800-1855," offered some new interpretations and attempted to place the Conners in the broader historical context of the unfolding American saga. The authors revealed the fascinating parallels in the life experiences of father Richard Conner, his son William Conner, and William's first-born, half-blood son John, all of whom were involved in trade, Indian relations, and the advance of white American civilization at different times and on different frontier stages. Likewise, there was the ongoing triple alliance of the Moravian missionaries, the Delawares, and the Conners which persisted from Ohio into Michigan and Indiana. Finally, the authors explained how the Conners served as liaisons between the advancing white society and the Indian tribes who had agreed to relocate to the Indian Territory of the Far West. Consequently, just as Thompson had accomplished five decades before, these authors demonstrated that it did not harm the Conners' story to consider new evidence. Rather, it served to illuminate and describe more completely how the

Conners participated in the commercial penetration and political development of Indiana and the American West.

We remember William and John Conner and their families not to elevate them to the level of the nation's Founding Fathers nor to perpetuate the romantic legends of frontier and Indian life, but rather to recognize the contributions of these individuals to the advancement of American society and their involvement in the displacement of native Americans in the face of the moving frontier. John Conner was a trader, merchant, Indian interpreter, and government representative. William Conner was a trader, Indian interpreter, livestock broker, land speculator (owning upwards of 4,000 acres of land in Hamilton County in 1837), town planner, financial agent, and capitalist. Both men acted out on the stage of the developing American West what was normal for and expected of the American pioneer in the vastness of recently opened lands. If we recognize and acknowledge this, then we will be rewarded by a deeper understanding of the Conners' presence and involvement in the beginnings of our local community and the state of Indiana.

*   *   *

With this reprint edition, we commemorate not only the dedication of Eli Lilly in his restoration of the William Conner house during the 1930s and the devotion of Charles Nebeker Thompson to the compilation of the Conner biography, but also the mission and vision of Conner Prairie in seeking to carry forward the Conner story as an example of life in the American West of the early nineteenth century. It remains the challenge for historians to search for new information and offer new understandings about the Conners and for Conner Prairie to preserve their story for future generations. Historian Francis Parkman was absolutely correct when he wrote, "These sons of the wilderness still survive."

David G. Vanderstel, Ph.D.
Senior Historian
Conner Prairie
Noblesville, Indiana
30 March 1988

CHAPTER I

The Northern Ohio Valley, 1750-1814

MORE THAN one hundred years have passed since the final scenes of the stirring drama of settlement in the Ohio Valley. The actors were men and women with iron wills and steel nerves forged in the flames of Indian wars. They led lives of hardship incredible to us in this softer age. Before giving an account of a family of the period, it is well to recall some of the major events in the beginnings of what is now the Middle West.

By 1750 the Ohio Valley was the refuge of many Indian tribes. Pushed back from the Atlantic seaboard by the advancing tide of immigration, the Six Nations, who first inhabited the northwestern part of New York, were living in greater numbers in the upper Ohio country than in their original country. The Delawares and Shawnee had left their hunting grounds on the north and west branches of the Susquehanna and had sought lands in the Ohio Valley. The Wyandot, fleeing westward in the early part of the eighteenth century, had settled near Detroit and had finally established towns along the Sandusky River.

This exodus was not without bitterness. These Indians had watched their lands pass from them through the large purchase of William Penn in the latter part of the seventeenth century, and the tricky Walking Purchase of 1737, and there were among them prophets of disaster. There were ominous signs that the pressure from the East had not ended but had just begun. The Indians were fearful and resentful.[1] But the Ohio Valley toward which many tribes were turning was a fair country. The forests were virgin, the streams abounded in fish, and the woods in game. There were great plains, sheltered valleys, navigable rivers.

The Shawnee, among the most savage of the Indians, had established their towns along the Scioto River from its mouth to the Pickaway Plains. They had also a group of towns on the Muskingum River, near the present town of Dresden, in

(1)

Muskingum County. The capital of the Delaware nation was on the upper waters of this river, first near what is now New-comerstown, later at the present town of Coshocton. To this more peaceful tribe of Delawares came the Moravian mission-aries with their group of Christian Indians from Pennsylvania in 1772.[2] The Chippewa and Ottawa were farther north around the Great Lakes. The Miami, the Kickapoo, and the Potawatomi occupied the country west of the Scioto River to the Illinois River, including the southern part of Michigan.

In 1750 this entire country was an uncharted wilderness reached only by watercourses and trails made by Indians. Few white persons ventured within it except for purposes of trade or exploration. With the Indians there was a considerable group of white captives taken by them in their murderous raids in Pennsylvania and Virginia. Some of these had been cap-tured when they were infants or small children and had grown to be indistinguishable from the Indians in manners and ges-tures. A few had become agents or intermediaries between the settlers and Indians, interpreting the language of the latter and exchanging their peltries for goods. They frequently mar-ried Indian women. Some became leaders in the tribes which adopted them.

The only European nation that in 1750 had any posts in the rich hunting and fishing region which extended from Canada to Louisiana and as far west as the Mississippi, was France. It had a population of not more than one hundred thousand in all this domain, but it was a homogeneous group.[3] A thin line of outposts and forts had been established from the northern to the southern boundary. These forts had been built in the wake of missionaries, explorers, and traders as symbols of the authority of France over this territory, and to further their work. Stockades around small settlements or the comman-dant's house, were in some instances the only fortifications. The French were primarily traders, not settlers, and their pur-pose was not to disturb the Indians' hunting preserves but to protect them in the interest of the fur trade. The Indians ap-preciated this arrangement, for the trade brought many con-veniences to them. Gaily the French flag floated over these make-believe forts, and in 1749 Céloron de Blainville, in the name of the French government, planted plates of lead along the Ohio, claiming title to the land in the name of France.

These were grandiose but puny gestures of authority in the face of approaching eventualities.

More than a million people, English, German, Dutch, Scotch-Irish, and Scandinavian, had settled on the Atlantic slope. Each ship from Europe brought more. These colonists and the mother country, England, were not unaware of the rich trading possibilities of the Ohio Valley, and they were not content to see it monopolized by France, their traditional enemy. The wealthy classes in Europe were demanding furs, the poor classes, skins. English financiers were ready to lend money, and English merchants were willing to extend credit to further a profitable trade. There were not lacking reckless and desperate characters to act as agents beyond the mountains. By 1750 Pennsylvania traders had invaded the principal Indian villages even to the country near the Wabash and Maumee rivers, nearly five hundred miles beyond the settlers' frontier.[4]

The Virginians did not like the aggressiveness of the Pennsylvania traders. Virginia claimed the land under its charter of 1609, and desired access to it for settlement as well as trade. In 1748 the Ohio Company had secured a grant of land of five hundred thousand acres situated on the upper Ohio on condition that it should be colonized within a fixed period. Christopher Gist, a surveyor, was employed by this company to explore and report upon this land the year after Céloron on behalf of France had planted his plates on the Ohio. Squatters as well as traders now broke through the mountain barriers. Some of them were lawless and brutal, and their movements alarmed and angered the Indians. France, too, became increasingly disturbed.

Meanwhile, in Europe, England and France had been engaged in a struggle which finally culminated in the Seven Years War beginning in 1756. It was this conflict, spreading to America, that became the French and Indian War. The French had strengthened their position in 1753-1754 by building forts nearer the scene of possible conflict, at Presqu'Isle, Le Boeuf, and Venango in western Pennsylvania. They had the advantage of friendly contact with large numbers of Indians from Pennsylvania to the Illinois River. These now became active allies of the French, exciting terror among the white settlers.

When Washington withdrew from Fort Necessity in 1754,

only the fleur-de-lis floated in the valley of the Ohio. A year later Braddock's defeat left the frontiers of Pennsylvania, Virginia, and Maryland defenseless, and the settlers in despair. The Indians, stimulated by the success of the French and disgusted with the weakness of the English, arose with one accord against the enemies of France. The next year the frontier reeked with the burning of homes, the massacre and scalping of settlers. Survivors were usually taken captive.

At last the tide turned. The flimsy forts fell one by one into the hands of the invading British, who rebuilt them and constructed others. In 1762 the French held only Forts Vincennes and Chartres in the Illinois country. Hostilities between France and England ceased in 1763 after seven years of horrible warfare. On the tenth of February of that year, the treaty of peace was signed in Paris. France ceded Canada and the land east of the upper Mississippi to England, and transferred Louisiana to her ally, Spain.

The Indians, however, did not readily accept subjection to the English. They were not satisfied with vague promises that settlements beyond the Alleghenies would be restricted. The French traders and settlers chafed under the loss of their rich fur trade. In May of 1763, Pontiac's War, which had been brewing for over a year with the aid and abetment of the French traders, opened with a furious attack on Detroit. While that fort was besieged for three months by savage hordes, other bands were attacking Forts Sandusky, St. Joseph, Michillimackinac, Ouiatenon, Miami, Presqu'Isle, Le Boeuf, and Venango. This was a general uprising, attended with all the horrors of Indian warfare. The Indians penetrated to the interior of Pennsylvania, threatened Fort Ligonier and Fort Bedford. Settlers on the frontiers of Maryland and Pennsylvania fled at their approach.

Fort Pitt, though hard pressed in three assaults, held out. The Indians were decisively defeated by Colonel Henry Bouquet, a Swiss officer in the British service, who was assailed by them as he was marching with about five hundred men to its relief. This was the Battle of Bushy Run, August 5, 1763. After relieving Fort Pitt, Bouquet marched into the Ohio Valley and compelled the Shawnee and Delawares to sue for peace. He also demanded the immediate return of all white prisoners.

The conspiracy of Pontiac was a flare-up of the smolder-
ing hatred of the Indians against the English, whose parsimon-
ious methods in trade and land dealings irritated them. They
also feared that the onrush of settlers would deprive them of
still more land. The immediate conflict was now at an end,
but the bitterness was still there.[5]

From 1765 to 1774 there was a period of comparative
peace. French influence was rapidly diminishing even in the
Illinois country, for Bouquet had inculcated fear and respect
for the English. Both the English and the Indians wished to
renew a mutually advantageous trade, and the territory for
operations was now vastly increased, extending as far as the
Mississippi. There was conflict, however, between the traders
and the settlers over supplying such disputed articles of trade
as guns, ammunition, and rum to the Indians. The firearms
which facilitated the killing of fur-bearing animals were turned
too frequently on the settlers; whisky maddened the Indians
and increased their natural ferocity, but the traders insisted
upon supplying both for the sake of profit.

The British government tried to restrict the sale of these
articles. As it had taken the management of Indian affairs
out of the hands of the colonists, Britain had a free hand, but
the imperial methods at their best did not satisfy the Indian,
the trader, or the settler.[6] The great merchant firms of Europe
and the colonies were losing money in the Indian trade. Cara-
vans of goods moving westward to supply the Indians were
destroyed by irate settlers. The traders were chiefly from
Pennsylvania; the settlers were chiefly from Virginia. The
situation between them became acute. In addition, the drain on
the British treasury for the management of Indian affairs was
becoming serious. When at peace, the Indian must be constantly placated by expensive gifts. When at war, he took a
frightful toll. This cost on the frontier was one of the causes
of the movement to tax the colonies.[7] Clearly, some roots of
the Revolution lay in this Ohio country.

Still the westward tide of immigration increased, reaching
its height between 1770 and 1774. In the latter year, a daring
rogue, Dr. John Connolly, agent of Lord Dunmore, then governor of Virginia, took possession of Fort Pitt as a part of
Virginia territory. The Indians were restive, and Connolly

was ruthless in his dealings with them. Another uprising was feared by the settlers and Connolly urged them to arm. White borderers attacked and massacred unoffending Indians, among them the family of Logan, a Mingo chief long friendly to the whites.

This started Dunmore's War which is said to have been the opening to the drama that closed at Yorktown.[8] Lord Dunmore's chief motive in this war seems to have been the acquisition of territory. His war was of only two months' duration and ended with the battle of Point Pleasant at the junction of the Ohio and Great Kanawha rivers, nearly opposite the present Gallipolis, Ohio. The Indians, mostly Shawnee, while not victorious, made a masterly retreat. Peace was concluded in 1774 at Camp Charlotte, near the present town of Circleville, Ohio. As usual, a condition of peace was the return of all white captives held by the Indians.

On the return of the Virginians from this conference they halted at Fort Gower and in writing promised allegiance to the British king if he "reigned justly" over them, with the reservation that "first, however, came their love for America."[9] This had no significance to the stubborn, shortsighted king and the group of incompetent ministers in England. The War of the Revolution had opened in this western country.

During the war the Ohio Valley Indians chiefly supported the British. The only exception was a group of Delawares which was influenced by the Moravian missionaries to maintain neutrality. The American forces held Fort Pitt and Fort Henry. The British held Fort Detroit. The country between was traversed frequently by Indian war parties led by British agents and was the scene of many clashes with the American forces. Forays upon outlying settlements were frequent, and a state of fear and unrest existed in the entire valley. It was difficult to maintain trade or communication. The British in this region progressed gradually from a passive to an active hostility. Lieutenant Governor Hamilton of Detroit gave standing rewards for the scalps of Americans without regard to age or sex, and incited murderous expeditions composed of the greatest number of savages the frontier had ever known. He planned an expedition to reduce all of Virginia west of the mountains in a great carnage of blood and fire. This program was defeated in 1779 when George Rogers Clark at Vincennes took Hamilton prisoner. He was later incarcerated in a cell in Virginia as an "unprivileged" prisoner.[10]

By the treaty of peace in 1783 between the United States and Great Britain the jurisdiction of the territory northwest of the Ohio was granted to the United States. The Governor General of Canada, however, refused to give up the forts of Niagara, Presqu'Isle, Sandusky, Michillimackinac, and Detroit and a few less important posts—all within the territory of the United States. They were kept with the approval of the British government on one pretext or another, in order to conserve her valuable fur trade. Detroit was the most important of these posts. Instigated by British agents, now actively hostile and brutally insolent, Indian war parties gathered on the Maumee, the Wabash, and the Miami rivers. Arms and ammunition were supplied them by the British, and the ravages by Indian war parties continued.

The settlers in the Ohio Valley were beginning to feel that the government was neglectful and indifferent to their interests and safety. Loud demands were made for immediate and vigorous measures to save American settlements from being broken up by the savages. To meet this situation, the governor of the Northwest Territory, General Arthur St. Clair, marched with a volunteer army into the Indian country in what is now northwestern Ohio. He was disastrously and humiliatingly defeated on November 3, 1791, by twelve hundred Indians led by Little Turtle, Blue Jacket, and Buckongahelas.

The Indian war spirit now became increasingly vindictive. Another attempt to crush it was necessary. In 1794 General Wayne, appointed commander of the army by President Washington, headed an expedition against the Indians, and in the Battle of Fallen Timbers, not far from Toledo, he defeated them. The Treaty of Greenville, concluded the next year, brought tranquility for a decade and a half to the frontier,[11] but the contest was not yet ended. The interim was used by the Indians and British only to gather forces for a new attack—this time farther west, in Indiana. There the Shawnee, Winnebago, Kickapoo, and Potawatomi were rallied by Tecumseh and his brother the Prophet. At the Battle of Tippecanoe in

1811 the Indians were again defeated, but not decisively enough to prevent them from allying themselves with the British in the War of 1812. In the first year of the war the Miami met with defeat at the Mississinewa. The power of the Indians in the Northwest was finally broken by General William Henry Harrison at the Battle of the Thames in 1814. It was not until this event that the fear of incursions of hostile Indians subsided in Indiana. These Indian wars had outlasted the War of the Revolution by more than thirty years, obstructing the development of the Ohio Valley and inflicting "heartsick cruelties" upon the settlers. At last general peace came to Indiana. In 1820 began the departure of the remaining tribes of Indians to the region west of the Mississippi.[12]

The march of Anglo-Saxon civilization for the conquest of the rich wilderness of the Ohio Valley had progressed relentlessly westward since its beginning in the early part of the eighteenth century. At times it faltered. At times it blundered. There could be only one result. The vast but frail French empire in this new continent crumbled before the slow moving but determined advance. Without fully comprehending the issues involved, the Indians under Pontiac undertook to drive the English into the sea. But they themselves were only driven further west. The decree of civilization was inexorable. The Indians were too few for this extensive area. The home seekers were too numerous. Tecumseh, the last great Indian leader, grossly misled by the British, tried vainly from time to time to rally the savages to withstand these forces of civilization. His death at the Battle of the Thames ended Indian warfare in this area.

This book contains the story of a family which like many others was caught in the maelstrom of this great struggle. William and John Conner were born when the struggle was at its height. Richard Conner, their father, was in the heart of the Ohio country from 1767 to 1782; their mother was from childhood a captive of the Shawnee Indians. They were preserved to become the earliest settlers in central Indiana and to have a part in the final scenes of this great drama. These momentous events which finally closed the War of the American Revolution, lifted this family from obscurity. To Indiana, its achievements have historical significance.

CHAPTER II

RICHARD CONNER AND MARGARET BOYER— THE MORAVIAN MISSION

WRAPPED in the vivid cloak of romance is the story of Richard Conner and his family as it has come down by word of mouth from one generation to another. Most of it has historical basis; parts of it are supported by tradition only. Even without the embellishments of tradition and the embroidery of imaginative narrators, it remains a story of thrilling and adventurous action. This recital will set forth the sources of both the traditional and historical elements.

A persistent tradition in all branches of the Conner family in Indiana, Michigan, New York, and Pennsylvania, has it that three young Irishmen, John, William, and Richard Conner, emigrated to America early in the colonial period from Castle Pollard, County of Westmeath, Ireland. It is said that John settled in New York, William in Virginia, and Richard in Pennsylvania or Maryland. Two hundred years make a very misty past when there are few, if any, beacon lights. This Irish-born Richard Conner may have been the planter of Prince George County, Maryland, who died about 1721, leaving a son Richard. Sometime before Maryland became a royal province, while it was still under proprietary rights granted by Charles I to the Calverts, a native son of Irish descent, Richard Conner by name, is known to have been living with his brothers near Frederickstown. He may have been the son of the planter of Prince George County, but one indubitable fact stands out— that Richard Conner of Frederickstown was born in Maryland. The exact date of his birth is uncertain, but it was probably in 1718.[1]

Subsequent to 1763 Richard Conner was ranging through the Ohio country, for what reason or on what business is not clear. He may have been a fur trader or an agent for Indian traders at Lancaster, Pennsylvania, although there is no available record to show that he was licensed to trade. He may have been an adventurer. If he had in mind settling in this country he was stepping into a dangerous situation, for the government of Pennsylvania had promised the Indians at the Treaty of Easton in 1758 that no settlement should be made west of the Alleghenies, and after Pontiac's uprising the king issued a proclamation setting this same boundary.[2]   Conner may have been a prisoner and adopted into some tribe of Indians, as were many white men of this time.   His exact status is unknown.   But while with the Shawnee in the Scioto country in what is now the state of Ohio, he met a white girl who had been taken captive by this tribe when a child.   She was said to be beautiful and her name was Margaret Boyer.[3]

And who was Margaret Boyer?   Who were her parents? Where was she taken captive?   These are questions that have never been fully answered, either in the histories of Indiana or Michigan.   Two stories, half traditional, half historical, have survived, one in the Conner family, one in the Boyer family. One begins where the other leaves off, but each has certain elements that strengthen the other, and taken together they make a credible, fairly convincing whole.   According to the account handed down in the Conner family for more than fifty years, Margaret, when a little girl about six years of age living with her parents in Pennsylvania, was taken captive by the Indians.   Her sister was also captured.   Their father was in a field when he discovered the approach of the Indians.   He hid the children and swam the river in attempting to flee for aid. As he ascended the opposite bank he was shot and killed.   The children were taken away by the Indians.   Margaret's sister married an Indian chief, whose name is not known.[4]

The story told in the Boyer family is more detailed.   It begins during the French and Indian War, when Indian raids in eastern Pennsylvania were a common occurrence and forts were hastily constructed by the terrified inhabitants for their protection.   There was at that time among the settlers owning and tilling land near Fort Lehigh, a farmer by the name of Boyer.   His family was of German extraction, and the original spelling of the name was Beyer or Bayer.   Andreas Boyer emigrated from the Rhine Bavaria with four sons, John Jacob, John Philip, Philip, and Martin, landing at Philadelphia on September 5, 1738.   John Jacob settled near Lehigh Gap, acquiring land at the foot of the Blue Mountains in 1755.   Here he erected a log house which served not only as his home but also for the protection of his family and near-by settlers. His plantation, the only one in the vicinity, lay about one and one-half miles east of Fort Lehigh, which commanded the Gap. When Indian attacks were frequent or imminent Boyer kept his family in the farmhouse at the fort. One day in the summer of 1756 he took his thirteen-year-old son Frederick and his two little daughters, probably four and six years old, to the farm, leaving his wife at the fort. While Boyer plowed and his son hoed, the younger children played near by. Suddenly and quietly, a party of perhaps three Shawnee Indians came into view. Boyer called to Frederick to run, and he himself endeavored to reach the house. Finding that he could not do so, he ran toward the river in a vain attempt to draw attention away from the children, but he was shot through the head as he reached the other side. The boy escaped to the wheat field but was brought back by the Indians, who then scalped the father in the presence of the children. The horses were unhitched from the plow and taken with the children to Stone Hill in the rear of the house, where a band of Indians met them and took them away.

Sometime after their capture the two little girls were separated from their brother. Frederick spent the next five years as a prisoner with the French and Indians in Canada, but was released at Philadelphia at the end of that time, and returned to Lehigh Gap. He secured his father's farm, married, had eight children, and died on October 31, 1832, aged eighty-nine years. His captive sisters were not released. One married an Indian chief and in later years she once visited her brother Frederick, perhaps with her two little Indian boys. She went back to her husband because he had been very good to her and she had promised to return. The other sister was never accounted for.[5]

There is no absolute identification of the lost sister of Frederick Boyer with the Margaret Boyer who captivated Richard Conner, but the main events and the time elements of the two stories fit together so well that one ventures to assume that they relate to the same person.

2.

It was to this beautiful young captive that Richard Conner

gave his heart. His application to the chief of the tribe for permission to marry her was granted, but there were conditions to be met.[6] First there was money to be paid. It is said that the sum was two hundred dollars. This payment must have taxed the young adventurer, who, doubtless, had come to this virgin country not with his fortune but to make it. But his warm Irish heart had been moved by beauty in distress and somehow he secured the money. Another condition, harder to meet than the first, was that the first-born son was to remain with the tribe. The marriage contract agreed to, Richard claimed his wife. Gallic and Teutonic strains were mingled in an Indian village in the heart of an almost trackless wilderness.

After their marriage the Conners lived for a time with the Shawnee.[7] Richard was not the type of man to remain long without asserting his leadership, and it is not surprising to learn from a Baptist missionary who was traveling in this country in the winter of 1772-1773 that Richard Conner was established in a Shawnee town named for himself—Connerstown. The missionary, the Reverend David Jones, describes the place as being a day's journey from where Salt Lick Creek empties into the Muskingum, in the country between what is now Lancaster and Newcomerstown in the state of Ohio. The illuminating and interesting entry in Jones's *Journal,* which is one of the earliest written records of the Conner family, is as follows:[8]

"THURSDAY [1773. Feb.] 11, set out for a small town called Conner's, a man of that name residing there.

"Our course was near northeast—the distance was less than the preceding day's journey, so that we arrived to town some time before sunset. Travelled this day over a good country, only wanting inhabitants. This town is situated near no creek, a good spring supplying them with water—the land about it is level and good, the timber being chiefly blackoak, indicates it will produce good wheat, if a trial was made. Mr. Conner, who is a white man, a native of Maryland, told me that he intended to sow wheat in the fall following, and was resolved to proceed to farming at all events. 'Tis probable that he will be as good as his word, for he is a man that seems not to fear GOD, and it is likely that he will not regard man. His connections will favour his attempts, for according to their way, he and the chief Indian of this town are married to two sisters. These women were captives, and it is likely from childhood, for they have the very actions of Indians, and speak broken English. It seemed strange to me to see the captives have the exact gestures of Indians. Might we not infer from hence, that if Indians were educated as we are, they would be like us? This town consists of Shawannees and Delawares; and some of them dwell in pretty good log houses well shingled with nails. Mr. Conner keeps a sort of a tavern, and has moderate accommodations, and though he is not what he should be, yet he was kind to me."

About the time of the sojourn of Jones, a missionary of a different denomination had visited the Conners. This was the Reverend David Zeisberger, a Moravian missionary of fine ability, unselfish devotion, and deep spiritual power, who was destined to influence the fortunes of the Conner family profoundly for years to come. Zeisberger had been a missionary among the Indians in America since 1745, first among the Iroquois in New York and later in Pennsylvania. By 1765-1766, the Moravians had given up their work among the Iroquois and were confining their efforts to the Delawares and eastern tribes. Several mission stations had been established by them in Pennsylvania. These had suffered during the French and Indian War and in the subsequent Indian raids. By 1771 it seemed desirable to remove the Christian Indians from Pennsylvania, and the chief of the Delawares, Netawatwees, in 1772 granted them land on the Tuscarawas River near the Delaware capital, Gekelemukpechünk.[9]

The first town, Schoenbrunn, "Beautiful Spring," was founded in the spring of 1772 by the Pennsylvania Christian Indians under the leadership of the Moravian missionaries, chief of whom was Zeisberger. It lay near the site of the present town of New Philadelphia. The following autumn Zeisberger set out to visit the Shawnee towns in the Muskingum Valley in the hope that he might bring the gospel to them. On his way to the main Shawnee town, he stopped at Conner's house, which must have been known at that time as an inn for travelers and traders. He spent the night there, and contrary to Jones's experience, he found Richard Conner in a receptive mood for religious approach. They talked "half the night about salvation and all that is involved."[10] Margaret, Richard's wife, was also deeply interested and in the succeeding months often urged that they should move to Schoenbrunn. Zeisberger did not encourage that suggestion at this time, because of the difficulties raised by the close relation of the Conner family to the pagan Shawnee, and the stipulations of their marriage contract. A son, James, had been born September 17, 1771, and his parents were committed to leaving him with the Indians.[11] Then, too, the Moravian mission towns were confined to Indians. It would be a complication to admit a white family.

3.

Their deliverance, however, was approaching from an unexpected source. It was 1774—the year of Dunmore's War. There was uneasiness and concern among the Indians in the Ohio country. Chief Logan's family had been wantonly murdered by the whites. Dr. John Connolly, a British agent unfriendly to the Indians, was in possession of Fort Pitt. The Shawnee had been preparing for war, and the inciting cause was now not lacking. Richard Conner, in the interest of safety no doubt, had abandoned his home at Connerstown and was living at the Shawnee village of Snakestown upon the Muskingum, named for John Snake, a Shawnee captain.[12]

By October 17, 1774, Dunmore's War was over and the Shawnee in full retreat. A military camp was hastily arranged by Lord Dunmore and his soldiers under a great elm tree on the Scioto Trail near the site of the present town of Circleville, Ohio. It was named Charlotte in honor of the English queen. The Indians were well represented by their chiefs—all except Chief Logan, who refused to come. Colonel John Gibson was commissioned to go after him and finally brought him in to make his famous speech. This was a momentous day for the Conners, for one of the treaty stipulations provided for the return of all white prisoners. Perhaps Margaret Boyer recalled the day in 1764 when Colonel Bouquet marched into the Ohio country and in his camp in the center of the Indian villages demanded of the Shawnee that they deliver up all their white captives. Was she delivered up then and did she return voluntarily because of the lure of this wild free life? Or did the Shawnee secrete her and refuse to give her up? There are no precise answers to these questions. But by the treaty of Camp Charlotte both Richard and Margaret were free.[13]

They spent the following winter in Pittsburgh.[14] It was a dismal little town of only about thirty houses, at the junction of the Monongahela and Allegheny rivers. There was a fort some distance from the town with a small garrison under command of the same Dr. John Connolly. Most of the inhabitants were traders or trappers, connected in some way with the chief business of the town, which was fur trade. There was no minister of the gospel here. Indians frequented it chiefly for the purpose of getting whisky. It was a rough, crude, frontier community. It sickened Margaret Conner, and she thought longingly of the peace and beauty of the wilderness. That was her home and there was another attraction there now, the little Moravian town of Schoenbrunn. She had not forgotten the night that David Zeisberger had spent with them in earnest conversation. In the town he had established was her opportunity for a fuller life—not here. But above all these considerations, there was her first-born, left among the Shawnee according to her marriage contract. How her heart yearned for him! How unthinkable to her, now that Zeisberger had given her a glimpse of another kind of life, that the child should grow up untutored and untrained. Richard listened and felt that she was right. On February 24, 1775, they arrived at Schoenbrunn.[15]

4.

This first of the Moravian towns in Ohio was now almost three years old. It was located on the Tuscarawas River, on both sides of which small lakes were interspersed in the bottom lands. There was a high bluff on the west and a smaller hill on the east. At the foot of the hill a spring of great beauty gushed forth to feed a lake nearly a mile long, which joined the Tuscarawas River. This lake and the river were navigable, and the Indians could paddle their canoes to the foot of the little hill or plateau on top of which was the town.

The town was built in the shape of an inverted T with forty lots, each about fifty by a hundred feet. There were sixty

houses built of logs and covered with clapboards, in addition to
huts and lodges. The church was forty feet long by thirty-six
feet wide, constructed of logs and surmounted by a cupola with
a bell. Open fireplaces provided heat for both houses and
church. The latter was built in 1772-1773, the first Protestant
church in the United States west of Pennsylvania. It stood
on the horizontal section of the inverted T-shaped plan facing
the broad vertical street, and could accommodate five hundred
persons. In appearance and position it dominated the town, as
it was intended to do. The church was clean. The services
were conducted in a reverent, orderly manner. The preacher
spoke in English, which was interpreted to the Indians. There
was no accompaniment for the singing, but it had volume and
expression. To an observing traveler this was surprising.
Near the church was the small log house of David Zeisberger.
The schoolhouse was on a corner opposite the church. It was
built of logs, with a fireplace also, sloping desks along two
sides, slab seats arranged in the center, and space enough to
accommodate about one hundred pupils. It, too, was equipped
with a bell. This was the first schoolhouse in the United
States north and west of the Ohio River.

Every lot in Schoenbrunn was fenced in, including God's
Acre, the burial ground in the northwest part of the town. A
fence enclosed the entire town. There were large cultivated
fields with rail fences, gardens, and fruit orchards as well as
cattle, horses, and hogs. Beyond the plain, which was five
miles in circumference, there was the familiar forest of oak,
hickory, chestnut, ash, and maple, while nearer the river were
huge sycamores, walnuts, cedars, horse chestnuts, and locusts.
These forests were rich in game, berries, and herbs; the streams
abounded in fish.

To such a town in such a setting did Margaret and Richard
Conner bend their steps on that February day in 1775. Small
wonder that it seemed to them an oasis, a promised land.[16]
Their arrival in Schoenbrunn, however, presented anew to the
missionaries the problem of whether they could permit a white
family to join their Indian settlement. While they considered
this question, Richard went to the country of the Shawnee
seeking his young son, James, to redeem him if possible.
Margaret stayed at the mission, charmed with its order, its

cleanliness, and its kindness. Here was the Indian environment in which she had grown up, but impressed upon it was the Christian ideal for which unconsciously her soul had hungered. When her husband returned without news of their boy, they both applied for membership in the Indian church, asking no favors to be granted to them above the Indians and cheerfully acquiescing in all the regulations. Zeisberger hesitated, fearful lest such a step might be misunderstood by the Indians and their confidence in him be lessened. The Indian members of the congregation were consulted and likewise White Eyes,[17] first war captain of the Delawares and trusted counselor of Netawatwees. White Eyes knew Richard Conner, and had discussed with him his intention of coming to live at the Moravian town. Evidently no adverse opinion was given, and Zeisberger, yielding at last to their importunity, accepted them on probation for a year. Richard set to work to build his house. The summer was thus pleasantly occupied and the house completed in time for a new arrival in the family, another boy, baptized by David Zeisberger, August 27, 1775, with the name of John.[18] He is the John of this narrative.

This little family had reached a peaceful haven at a very critical time in the country's history. Only a few short months before John's birth the battles of Lexington and Concord had been fought. The Continental Congress in July of this year determined upon an effort to keep the Ohio Indians neutral in the event of war, which seemed inevitable. As part of this movement, emissaries were authorized to carry belts as tokens of peace to all the tribes. In the fall of 1775, Colonel John Gibson, who had translated Chief Logan's speech at Camp Charlotte, came to Schoenbrunn during his tour of the Indian country bearing the "Congress Belt." It was six feet long and half a foot wide—an emblem of neutral friendship to which the Indians had agreed.[19] Richard Conner embraced the opportunity to accompany Colonel Gibson on his visit to the other tribes, with the thought always in his mind of recovering his little son James, who was still somewhere with the Shawnee. This time he was successful. On the return journey in the following spring he found his boy among the Shawnee and after sundry tribal conferences was able to ransom him for forty dollars. The little boy's head was shaved like an Indian's.

What a day of rejoicing in Schoenbrunn was March 18, 1776, when he was restored to his mother's arms![20]   Peace and joy filled the heart of Margaret Conner, now familiarly known in Schoenbrunn as Peggy. Her family circle was complete. In addition she had formed a warm friendship with Mrs. Jungman, the wife of one of the Moravian teachers.[21]

5.

Schoenbrunn was not the only town established by the Moravian missionaries in 1772.   In the fall of that year, another town for Christian Indians, especially the Mahican, was established about ten miles south of Schoenbrunn on the Tuscarawas River, and called Gnadenhütten, or "Tents of Grace." The latter was never as large as Schoenbrunn, but both were flourishing communities from 1772 to 1777. Nine tribes were represented in these mission towns, the Unami, Unalachtigo, and Munsee (all Delawares) ; the Mahican, Nanticoke, and Shawnee (tribes descended from or adopted by the Delawares) ; Conoy, Mingo, and a Cherokee. At the earnest request of the Delawares a third town was established a few years later about three miles below the site of the Delaware capital, on the east side of the Muskingum. It was called Lichtenau, or "Pasture of Light," and was established by David Zeisberger and his valiant assistant, John Heckewelder, on April 12, 1776. By January, 1777, there were four hundred and fourteen believing Indians in the three towns. Colonel George Morgan was a visitor at these towns during this period and was "astonished and delighted, in observing such order, regularity and industry."[22]

The war clouds of the American Revolution were beginning to thicken over this little center of civilization in the Ohio wilderness. Both English and American leaders in the struggle were at first anxious to keep the Indians in this territory neutral, and the strategic position and influence of the Moravian towns were clearly seen by both. The Moravians by the tenets of their religion were against war and more than willing to throw the weight of their influence to keep the Indians out of the conflict. But that task grew increasingly difficult. The Indian tribes were easily incited to war, which was a natural pastime for them. A few of their chiefs sensed that their future was at stake in this war.

When the English realized that they faced not a slight colonial insubordination to be easily put down, but the rising of a people intent upon securing their liberties, they turned for reinforcements to the Indians. In 1777 the Shawnee joined the English; later, the Iroquois and the Wyandot did likewise. From Detroit, British military headquarters in the West, came three men who had great influence with the Indians. These three were Alexander McKee, Matthew Elliot, and Simon Girty. They were malignantly and wickedly bitter against the Americans. Elliot was a renegade royalist. McKee was a Pennsylvanian with a treasonable record. Girty, a half-breed, was illiterate, depraved, brutal. This despicable trio effectively incited the tribes in the Ohio Valley in the interests of the British and against the Americans.[23] Colonel Matthew Elliot, as he became by promotion in the British service, and Simon Girty will appear later in this narrative.

On the eastern rim of this valley, Forts Pitt and Henry were garrisoned by Americans. The Delawares, under the wise guidance of Chief White Eyes and undoubtedly influenced by the Moravians, held out the longest for neutrality. But one tribe of the Delawares, notably, the Munsee, forsook them and joined the English. This disaffection spread to Schoenbrunn, and before the missionaries were aware of it there was a party of apostates in this peaceful little town, led by a recent convert, Chief Newallike. Zeisberger was too much of a statesman to hesitate in a crisis where the lives of both missionaries and believing Indians were threatened. Unable to move the apostates, he decided to abandon the much-loved town of Schoenbrunn and remove the congregation to the new town of Lichtenau, located near the capital of the friendly Delawares who had promised them protection.

Richard Conner was received into the church on March 27, 1777; his name was the last one written on the list of members of the congregation at Schoenbrunn before April 19, 1777, the day the town was abandoned and the chapel razed. The town was left in the hands of the hostile Munsee. The Conner family with the Jungmans and others had fled to Lichtenau earlier in the month. They had been driven out of their comfortable log houses at Schoenbrunn into a wilderness, to face the raw winds of April without any sort of shelter or assurance of protection. This change was a difficult and anxious one, a prelude to a still more critical period. The missionaries at Lichtenau were Zeisberger, the Jungmans, and William Edwards. By August, 1777, the Jungmans, at the urgent insistence of Zeisberger, left to return to Bethlehem, and Margaret Conner was thus deprived of her friend as well as her home at Schoenbrunn.[24] It is probable that at this time the Conners had three small boys, James, William, and John, although there is no available record of William's birth.[25]

6.

The Delawares had encouraged the establishment of Lichtenau and had promised to protect it from war parties, but the situation of the congregation in this town was now precarious. The English had become suspicious of the motive of the missionaries in keeping the Delawares neutral. Hostile tribes were making constant attempts to break down this neutrality of the Delawares. Skirmishes between the hostile Indians and the Americans were more frequent, and Lichtenau was in the path of war parties from both sides.

In August, 1777, the Half King, chief of the powerful Wyandot, who had allied themselves with Great Britain, came to Lichtenau with eighty-two warriors and stayed in the neighborhood for two weeks recruiting Indians of all tribes. This was a very trying time for the inhabitants of Lichtenau. The warriors were noisy, dancing and begging for bread before every house, and becoming drunken and rowdy under the influence of rum imported from Pittsburgh. The missionaries and Christian Indians tried to give them no offense and to treat them with kindness, but this attitude was misinterpreted by the American white settlers on the Ohio as an evidence of friendliness toward the British.

Rumors of all kinds were current, especially one relating to an invasion by the Americans. The Christian Indians in the two towns of Lichtenau and Gnadenhütten prepared for the worst. A site was selected on the Walhonding River as a place of refuge for both congregations. On September 17, 1777, frightened by a false rumor of an attack by the Americans, they all fled to this place, but later returned to their towns when their fears were allayed. It was in this period of fear and unrest that Margaret (Peggy) Conner was received into full membership of the congregation.[26]

It was finally decided to combine the two congregations, and the Christian Indians of Gnadenhütten were brought to Lichtenau in 1778. This was another hard experience for the inhabitants of Lichtenau, at least until houses were built for the newcomers. Even then the little town was overcrowded. Furthermore, the friendly Delawares were wavering in their neutrality. The United States was urging them to make war on the Indian allies of the British, but they resolved, instead, to join the English, and thus became the enemies instead of the friends and protectors of the mission congregation.

The situation of the mission station at Lichtenau was now critical. It was no longer advantageous to be near the Delaware capital. War parties of Indians made it a point to pass through Lichtenau to annoy the inhabitants and raid them for provisions. Zeisberger was not ready to give up the enterprise, but he recognized that a change would have to be made. As greater success had attended his efforts when the communities were small, he decided to divide the congregations into three towns again. He prepared to select the site of a new town and took with him, in the spring of 1779, a part of the congregation to a place across the river and a mile west of the site of the first town, Schoenbrunn, now completely destroyed. The members lived in huts for the greater part of the year and worshiped in the open until the new town was completed in December of that year. He named it New Schoenbrunn—with what nameless hopes and fears! Whether the Conner family went with him in April, 1779, and had a part in the choosing of the site, or whether they went later when the town was completed, is not known. On October 7, 1780, another son was born to the Conners at New Schoenbrunn. This child, Henry, was a fair-haired little boy. In later years he was known by the Indians as Wahbeskendip or White Hair.[27]

Before the third town of Zeisberger's new plan was established, Lichtenau (the last of the original trio of Schoenbrunn, Gnadenhütten, and Lichtenau) was finally abandoned on March 30, 1780. Those who had come there from Gnadenhütten returned to that place. The rest formed the inhabitants of New Schoenbrunn. On April 6, 1780, John Heckewelder, with a party of converts, established the last town of the Moravian Indians in this period—Salem, which was located only a few miles from Gnadenhütten. Zeisberger's plan for three towns was now realized. They were Gnadenhütten, New Schoenbrunn, and Salem. He had formed his ranks for the impending conflict.

CHAPTER III

Removal to Michigan with the Dispossessed Moravians

THE FORCES of disaster were rapidly closing in on the peaceful Moravian settlements. In the East and South the War of the Revolution was entering its last phase, but the outcome was still uncertain. The British had been content up to this time to use their Indian allies only for the purpose of harrying the settlers on the frontier in an attempt to break their morale. Companies of Indian warriors under white leaders were now incorporated into the British army. One field of action for these was the Ohio Valley. The British had resolved upon the destruction of the Indian congregations. Unfortunately for the security of the missionaries, many of the Americans in the Ohio Valley were convinced on their part that the Moravian Indians were giving secret aid to the Indian allies of the British.[1]

Colonel Daniel Brodhead, in January, 1779, had assumed command of the American headquarters at Fort Pitt. During that year he received from Heckewelder information concerning the hostile movements of Simon Girty and his Indians, and in the next year other messages were sent to him from Heckewelder and Zeisberger relating to the movements and actions of these Indians, among whom were now the Delawares. In 1781 the Indian war became general. Not a single tribe in the country beyond the Ohio remained friendly to the Americans. In January of that year Richard Conner, on one of his trips to Fort Pitt, gave information to Colonel Brodhead about the state of affairs among the Delawares, and Brodhead expressed the hope that the Christian Indians would not furnish cattle and swine to the enemy.[2] In March, Colonel Brodhead wrote to General Washington that he had learned from the Moravians that the temper of the Indians was unfriendly and that a general Indian war was at hand. Acting upon this advice, Brodhead a month later attacked and defeated the Indians at the Delaware capital, Goschachgünk, in what is known as Brodhead's Expedition. The Delawares abandoned their capital and went to the Sandusky country to be near their British allies. A prominent chief of their own tribe, Captain Pipe, had removed his village there in 1778 and allied himself with Half King of the Wyandot. These two were soon to make common cause against the Moravians.[3]

2.

On August 18, 1781, Zeisberger, realizing the gravity of the situation, sent a message to Fort Pitt that about two hundred and fifty Indians, Wyandot, Delawares, Munsee, Shawnee, and Mingo, led by the British captain, Matthew Elliot, were approaching to attack the Americans at Fort Henry (Wheeling, West Virginia) and other posts. This and later information was forwarded to Fort Henry, so that when the Indians started their attacks the defense was ready for them and they were compelled to retire. The British Indians learned from white prisoners that the Americans had been warned by the Moravian missionaries, and this discovery exasperated them. The incident confirmed their strong suspicion that the Moravians were sending information to Fort Pitt. Undoubtedly as a result of this, Elliot and his Indians were given instructions to take the Moravians and the Christian Indians prisoners, and to break up the missions. The Indians arrived near Salem on August 10, 1781, led by Half King (Wyandot), Captain Pipe (Delaware), Wenginund (Delaware), Captains John and Thomas Snake (Shawnee), Abraham Coon or Kuhn, Matthew Elliot, and Alexander McCormick. They carried a British flag. More warriors came, until about three hundred encamped west of Gnadenhütten. The gravity of this situation was increased by the fact that the Indian leaders expected to be joined by an army of one thousand British and Indians who were on their way to stop George Rogers Clark from going down the Ohio and then (so they understood) up to Detroit.[4]

Meanwhile, in a rough log cabin in the recently built village of New Schoenbrunn about ten miles away, Richard and Margaret Conner faced all the implications of this situation for themselves and their four boys, James, William, John, and Henry—the eldest ten, the youngest a baby. As they were Moravians by choice and close friends of the missionaries who were hated and whose lives were sought, it was possible that their family too, was on the edge of destruction. This must have been in their thoughts, but to their credit they made no effort to disentangle their own fortunes from those of the missionaries who had befriended them and were now in trouble. The British Indians had determined to remove the Christian Indians and to break up the mission settlements, and, if necessary to accomplish this, murder all the missionaries. Besides the missionaries and the Conners there was one other white family in these Moravian towns, that of John Leith.[5] So great was the hatred of the Americans that their lives, too, were in danger.

Zeisberger was in great distress of mind, not because of his personal safety but for the future of his Indian missions. He asked for delay until the crops were garnered. He pleaded for a continuance of his work. Council after council was held by the Indians to determine the fate of the missionaries and converts. A sorcerer was called. When the proposal to kill the missionaries was submitted, he dissented on the ground that the native assistants would take the place of the missionaries. When it was proposed to kill the assistants he dissented again, for that would involve killing their own people, their relatives and friends. To fortify his position, he threatened dire calamity if his words were disregarded. Finally, on September 1, the council decided to spare the missionaries' lives and take them prisoners. The ultimatum was given on September 3, when, for the last time, Half King and his captains asked the missionaries to leave their towns and go with them to the Wyandot country. They refused. That afternoon Zeisberger and Heckewelder were taken to Elliot's tent as prisoners. Simultaneously a band of thirty warriors set out for Salem and another party of warriors went to New Schoenbrunn to capture the remaining missionaries and their families. During a night of heavy rain they were taken from their beds in their sleeping clothes, and at dawn they were on their way to the camp near Gnadenhütten, their captors singing the death song and shouting scalp yells. The missionaries were imprisoned for three days, at the end of which time they yielded to the demands and agreed to abandon the mission towns. They were then released from their confinement. Meanwhile, the Indians had plundered the mission house, the houses of the inhabitants, and burned the books and writings of the teachers. A company of Indians had entered Salem and committed such outrages as could only be expected of madmen. No attempt was made by Elliot or Half King or Pipe to curb the excesses of the savages.[6]

The Conner family was in imminent and great peril. Their fate was bound up with that of the Moravian teachers. The Christian Indians on the other hand were countrymen and relatives of the hostile Indians. British agents and Indian chiefs both clung to the belief that if the missionaries were disposed of, the Christian Indians, including the assistants, would return to their tribes and savage lives. Once more subservient to their chiefs, they would become allies of the British, and the future of the Moravian missions would thus be ended. But it was just this that Zeisberger refused to do, to be separated from the Indians whom he had nurtured in the faith and who needed still to be strengthened lest they fall away from it. His decision meant the triumph or failure of his lifework.

3.

On September 11, 1781, the whole body of Christian Indians, with the Moravian missionaries and their families, the Conner family and the Leith family, left Salem, the place appointed by Zeisberger for the assembling of the inhabitants of the three towns. They were closely guarded by Delaware and Wyandot warriors commanded by Elliot. As the cavalcade of four hundred Moravian Indians left Salem there were sad hearts and perturbed minds. They were giving up rich plantations, thousands of bushels of unharvested corn, herds of live stock, poultry of every kind, gardens with abundance of vegetables, three flourishing towns, homes, implements of agriculture and of domestic use—all for an unknown wilderness where food and shelter would be uncertain. It was a dark, disheartening outlook, which was not softened later by stern reality.

The expedition traveled in two divisions—one in canoes on the Tuscarawas, the other on land, driving a large herd of cattle. The river was low and driftwood obstructed its current so that at times a passage had to be cut through it. At Goschachgünk Elliot left them. They went by land through the forsaken Delaware capital to the Walhonding River, then proceeded partly by water and partly along the banks, spending six days in camp at two different places on the borders of this river. During this period they encountered a terrific storm of rain, wind, thunder, and lightning. Half King, who had recently overtaken them with his troops, gave orders for them to lie by for the day in order to dry their clothes and get their things in order. In this storm two canoes were lost and many provisions. The camping site was flooded and no campfire could be made.

The Indians treated their captives with indignities and at times with harshness. The Conners were stripped of all their belongings, even to a kettle for cooking. Richard bore one and then another of his little sons, and his wife carried the baby, Henry, in Indian fashion. Tradition has it that the mother darkened the bright hair of her babe in order to make him appear more like an Indian and to attract less attention to the fact that they were a white and not an Indian family.[7] The Indians drove them forward like a herd of cattle, striking their horses to make them go faster, refusing to allow mothers time to nurse their babies. Mrs. Zeisberger was twice thrown from her horse. Michael Jung received a sharp blow to hasten his steps. Their shoes were worn off their feet before they reached the Sandusky River at noon of October 1. They had traveled one hundred and twenty-five miles in twenty days on sore and lacerated feet. At this point Half King with his warriors left them without explanation or offer of assistance, only announcing that it was his intention to organize them into war parties to fight the Americans. Left stranded in a country totally unfamiliar to them, a desolate and wild land compared to the fruitful valley they had left, their situation was critical, their spirits at the lowest ebb. Their first camp was about ten miles from Half King's town, near the deserted Wyandot village of Upper Sandusky Old Town. During the next week they found a more desirable town site with timber accessible, and at once began to build small log houses. Too disheartened to give the site a name, lacking both clothes and food, they camped in this nameless place which was afterwards, for purposes of identification, called Captives' Town.[8]

4.

The missionaries were soon summoned to Detroit for trial.[9] After a journey of great hardship, lacking provisions and equipment, they arrived hungry, friendless, and weary at the house of Major de Peyster, commandant.[10] They were without guard, for the two Delawares (Pipe and Wenginund) who had delivered the message of the commandant to the missionaries failed to return with them. They were ungraciously received by Major de Peyster and their hearing was postponed until Pipe, who was carousing in a camp on the Maumee, should arrive. The British agent, Elliot, who had persuaded De Peyster to the capture of the Moravians at Salem on September 11 was distributing rewards to Pipe's Indians.

Five days later Captain Pipe made a spectacular entry into Detroit with two of his councilors and a band of Delawares whooping the scalp yell. The next day, November 9, he appeared with his savage retinue in the council chamber of Commandant de Peyster. It was a cold, gloomy, scantily furnished room. De Peyster sat at the head of the table. On one bench facing him were the missionaries, charged with giving aid and information to the enemy—the Americans. On each side of them sat their accusers, Pipe and his Delawares on one hand, Mingo and Indians of various other tribes on the other. Behind the commandant, his secretary, and his Indian agent, were grouped British officers, interpreters, and servants.

It was a solemn occasion. Pipe was the first to make a speech. He outlined the part played by the Delawares in the French and Indian War, in Pontiac's War, and the reasons for their present alliance with the British. Now and then he referred with biting sarcasm to the British, and, in the same breath, made protestations of loyalty to them. At this point he delivered to De Peyster, who was somewhat of a gentleman and scholar, a stick on which hung human scalps, and other chiefs presented like evidence of their loyalty. These gruesome and repulsive tokens of achievement were received according to the British rules of warfare and placed in a corner of the room. The prideful Pipe then sat down.

Major de Peyster, with the stern dignity becoming to the occasion, arose and rehearsed the charges that Pipe made and then asked him directly whether the Moravians had given information and aid to the Americans. Pipe had had an active part in the deportation from Salem which had been ordered by De Peyster on the basis of this and similar accusations. His mind did not act at this moment and his tongue was confused. He answered evasively, and, whispering to his councilors, urged them to speak, but they hung their heads. Perhaps memories were arising in the minds of all of them of the kindness of these teachers who had come among them at their own request—of the occasions on which they had been fed and sheltered, consoled and taught by them. De Peyster, soldier that he was, standing with military bearing, his eyes fixed upon Pipe, was awaiting the answer to his question. The tense silence of the room was broken only by uneasy shuffling of feet and slight restlessness among the Indians. Suddenly Pipe sprang to his feet and declared that the accused were innocent and that what they did in writing letters to the Americans they were compelled to do. Striking his breast with his clenched fists, he exclaimed: "I and the chiefs at Goschachgünk are responsible."

The trial ended with the acquittal of the missionaries, for by the lips of De Peyster's own witness the incriminating evidence was turned not against the accused but against the accuser. If De Peyster did not know that the British-Delaware alliance was based on force rather than friendship he learned it from Pipe's speech at this trial. Perhaps he had no notion of testing the strength of that alliance at this critical time by convicting the missionaries in the face of Pipe's statement that they were innocent. Both Zeisberger and Heckewelder had written letters to Fort Pitt giving information concerning the movements of the Indians. The Moravian villagers had fed Colonel Brodhead's soldiers and furnished them horses at the time of their attack upon the Delaware capital at Goschachgünk. They, as well as Conner, although situated in a country bristling with British agents and hostile Indians, were in sympathy with the Americans but could not openly espouse the American cause and hope to escape the penalty. Doubtless the letters that Pipe referred to were written as he stated, but there was other evidence which might have implicated the missionaries in the charges that were preferred against them.[11]

Whether or not this was known to De Peyster is not clear from the record.

The fate of the Conner family at this time was dependent on De Peyster. His was an awkward position in a serious situation. After inflicting indescribable sufferings and misery on more than four hundred human beings by ordering the raid on Salem, he now dismissed the whole proceeding without pressing the charges against the missionaries. The loyalty of the Delawares to the British was not free from doubt. De Peyster was convinced of the friendly relations between the accused missionaries and the Americans at Fort Pitt and Fort Henry, and had ordered the Salem raid for the purpose of segregating the white Moravians from their followers and from the Americans. In less than ninety days from this time the four hundred Moravian Indians had returned to their tribes. The joker in De Peyster's apparently friendly and generous ruling was that the missionaries were not released from his control. By allowing the Indians to slip away he accomplished his purpose and broke up the mission so that it was no longer a menace to the British. Shortly he wrote to McKee that the missionaries seemed "to be harmless people" and that upon Pipe's application he had allowed them to return to their families.[12] By one clever stroke he had shorn them of all their power because he had in this way taken away their Indians. The missionaries, as an expression of gratitude for their deliverance, built and dedicated a house of worship at Captives' Town. Their perceptions of the real situation were blurred by sufferings and apprehensions. Shortly the stark truth would be disclosed to them.

5.

Richard Conner, meanwhile, had become convinced of the hopelessness of trying to maintain his little family in the barren location of Captives' Town. In the swiftly flowing current of events, the fortunes of this little group were only a small eddy. The village was overcrowded and there was not enough food to go around. It was unlikely that it would be anything more than a temporary abiding place for the Moravians and their Christian Indians, and to attempt to develop it as a town or as an agricultural community would be folly. In

fact, Conner did not take his family there at all, but remained
at the Wyandot village at Upper Sandusky Old Town and
prepared to move them to Lower Sandusky, now Fremont,
Ohio, where there was a trading post and a small Wyandot
village. He had accomplished this removal by December 1,
1781. The warriors at Lower Sandusky were abroad fighting
the Americans. Ships from Sandusky transported troops up
the river to this point. French and English traders brought
their wares here by boat. Zeisberger, visiting Conner on
March 19, 1782, realized that Conner could better maintain
himself here than at Captives' Town. The family was subject
to any disposition the Wyandot, acting under the orders of the
British commandant at Fort Detroit, wished to make of them,
but for the present their movements were not restricted so long
as they remained within the Wyandot country.[13]

The winter following, however, was one of suffering and
distress among the missionaries. The weather was intensely
cold, their huts furnished inadequate shelter, and they were
without the actual necessities of life. Girty and Half King
were openly antagonistic. As the famine increased one hundred and fifty Christian Indians were allowed to go back to
the Muskingum Valley to gather the ungarnered corn in their
fields. The remainder straggled back to their friends in other
tribes. Converts that Zeisberger had so toilsomely gathered
together and who had so loyally supported him were dis-
persing because to stay meant starvation. By the end of
February nearly all of the inhabitants of Captives' Town were
scattered.[14] The teachers and a few old people were all that
were left. Richard Conner had been shrewdly right. The
town could not be supported in this location. He was still at
Lower Sandusky.

6.

Early in March, 1782, word came to the missionaries that
De Peyster wished the teachers and their families to return to
Detroit. It sounded like a message of deliverance, but to
Zeisberger it was a message of despair. The invitation did not
include his Christian Indians, and if he left them now in the
midst of disaster he felt he could never rally them and his
work of forty years among them would be brought to naught.

He had hoped even in this unpropitious place to build a community for them and gradually to win them back. He had no choice, but he could not leave without an explanation to his Indian children, so he sent messengers to them scattered as they were throughout the Ohio Valley bidding them meet him in Captives' Town. There he held a farewell service on March fifteenth, while anguish filled his soul.[15]

One group was not represented in this little company of the faithful, and that was the party who had gone back to Gnadenhütten for the ungarnered grain. Word had reached Zeisberger that this group had been captured and put to death by the American militia, but he did not believe it, so great was his faith in the Americans. Four days later when the missionaries were waiting at Lower Sandusky for a boat to take them to Detroit, he learned the truth. Ninety Christian Indians at Gnadenhütten had been foully murdered by Pennsylvania and Virginia militia under the command of Colonel David Williamson. They had been packed into houses and slaughtered like animals—men, women, and children. The frontier settlers had been outrageously treated by hostile Indians, but to revenge themselves in this manner on peaceful, unarmed Indians who had not wronged them in any way, was an unspeakable crime. This act was the Nemesis of the Americans in the years to follow.[16]

David Zeisberger's cup was full as he set sail for Detroit. It can be assumed that the Conner family at Lower Sandusky did what they could to assuage the grief and despair of their friends, the missionaries, during the four weeks they spent there waiting for the boat and that they saw them depart with a deep sense of loss.

When Zeisberger and his assistant missionaries arrived in Detroit, April 20, 1782, De Peyster welcomed them cordially and offered to let them stay in Detroit or go back to Bethlehem. He had brought them here at the behest of Half King and Girty, who were still determined to break completely the power of the missionaries over the Indians. Half King, in his cruel untutored mind, held them responsible for the death of his two sons who had been killed in a raid on the white settlers on the Ohio at the time of the Salem attack. The commandant, naturally humane, was now disillusioned as to his Indian allies. He could see no reason for inflicting further punishment on these people because they were hated by Girty and the Half King, and he thought it advisable to remove them from a dangerous situation. He, therefore, induced the Chippewa to give them permission to settle on the Huron (now Clinton)' River about twenty miles north of Detroit.[17]

7.

By June following, Lower Sandusky was filled with rumors of war. The tragic sequel of the massacre at Gnadenhütten was now to follow. Major William Crawford, Virginia landowner and friend of Washington, was commissioned to lead an army to Sandusky to punish the Wyandot, Seneca, and Shawnee for their murderous raids against the Pennsylvania and Virginia settlers. Colonel David Williamson, who led the expedition against Gnadenhütten, was a field marshal in this campaign. This army was badly defeated in a desperately fought battle at Sandusky lasting from June 4 to 7. Major Crawford was captured and burned at the stake. Williamson, the real culprit, escaped.[18]

The Conner family was caught again in the midst of exciting and terrifying happenings. Richard's anxiety for their safety was very great, and as soon as it was practicable he determined to follow the missionaries to Detroit, thus evading the backwash of the brutal Indian triumph. The Conners arrived in Detroit about the middle of June. Zeisberger, meanwhile, had made preparations for the establishment of a Christian Indian settlement on the banks of the Huron River. On the twenty-second of July, with a little band of Indians, he selected the site for the town, which he named, with hope, New Gnadenhütten. It consisted of one street of more than twenty log houses and a church. The site had some points of resemblance to the first Moravian town in Ohio—the beloved Schoenbrunn. These were the river, the plateau with "springs of limpid waters gushing from its base," the dark fringe of woods filled with huge forest trees so familiar to them. But the forest was not as inviting as the one they had left. The ground was covered with a dense growth of bushes which hid from the eye of the unsuspecting traveler the treacherous marsh. Berries were plentiful, however, and wild flax grew abundantly. There were possibilities here to satisfy the needs of a growing community. By the end of the year there were fifty-three members in this little colony.[19] There was magnetism in Zeisberger's unselfish devotion.

Richard Conner remained in Detroit for nine months, probably because he had found means of supporting his family there. He came to know De Peyster and was employed by him on business with the Indians in their country. On one occasion, in July, 1782, he used this opportunity at the request of Zeisberger, to tell the Christian Indians whom he met about the new town that Zeisberger was building, urging them to come back to it. Many returned as a result of this solicitation. Conner himself desired to join Zeisberger as soon as he could, and in the spring of 1783 removed his family to New Gnadenhütten. As Detroit was not far away, communication was easy and frequent, and until they could clear the forest and place the land under cultivation they could depend upon Detroit for provisions. De Peyster apparently furnished provisions for the entire mission station for a time, but in July, 1783, the supplies were discontinued and everyone was compelled to buy his food.[20]

During the previous winter (1782-1783) the inhabitants had made maple sugar, canoes, baskets, brooms, bowls, had gathered berries and caught fish—all of which had a ready market in Detroit. But the winter following the arrival of the Conner family was unusually cold. Famine hovered over the little community until a herd of deer wandered unexpectedly into the vicinity. Many, however, on account of inadequate provisions were compelled to go to Detroit to earn their livelihood.[21] For a time there were only the missionaries and the Conners living in the village. It was during this cold winter, December 16, 1783, that a daughter was born in the Conner household, and was baptized with the name of Susanna.[22] The family now consisted of four boys and one girl. During all their hardships and perils, not one of this family had been lost.

The harvest of 1784 was abundant, but a new set of difficulties confronted the community. Though a cessation of hostilities between the British and Americans had been proclaimed early in the spring of 1783, a general treaty of peace was not signed until September 3. The future government of the country in Detroit and adjacent territory was unsettled. The British wished to hold it as long as possible. The Chippewa, irritated by the presence of the Moravians among them, said that they had granted the land to them only until the end of the war. The British governors who succeeded De Peyster at Detroit did not encourage the Moravians to remain. Major Ancrum, commandant, and John Askin, a Detroit merchant, offered to buy the improvements in their village (excepting those of Richard Conner who had decided to remain) for four hundred dollars. Under these conditions it was decided to abandon the mission and seek another site on the other side of Lake Erie.[23]

8.

Richard Conner, now advanced in years, felt that he could no longer follow the Moravian missionaries in their transitory locations, and remained with his family on the homestead he had provided for them. This ended the connection of the Conner family with the mission settlements of David Zeisberger, whose effort to establish a permanent location was to be again frustrated. The Conner family was now the only white family in New Gnadenhütten. The Chippewa Indians were their only neighbors until 1799 and perhaps a year longer. Why the Chippewa made an exception of Richard Conner's family is not known. Probably it was for the reason that this family who had lived for many years among the Indians understood the language and customs of even the uncivilized Chippewa. The Conner children were reared on this land, which came to be known locally as "Conner Farms." Their dwelling had the distinction of having a cellar. Near by was a field of Indian corn and a garden. At last, the wilderness was beginning to blossom at the hands of Richard Conner.[24]

Records touching on the Conner family are meager between the years 1786 and 1800. They lived in a more primitive way after the Moravians had left. Detroit, only twenty miles away, was then a trading as well as a military post. Farms adjoining it had been cultivated since the date of its founding in 1701. There was the mingling here of both French and English. The Catholic church was the dominant one, and while the Conners had been Irish Protestants from the beginning, it was only natural that under these circumstances some of their children should drift into the Catholic church. The family had both business and social relations in Detroit. Richard was essentially a farmer, and he became an extensive landowner in Macomb County, where he was the first white settler. Mt. Clemens, the county seat, was laid out in 1803 on land purchased from him. After his death on April 22, 1807, his widow and children proved their claims to over four thousand acres of land. When in 1796 the British government, under Jay's treaty, had surrendered possession of lands in Macomb County, the titles were adjudicated on proof that improvements had been made by the claimants prior to 1796, and patents were issued by the United States upon such proof. Indian titles were not recognized.[25]

Richard Conner's family lived in or near Mt. Clemens until the War of 1812. After the massacre at the River Raisin—a bloody chapter of British perfidy—the Indians assumed a threatening attitude. Margaret Conner was then living with her daughter, Susanna, who had married Elisha Harrington in the year of her father's death. Harrington was in the army, as were the Conner sons, and for personal safety his family, including Margaret Conner, fled with other settlers living near Detroit to that town. The Conners Creek home of Henry Conner was opened to his relatives while he was at the front fighting. Savage marauders stole everything they could lay their hands on, particularly poultry, cattle, and horses. Even in this last year of her life Margaret Conner's soul was not to be unharried by brutalities. It is said that the Indians displayed scalps of white victims taken in the recent massacre and claimed that one was that of her son, Henry Conner. It was not true, but how the exhibition must have wrung the mother's heart! Six months later, in June, 1813, Margaret Conner died in Henry Conner's home at the probable age of sixty-three years.[26] She was buried in Detroit—a worthy mother of pioneers.

This narrative will henceforth be confined to the adventures and achievements of two of her sons, William and John, pioneers in the region now known as the state of Indiana.

CHAPTER IV

JOHN AND WILLIAM CONNER, TRADERS ON THE
INDIANA FRONTIER

WHEN THE Moravian mission at New Gnadenhütten, Michigan, was abandoned in 1786, James Conner was fifteen, William about thirteen, John, eleven, and Henry, six years old. They had spent their childhood and youth among the Indians. Their mother and father, both adopted members of the Shawnee tribe, had familiarized the children with its language. Shawnee dialects were probably used in common with the English language in the household. The most impressionable years of these boys had been spent in the Moravian mission towns in Ohio and Michigan, where the children of the mission heard German as well as English.[1] Hymns and the Psalms were taught in the German language. Delaware Indians and representatives of other tribes composed the mission towns, and parties from neighboring bands were constantly passing through on one errand or another, sometimes staying for days at a time. Naturally the Conner boys became familiar with the dress, the customs, and the language of many different tribes. When the Conners were held virtually prisoners in the Sandusky country, they were close neighbors of the Wyandot and had intimate association with them. Later, in Michigan, they lived among the Chippewa. No wonder a tradition persists to this day in Mt. Clemens, that the children of Richard Conner dressed and acted like Indians.

It was a natural sequent that the four boys became well-known Indian interpreters. There were three dialects in the Delaware language, the Unami, Munsee, and Unalachtigo. It is certain that William and John knew all of these, and could speak the Shawnee, Chippewa, and probably the Wyandot languages. As the school was next in importance to the church in the mind of David Zeisberger, it can be assumed that the boys learned the rudiments of reading, writing, and arithmetic under the tutelage of that able man.[2] Whether their education was continued in Detroit after the abandonment of the New Gnadenhütten mission is not known. If it was, there

is no record of it.   But by this time they were familiar with
more languages than most boys of the same age today.

In addition they had learned the secrets of the forests, and
acquired a sound practical knowledge of frontier trading operations.   An Indian trail was almost as easy for them to follow
as a modern road for the youth of today.[3]   Every sound of the
forest had a meaning to their ears.   The tracks of beasts, the
flights of birds, the changing colors of the woods and sky and
water were full of significance to them.   The cult of the Indian
was inbred in them.   They had observed the methods of both
French and English traders while they were at Sandusky and
later at Mt. Clemens.   Some knowledge of the French language
was thus acquired as they became friends of the rough traders
and learned the value of the pelts from them.   From its beginning Detroit had been coveted by three nations for its strategic
position in the fur trade.

The boys' father, Richard, was essentially a farmer.   Lov-
ing the soil and its cultivation, he had acquired vast acres for
his family, but two of his sons were not content to remain
there any longer than was necessary to establish a title.   By
July 1, 1796, both William and John were in possession and
occupancy of land in what is now the state of Michigan, given
to them by their father.[4]   Soon after that date the two young
men were off to the Indian country.   What urge for adventure
or new opportunities incited them is not entirely clear.   It
appears, however, that at this time they definitely rejected a
settled agricultural existence for the freer and more exciting
life of the Indian trader.

It may have been that the political situation at that time
had a bearing on their decision.   Although with the ratification
of the treaty of peace following the War of the Revolution,
title to the post at Detroit passed to the United States, the post
itself was not surrendered until July 11, 1796, in accordance
with the Jay treaty of 1794.   By that time all of Michigan was
in the hands of the Americans.[5]   The English had held on
stubbornly to this trading center.   English governors were in
control of the territory surrounding Detroit until 1796.   Title
to the land was uncertain.   Laxness and irregularity governed
the fur trade too, and these conditions continued for some years
after the United States took control.[6]

Detroit at this time was totally uninviting. It is described by a writer three years later (1799) as "filthy beyond measure—calculated to accommodate a few traders." Small houses crowded together in a small space less than four hundred yards square, narrow streets with only one of sufficient width for "a cart to turn about in," a so-called citadel which consisted of soldiers' barracks and parade ground connected, so it is said, by a covered passage to the inadequate fort at the back of the town; pickets separating the citadel from the dwelling and pickets surrounding the whole town—this was Detroit. Soldiers, traders, Indians, and a citizenry to minister to the needs of all three constituted the inhabitants of this rough uncouth town which was not much more than an overgrown trading post, over the rich trading possibilities of which French, English, Indian, and American had contended.[7] From a similar town—Fort Pitt—Margaret Conner had turned with great disgust in 1775 and set her face to the wilderness. Now, her sons, standing on the threshold of a new century, turned their backs in like fashion upon just such a sodden community and their steps to a new wilderness farther west.

It is difficult, if not impossible, to pick up the trails of the traders who went into that vast area denominated the Indian country. Under the provisions of the Greenville Treaty with the Indians, August 3, 1795, what was colloquially known as the Indian country was, broadly speaking, land reserved for Indian tribes, extending northward from the Ohio River, eastward from the Mississippi River, and southward and westward of the Great Lakes, including in Ohio, however, only the northern section west of the Cuyahoga River. All claim to this large area, less a number of small special cessions, was "relinquished" by the United States to the Wyandot, Miami, Shawnee, Delawares, Ottawa, Chippewa, Potawatomi, Wea, and other tribes of the region. This treaty confirmed the Indians' rights to all the land within the present limits of Indiana except the Gore (a wedge-shaped area between the treaty line and the present Ohio boundary), one piece six miles square near Fort Wayne, one piece two miles square lying eight miles west of Fort Wayne, one piece six miles square near Ouiatenon, 150,000 acres in Clark's Grant, and the post of Vincennes and land adjacent, to which the Indian title had been extinguished.

After the cession to the United States of their lands in Ohio, most of the Indians living in that section moved to other parts of the Indian country. Large numbers of the Shawnee and Delawares came to what is now Indiana.[8]

William Conner left his father's homestead in Michigan sometime after 1796. A frequently recurring tradition is to the effect that he went to the Saginaw country in Michigan as an Indian trader, backed by some Frenchmen; that he was there for some time until there were signs of trouble. Warned by friendly Indians, he left, while the white men who disregarded the message were killed in an Indian uprising. There is no contemporary record supporting this tradition. The events may have happened as stated, for the years from 1796 to 1800 are not otherwise accounted for as far as William Conner is concerned. In 1800 he went again to the Indian country and it is of record that this time it was to the region now within the state of Indiana. It is said by one writer that he came to the mouth of Fall Creek, on White River, a crossing point for many trails, where Indians were likely to congregate. The rumor had reached him that a Frenchman was trading at this place.[9] John Conner left the paternal home in 1797 with no more definite destination in view.[10] They never returned to Michigan for permanent abode.

It is no more apparent from the written records why John and William Conner came ultimately to Indiana than it is why their father emigrated from Maryland to Ohio. There may have been the same desire for adventure and new scenes. There may have been another reason in the case of the sons. In a very few years both were married to Delaware Indian wives. Is it not likely that these Indian women were friends of an earlier day, perhaps of their childhood in Ohio, and that they sought them out in the White River country to which the Delawares came after the Treaty of Greenville? A less romantic possibility is that the Conners followed this friendly tribe of Indians whose language and customs they knew so well for the purpose of trade, and that they intermarried in the tribe to facilitate their trading operations—a custom quite common among traders at this time.

2.

When a division of the Northwest Territory was made by act of Congress, May 7, 1800, the section designated as Indiana Territory comprised the present states of Indiana, Illinois, Michigan, and Wisconsin, and parts of Ohio and Minnesota. Vincennes was the capital and William Henry Harrison was made governor. John Gibson was appointed secretary. This is the same John Gibson who was present at the treaty of Camp Charlotte when the parents of John and William were released from the Shawnee. He had also been a visitor many times at the Moravian towns in Ohio and knew their family.[11]

In the entire Indiana Territory there was a white population of about five thousand; in what is now Indiana the white population was about twenty-five hundred, divided between the southern part near Vincennes and Clark's Grant. There were also white traders scattered along the Wabash.[12] The country embracing what is now central and northern Indiana, was a continuous primeval wilderness with the exception of extensive prairies in the northwest part. There were no roads other than Indian trails and buffalo traces, no boats except the softly gliding Indian canoes, no towns other than straggling Indian villages, no inns between the white settlements. It was necessary for travelers to carry camp equipment and they were never secure against Indian attacks. It was veritably the haunt of wild beasts and savage men.

The Miami Nation or Confederacy claimed the whole of what is now Indiana. This Confederacy consisted of the Miami or Twightwees, situated on the headwaters of the Maumee River near Fort Wayne; the Eel River Miami; the Wea or Ouiatenon, whose more important villages were on the banks of the Wabash near Fort Ouiatenon; and the Piankashaw who lived on the banks of the Vermillion River and on the river Wabash between Vincennes and Ouiatenon. The Potawatomi, Kickapoo, Shawnee, and Delawares were allowed by the Miami to occupy various portions of this territory. As far back as 1770 the Delawares who were then living on the Muskingum River in Ohio had received permission from the Piankashaw (probably from the Miami Confederacy) to occupy the country between the Ohio and White River in the

present state of Indiana.[13] In 1781 Buckongahelas, a war
chief of the Delawares who realized the dangerous situation of
the Christian Delaware Indians on the Muskingum, caught as
they were between the opposing British and American forces,
had urged them to move westward. He was strongly pro-
British and anti-Christian and wished to break up the mission
and ally the Delawares with the British.[14] He failed in his
undertaking at that time, but he left a parting warning to the
Moravian Indians that the Americans were a bad lot and not
to be trusted. His words proved to be prophetic; incredible as
it seemed at that time, it was only six months later that the
massacre of Indians at Gnadenhütten shocked the western country. The Delaware tribe never fully recovered from this blow.
It was always a source of great bitterness to their leaders.
Many of them had joined the British cause and the Christian
Indians were dispersed in Indiana and Ohio.

At least as early as 1798, after the Treaty of Greenville,
the Delawares began establishing towns on the West Fork of
White River on the land granted to them by the Piankashaw.[15]
In the next few years there were nine settlements of Delaware
Indian families strung along both banks of White River. The
easternmost town was that of Chief Buckongahelas on the present site of Muncie, Indiana. The westernmost town was the
Lower Delaware town south of the present site of Noblesville,
Indiana. Several were the abodes of noted Delaware chieftains,
including besides Buckongahelas, Tetepachsit, Hockingpomsga,
and William Anderson.[16]

It was to this group of Delaware towns on White River
that John and William Conner came when they left Michigan.
They were here in May, 1801, when the Moravian missionaries,
Abraham Luckenbach and Peter Kluge, came to found a mission on White River similar to those David Zeisberger had
established in Ohio. History sometimes repeats itself. In the
same community there were co-operating after the lapse of a
quarter of a century, Delawares, Moravian missionaries, and
the Conners. The missionaries had come on the invitation of
the Delawares, who wished to enjoy again the civilizing influences of the mission. That may have been the sincere desire
of some of those who had earlier in their lives been touched by
this influence and longed for it again. But there were also

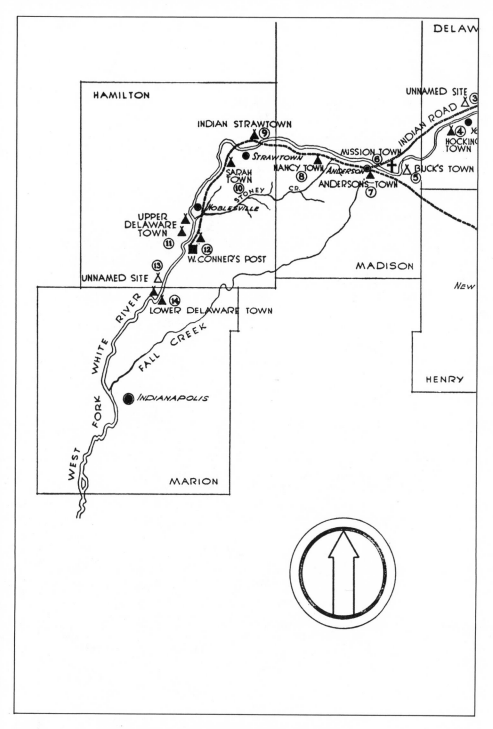

INDIAN TOWNS NEAR MORAVIAN MISSION
AND CONNER TRAIL

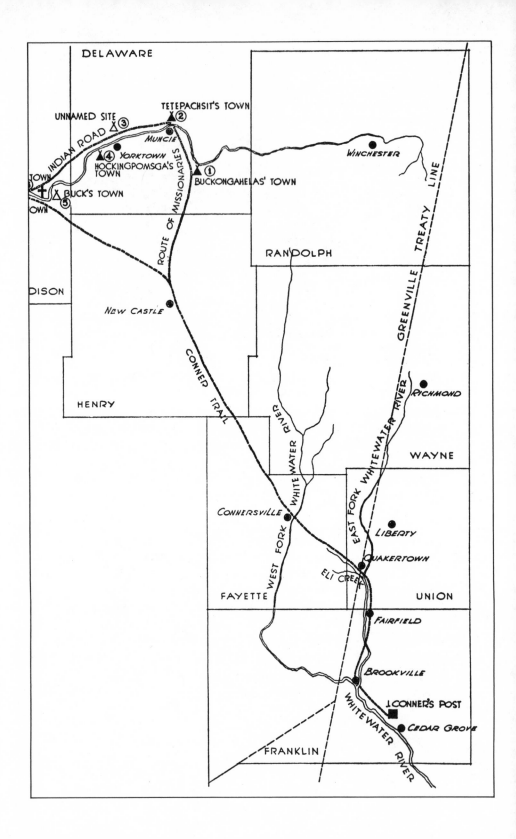

among them those like Buckongahelas who, unfriendly to the Christians, agreed to the invitation solely in the hope that the missionaries would bring with them a considerable number of the Delawares who were living in Ohio with Zeisberger, thus making their relatives in Indiana more contented and increasing the size of the Delaware nation here. What was the disappointment and chagrin of this group when only fifteen Delaware converts from Ohio arrived with the missionaries and some of these returned shortly to Ohio![17]

3.

The missionaries found John Conner established as a trader in Buckongahelas' Town. On their arrival Conner and his Delaware wife gave them some assistance in settling. The Indians granted land to the Moravians for their mission town on the bend in White River, eight miles downstream from Hockingpomsga's Town and three miles upstream from Anderson's Town. They were not permitted to follow Zeisberger's sound advice against settling within ten miles of an Indian town, and they were soon to experience the evil consequences which he had foreseen. William Conner probably was living at this time at Wapeminskink, the town of Chief Anderson, whose daughter, Mekinges, he married at an unrecorded time.[18]

An interesting sidelight upon the relation of the Conners to the Indians emerges in an incident related by Abraham Luckenbach. John Conner invited Luckenbach, who was about his age, to accompany him to an Indian dance. "In every Indian town," says Luckenbach, "there was a so-called long-house, about forty feet in length and twenty feet wide, in which the savages held their sacrifices and dances. It also served as a Council House. These houses were built of split logs set together between dug-in posts, and were provided with a roof, consisting of tree-bark or clapboards, resting on strong pillars dug into the earth. The entrance was at both gable-ends, and there was neither floor nor ceiling. Near both ends and in the middle, there were three fires over which hung large kettles in which corn and meat were boiled for the guests and always kept in readiness for them to eat, when finished with the dance. In the roof there were openings over every fire, so that the smoke could escape. Along the inside of the house there were seats or elevations from the ground about a foot high and five feet wide. These were first covered with the bark of trees and then with long grass. On them the guests sat, or, if they felt like it, lay down and smoked their pipes, while the others were engaged in dancing."

Conner asked Luckenbach to stay all night at his house, and took him to view the dance given that night and probably on succeeding nights as was the custom. He introduced him to the Indians present. The dances were given in honor of the protecting deities who had revealed themselves in the dreams of various members of the tribe. The ceremony is somewhat as follows. The leading dancer relates his dream and the parts are emphasized with loud, discordant noises. During the processional the leader indulges in antics which to the savage mind are in harmony with the major noises; in this interpretation lies the skill of the dancer. When the leader has paid his respects to the deities he concludes that round with a shrill yell, then another dancer comes forward and the performance is repeated so long as the dreams last. Between performances the chiefs adjured the Indians to abstain from strong drink and other devastating vices, although they, themselves, did not always set good examples. Luckenbach watched with a critical eye and noted carefully all the details of this occasion. After commenting on the dance he says of his host: "he . . . appeared to be very much taken with it. He said that the Indians in this way sought to serve their god, and that he had learned to know many of them whose dreams had been fulfilled; in fact, their dreams, with few exceptions, generally came true. He himself danced with them and had not gotten much farther in knowledge than the heathen."[19]

If Luckenbach was sound in his judgment, John Conner at the age of twenty-six years not only wore the dress of the Indians but had adopted their manners, spiritual views, and ways of thought. It is true that the Conners, through their long and intimate acquaintance with the Indians, understood them and possessed their confidence. The Delawares, especially, trusted these two traders to a greater extent than any other white men. But they never became thoroughly Indian in character, outlook, or interests. Rather, when the opportunity came, they were in the vanguard of those seeking the benefits of civilization and contributing to its advancement. The Moravian missionaries in Indiana, on the contrary, failed to develop a sympathetic understanding of Indian traits, and this failure was a contributory cause of the disaster which attended the mission.

Another, and perhaps the major cause of the mission's failure was the proximity of the Shawnee Tecumseh and his brother, Lawlewasikaw, later known as Tenskwatawa or the Prophet. They had been living among the Delawares since 1798 and had gradually extended their influence while they were engaged in the ordinary pursuits of the Indians. They lived in one of the Delaware villages on White River within the present boundaries of Delaware County, therefore probably in Buckongahelas' Town or Hockingpomsga's Town. This was known as the headquarters of these leaders. Early in 1805 Tenskwatawa assumed the role of prophet, inveighing against drunkenness, intermarriage of the Indians and whites, release of Indian lands to the whites by sale, and the sin of witchcraft.

By this time Buckongahelas was dead.[20] Tetepachsit, now an old man, was charged with too great friendliness for the whites. He sometimes carried with him a string of twenty-seven dried human tongues which he proudly offered as grim and mute testimony that he was not a weakling.[21] A quaint picture of these two chiefs is furnished us by the diarist of the mission congregation on White River. Sometime in 1801 they arrived together at the mission. As Buckongahelas was not in sympathy with the work of the mission he was probably prompted by curiosity. Tetepachsit, however, was known to favor its civilizing influences. The visitors are described as "rather old and quite venerable looking. Both wore broad blue belts, a silver ring as a collar around the neck, and carried in their hands a turkey wing to chase away the flies."[22]

Partly because Tetepachsit entertained a friendly attitude towards the Moravians and partly because the Prophet believed that it was the old chiefs who were leading the tribes to sell their lands, Tetepachsit was secretly marked for martyrdom. On March 17, 1806, he was accused of witchcraft, tied to a stake, tomahawked, and his body consumed by fire within sight of the mission. Three others, Billy Patterson, nephew of

Tetepachsit, Joshua, and Caritas, all believing Indians, met a similar fate. Other Indians, including Chief Hockingpomsga, narrowly escaped. The execution of these unfortunates took place at or near Chief Anderson's Town.[23]

Neither John nor William Conner was in this vicinity during these terrifying days, though doubtless they knew very quickly of the events. John was trading in Wapicomekoke by May, 1801, and by November 30 both of them had secured licenses to trade in Buckongahelas' Town and Petchepencues' Town. During that year they sent their furs by pack horses to Fort Wayne. Detroit was the ultimate destination. In the same year at least five other traders were granted licenses to trade at the Delaware towns on White River.[24]

In August, 1802, William Conner left Chief Anderson's Town and established himself and his Indian wife on land four miles south of the present site of Noblesville, across the river and a little south of the Upper Delaware Indian Town. He had been attracted by the character of the country there during his wanderings, especially by the fertility of the soil and the abundance of game for food and furs. Here he built himself a double log cabin large enough for storage of pelts and to accommodate beads, lead, flint, steel, knives, and hatchets, used in trading. Years later he told how "on a beautiful moonlight night, August 12, 1802 . . . with only the aid of a French-Canadian," he finished the roof of his log cabin. Little did he realize at that time that his dwelling was to become a landmark in the new country—known as the Conner Trading Post, its door always open to wayfarer or settler, Indian or white, the chief market place in central Indiana for Indian tribes of the region.[25]

4.

Meanwhile, in 1802 his brother John had made a journey to the seat of government at Washington with some Indian chiefs for whom he acted as interpreter. They had passed through Goshen where the aged David Zeisberger still lived among his Indians, and John saw again the man who had baptized him as a babe.[26] This journey must have had a profound effect upon the young backwoodsman. It opened his eyes to a new and more refined way of living. It suggested to him another route over which his furs could be sent with less danger and perhaps with better profit than through Detroit. He was doubtless impressed with the growing power and the stability of the government of the United States. To come in contact with two such men as the devout Moravian missionary and the philosopher-president was an unforgettable experience. The Indian life was full of fascination and charm for him, but his eyes were opened as his mother's had been before him, to the advantages of another environment. In the long return journey he had much time for reflection.

The following year he was able to give information concerning a French spy who was visiting the Indian towns with hostile intentions against the United States. Had Thomas Jefferson aroused a latent patriotism in the heart of John Conner? From this time on he is allied with the forces of organized society. In this year (1803) or the year following, he decided to leave the town of Buckongahelas and go to the southeastern part of Indiana which had been ceded to the United States in 1795. He saw the advisability of locating upon and acquiring for trading purposes land to which the Indian title had been extinguished. The laws at this period governing the Indian trade were very lax. Licenses were not required of those who operated in the country where the Indian title had been extinguished,[27] and in his new location Conner would have certain advantages over the traders living in the Indian country. He could sell spirits without restriction, while the latter were prohibited from doing so.

Conner's Delaware wife and a small band of Indians accompanied him to this new location. He established a store three-fourths of a mile above Big Cedar Grove Creek near the present site of Cedar Grove village on the very fringe of the white population in the Whitewater Valley.[28] John Conner was a shrewd man. He was now established just outside the Indian country, accessible to the friendly Indian tribes and advantageously posted at the entrance of a section soon to be opened to settlement. A thin stream of white settlers was already moving up the valley. John Conner's store, like his brother William's trading post, became a landmark for both Indians and settlers. It was a log structure on ground that is said to have been since washed away by the Whitewater. It had puncheon floors and puncheon doors. At one corner stood a rain barrel, and inside the cabin a hominy mortar had a prominent place. It is said to have been a custom to toughen the Indian babies of the household by ducking them in the rain barrel, sometimes in weather cold enough to film the water with ice.[29]

This early trading post had its share of rough, frontier incidents. One day, it is said, an Indian visitor whom drink had made garrulous began bragging about his achievements. To the consternation and fury of the bystanders, he ended his recital by boasting of the scalping of a young white girl. As he proceeded with the lurid details there was a restless movement and a showing of knives, but an old gray-haired scout raised his hand to the indignant throng and said with significant emphasis, "Wait." When the Indian had finished drinking and had closed his tale, he was allowed to stumble from the post unharmed, but, the story ends, "the Indian was never seen again; none of the white men at the post ever questioned whither he had gone."[30]

Two Frenchmen, Michael Peltier (sometimes abbreviated or nicknamed "Pilkey") and Charles Telier, at an early date (traditionally 1804-1805) had a store just above the present site of Brookville. This store was apparently not competitive, but co-operative, with Conner's Post just a few miles south. As Conner's activities gradually took on a wider range as scout and interpreter for General Harrison and these duties involved long absences from home, he secured "Pilkey" to manage his post for these periods. Gradually it came to be known as the "French Store," the "Conner and Pilkey" or simply "Pilkey's." There is no record that Conner had any interest in the French store at Brookville.[31]

5.

William Conner collected furs from the Indians, dressed, stretched, and packed them. These skins were from the beaver, otter, raccoon, fox, mink, muskrat, skunk, wildcat, fisher (kind of marten), panther, deer, and an occasional bear or wolf. The fur of the weasel, the groundhog, and the opossum was used by the natives in their dress, but was not valuable in trade. Raccoons were especially plentiful. An Indian often

caught as high as five or six hundred in a winter. Indian
women helped with this catch.   These skins brought from
37½ cents to 40 cents and sometimes $1.00 a skin. The otter
and the full-grown bearskins brought the highest amounts,
from $4.00 to $5.00 each, although sometimes bearskins
brought only $1.50 to $2.00. One pound of beaver hair sold
for $1.00 to $1.25.   Deer- or buckskins brought $1.00 each,
but doeskins were less, from 67 cents to 75 cents. The fox,
cat, and fisher skins sold for 50 cents to 67 cents, mink for 50
cents, and full-grown muskrats for 25 cents. These were the
prices the traders paid to the Indians.

The Indians were adept in preparing these skins. Incisions
were made around the mouth and in the head, and the body
of a small animal such as otter, muskrat, or mink, was drawn
through these openings, which left the skin inside out. An oak
or hickory hoop, very strong, was thrust into the skin and then
it was stretched tightly over it. The method used for deerskins was different. The hide was pierced by little holes along
the edges into which strips of tough bark were run. Strings
attached to these were fastened to trees or saplings on all sides
and drawn taut. All the meat and fat had been carefully removed and the skins well cleaned, before stretching. The coon-
skins were made almost rectangular by sewing the skin of the
forelegs to the edges of the skin of the neck and head which
made the fore part of the skin the same width as the hind part.
Other skins were also prepared in this way. It is said that no
"white man could fix them as nicely as the Indians did." Beaver skins were sold by weight, and traders found that they were
not cleaned so well, since the added fat increased the weight.
Sometimes a piece of stone or metal was found tucked away
between the skins. The Indians were shrewd bargainers and
knew the value of their wares. The test of a pelt was in the
color of the skin side, not the fur. If yellow, the animal had
been killed at the proper season and the fur was fine. If bluish,
the skin was poor. These furs were packed in bales at the
trading post by a rude press operated by wedges. Each kind
of peltry was put in a separate bale. William Conner sent them
on pack horses to his brother. John, in turn, sent supplies of
all kinds to William to use in his trade with the Indians.[32]

These supplies were carried over an Indian trail which led

for sixty miles through thick woods, along banks of creeks, over hills and sometimes through swampy lowlands. Pack horses, heavily laden, were sure footed, but it was much more difficult for the pedestrian. After frequent rains he would sometimes find himself knee deep in mud. Old logs and fallen trees obstructed the path, as well as thick undergrowth. The Indian on the trail carried his gun on his shoulder, his toma-hawk and knife slung at his side, and a piece of dried deer meat fastened over his shoulder. Thus comparatively free from impedimenta, he was agile in leaping over all obstacles. This feat was not easily achieved by the newly arrived settler, who was forced to take a roundabout way and was likely to lose his sense of direction. At various intervals there were hunters' huts made from the bark of trees, but no white settlements. Cincinnati, the depot for trading supplies, was only thirty-five miles from Cedar Grove and the journey thence could easily be made by water along the Ohio and the Big Miami River until the mouth of Whitewater River was reached, thence up White-water to Cedar Grove.[33]

In addition to his trading post, John Conner established a mill at his Cedar Grove location about 1807, where the big dam stood in 1845. Only one mill had been built prior to his in the Whitewater Valley—John Hagerman's mill in Bennett's Bottom. Neighbors of John Conner at this period were John Lafforge and Anthony Halberstadt. The latter was one of the Hessians taken prisoner by General Washington at Trenton. An early settler in this region, doubtless well known to Conner, was Jabez Winship, who came from Connecticut with his wife Hannah (Forsythe) and his five children about 1805. They were Baptists and active in the affairs of the Little Cedar Grove Baptist church. His young seventeen-year-old daughter, Lavina, later became the wife of John Conner.[34]

The Grouseland Treaty of 1805 considerably reduced the hunting grounds of the Indians, for it opened a large area in southeastern Indiana to white settlement, pushing the Indians farther north and curtailing the traffic in furs. At this time Harrison made an attempt to purchase an additional strip west of the Greenville Treaty line, but was prevented by the obstin-acy of one of the principal chiefs. John Conner, in order to retain his strategic position at the boundary between white settlements and Indian territory, decided to move his trading post into this area, which he rightly anticipated would soon be ceded to the government. Up the river about twenty miles he went in 1808 and there, a little above the present site of Connersville, he established himself with his Indian family. It was a primitive location in which there were still numerous Indians and which was accessible to many more. Wild animals—an occasional bear or panther—roamed through it at will.[35]

An eccentric neighbor was Betty Frazier, the subject of many stories and legends. The wife of a helpless cripple, she had squatted with her little family on the land across the river from Conner, hoping to make enough to buy her land.[36]

In 1809 the famous (from the Indian viewpoint, infamous) Treaty of Fort Wayne was signed, by the terms of which the land locally known as the Twelve Mile Purchase was ceded by the Indians to the government. With the conclusion of this treaty Conner could look forward to acquiring settler's rights, which could be ripened into a title when land entries were permitted. This occurred in 1811.

William Conner, following a different policy, was maintaining his trading post on lands where the Indian titles had not been extinguished. William, however, was the husband of Chief Anderson's daughter, and that chief was influential throughout the White River villages. He was rearing a large family of lusty half-breeds and apparently he was assimilated into the tribe. At any rate he did not seem to be concerned about land titles at that time.

The transition period in the lives of William and John Conner was approaching. The War of 1812 was impending, and the results of that war were to bring momentous changes in their lives. They accepted and faced with courage a new situation with new responsibilities.

CHAPTER V

Interpreters and Scouts

THE principal cause of violent conflicts between settlers and Indians during the colonization of Indian territory, was land. The Indians claimed its ownership. The United States government assumed title as a result of the War of the Revolution and coveted it for the expanding population of the new republic. Lack of scrupulousness in dealing with the Indians increased the irritation.

Spain, France, and England in their successive conquests of parts of America now within the limits of the United States, regarded it as fundamental that the title of the soil was in the sovereign state which had made the discovery or conquest. There was no general nor uniform rule as to the rights of occupancy of native tribes, each sovereign state treating these rights in its own way. After the War of the Revolution, the United States, to whom much of this land passed, held as a theory, while granting to the Indians the right of occupancy, that the absolute right to the soil was vested in the government. For practical purposes, however, to ease the process of securing lands from the natives, the Indian claim to ownership of the soil was not questioned. It was, in fact, tacitly admitted, and language to that effect occurred in treaties made with them. As instruments to secure Indian titles, the tribes were regarded as sovereign nations. Formal treaties were made with them for cessions of land under the treaty-making provisions of the Federal Constitution. This was the practice, especially as to important treaties, beginning with the Wayne treaty at Greenville, Ohio, in 1795. Governor Harrison used and approved this method.[1] Indeed, it was the only expedient one, for if the government had treated the Indians as occupants merely and ignored them as owners, it would have ignited earlier the fires of war.

The admission by the United States that the Indians were owners of the land was not, however, satisfactory to their leaders. Cessions of land made by individual tribes followed one another so rapidly that far-seeing Indian leaders were alarmed at the great areas of land which were passing from their control. Joseph Brant, the famous Mohawk chief, as early as 1786 advanced the doctrine that all Indian lands were held in common by all the tribes and that no single tribe had the right of alienation. This theory of common ownership was to be used years later by another great Indian leader.[2]

2.

A great part of the present state of Indiana was involved in the dispute. It was a beautiful, level country unbroken by mountains but traversed by rivers which occasionally found a channel through slightly rolling country to the plains beyond. Much of it was covered with thick forests of walnut, poplar, maple, linden, cherry, and sycamore. There were broad meadows with only stubble undergrowth of bushes. The natural plains had been fertilized through the centuries by decomposed vegetation. The top soil of the woods lay deep with rotted leaves. On these plains, as in the dark, damp recesses of the woodlands, nature from the beginning had been enriching the earth. Its transformation into productive fields needed only the axe and the plow.[3]

That this fertile country in 1801 was almost wholly occupied by Indians gave President Jefferson concern. He envisaged the land divided into farms and cultivated by both white and Indian settlers, living peacefully together. He even suggested mixed marriages so that the blood of the Indians would run in the veins of the white people.[4] This suggestion was rooted in Jefferson's desire for a settled state which would be another strong prop in the West for the expanding union.

In June, 1802, he instructed Harrison to persuade the Indians, if possible, to transfer to the United States the cessions which they had made to the Wabash and Illinois companies. In February of the next year, he stressed the necessity of procuring cessions of large tracts of land from the Indian occupants to be subdivided into small farms. He feared the effect of the retrocession of Louisiana by Spain to France, from which might come mounting troubles for the United States. Harrison was accordingly given a general commission to treat with the Indians to the end that they become civilized or remove beyond the Mississippi. "The crisis is pressing,"

Jefferson wrote. "Whatever can now be obtained, must be obtained quickly. The occupation of New Orleans, hourly expected, by the French, is already felt like a light breeze by the Indians. You know the sentiments they entertain of that nation. Under the hope of their protection, they will immediately stiffen against cessions of land to us. We had better therefore do at once what can now be done."[5]

Harrison acted promptly and efficiently. His first effort was at Vincennes where an Indian conference was held September 17, 1802, in which the chiefs of the Potawatomi, Kickapoo, Eel River, Kaskaskia, Wea, and Piankashaw Indians took part. Negotiations were opened, but final action was postponed until the next spring.[6]

The Vincennes agreement had a very unfriendly reception by most of the Indians. The Miami refused to follow the lead of their chiefs, Little Turtle[7] and Richardville, who were designated to carry out the agreement, and it was decided by the protesting chiefs of the Delawares and Miami to take the matter to President Jefferson. In December, 1802, Tetepachsit with eleven other Delaware chiefs, the representatives of ten other nations, and John Conner as interpreter, appeared before President Jefferson at Washington and presented their address with a protest by Buckongahelas against the validity of the Vincennes agreement. Their grievance was the occupation of their lands by white settlers. The president replied that the agreement signed by the tribal chiefs had fixed the boundary of the land ceded. Under the rules of all nations such an agreement was binding on all members. This statement was short of an answer as far as the Delawares were concerned, for they had not signed the agreement. The president added, as a sop to Indian feelings, that if any white person settled on Indian lands he would be subject to punishment and should be seized by the Indians and turned over to any officer of the United States for punishment.[8]

Shortly after the failure of the delegation to secure presidential intervention against the treaty, Harrison took steps toward its ratification. The Indians opposed him vehemently. When the chiefs were asked to attend a conference at Fort Wayne on June 7, 1803, to which many came, they showed a rebellious spirit. Buckongahelas interrupted Harrison's presentation of his reasons for ratification and hotly declared that nothing done at Vincennes was binding. The Shawnee were insolent and left the meeting. Little Turtle, however, aided in securing ratification. Finally, with much grumbling, the Miami, Kickapoo, Potawatomi, Eel River, Wea, Piankashaw, and Shawnee chiefs signed the treaty and a very large tract of land and valuable salt-lick springs came into possession of the United States. Buckongahelas, notwithstanding his protest to Jefferson and his vehement opposition to ratification at this meeting, also signed the treaty, together with his brother Delawares, Tetepachsit and Hockingpomsga. It was of such acts of tribal chiefs that Tecumseh complained to Harrison in 1810.[9]

3.

Harrison realized that to accomplish the plans of the president it was important for him to have on his staff competent interpreters and scouts; men who knew and possessed the confidence of the influential tribes such as the Delawares, the Miami, and the Shawnee; men he could trust for their integrity and judgment. On his return to Vincennes after negotiating the Treaty of Fort Wayne, his attention was directed to John Conner by an interesting incident. There came to Vincennes a man, well mannered, and apparently well educated, but poor in appearance, who was thought to be a French spy. His mysterious appearance corroborated rumors that agents of the French or Spanish governments were trying to encourage hostile measures against the United States. Information concerning him came from a Miami Indian, Long Beard, and from John Conner, a young man who was described to Harrison as living with the Delawares on White River. The spy got away before Harrison received orders to arrest him, but the incident left upon his mind a favorable impression of Conner's acumen and loyalty.[10] At this time Joseph Barron was the governor's chief interpreter, and in his judgment and loyalty Harrison had full confidence. It was well to keep John Conner in mind. He needed men of his type.

When the Louisiana Purchase was completed in December of this year and all the French and Spanish aggressions had subsided, Jefferson had a new vision, this time concerning the settlement of all territory west of the Mississippi, which was included in this purchase, as part of the foundation of a future great republic. The policy of acquiring Indian lands was therefore urged as vigorously as possible. In about fourteen months after the Fort Wayne Treaty of 1803 which ratified the Vincennes agreement, Harrison made four more separate treaties for cessions of land in Indiana: with the Eel River and other tribes, August 7, 1803; with the Delawares, August 18, 1804; with the Piankashaw, August 27, 1804. The Delawares relinquished their rights to the large tract in southern and southwestern Indiana in what is commonly known as the "Pocket." The Piankashaw gave up their rights to the same tract by their treaty. The fourth treaty, held at Grouseland, was concluded with the Delawares and other tribes on August 21, 1805. The land ceded by this treaty was in the south and southeastern part of Indiana. Title to this region had now passed from the Indians to the United States. John Conner was for the first time appointed sworn interpreter and acted with Joseph Barron in connection with the Grouseland Treaty. By the close of the year 1805 Harrison had acquired approximately 56,240,000 acres of land in what is now Indiana, Illinois, Wisconsin, and Missouri. Unwittingly, Jefferson and Harrison in their zeal to acquire more land for the United States had laid the fuse which would soon ignite sporadic and bloody reprisals and ultimately an organized Indian uprising.[11]

4.

Aware of this rising indignation among the Indians, Harrison desisted from his efforts to acquire more land for a period of four years. He was not displeased when he heard that the Delawares had determined to remove beyond the Mississippi,[12] for he realized very clearly that Indiana Territory could not remain part Indian and part Anglo-Saxon.[13] If the two races were not amalgamated, one or the other would have to be eliminated. Nor did Harrison have any confidence that a chain of forts or even a cordon of one hundred thousand men would protect the settlements. Efforts to extinguish title of more Indian lands must eventually be renewed.

Since Jefferson shared these views, authority was given Harrison in July, 1809, to arrange for a treaty with the Indians at Fort Wayne in September of that year. Chief Anderson accompanied the Delawares to this gathering, with John Conner to act for the second time as their interpreter. Chief Winamac came with the Potawatomi; Little Turtle arrived late with a band of Miami and Potawatomi, but Richardville, the principal Miami chief, though he was especially sent for, did not appear. Minor chiefs were present from each of the above tribes and from the Eel River Indians. Other interpreters besides Conner were William Wells, Joseph Barron, and Abraham Ash. It was a difficult negotiation. The Miami resisted for days any argument which would induce them to sell their land. Their young men arrived loaded with British goods and buttressed by British warnings against the treaty. Harrison labored untiringly, day and night, arranging separate meetings, using all his powers of eloquence, persuasion, and knowledge of the Indian character. More convincing than any argument was his power to withhold the annuities until a treaty had been concluded. On September 30 the Indians capitulated, and a few days later the annuities were distributed. The land conveyed to the United States amounted to nearly three million acres in eastern and southern Indiana.[14]

It was about this time that a story born of falsehood and nurtured by Harrison's critics and enemies, and by the British, was circulated to the effect that he was securing lands from the Indians for his own advantage and that President Jefferson, in fact, had not wanted them. Harrison did not try to answer this charge, but when some of the chiefs expressed a desire to meet the new father (Madison) at Washington, he decided such an expedition would do him no harm and might mollify the Indians. He appointed John Conner to accompany them in 1809 and furnished him with drafts on the secretary of war to pay the expenses of the trip. For various reasons, this expedition was abandoned.[15] The winter before a group of leading chiefs of the northwestern Indians had been summoned to Washington to hear the farewell admonitions of the aged Jefferson before he retired from the presidency.[16] It is probable that John Conner accompanied Beaver and Captain Hendrick of the Delawares on this trip, although there is no record to that effect. By this time he was accepted as an interpreter for the Delawares and possessed not only their confidence but also that of Harrison.

5.

Indian opposition to white intrusion had been handicapped by the lack of a leader of sufficient ability to marshal the tribes effectively against the policies of Jefferson and Harrison. But now such a leader appeared. Tecumseh, a Shawnee chief, was uniting the tribes in a common cause against a common enemy. He was assisted by his brother, Tenskwatawa, called the Prophet, whom Jefferson characterized as more "rogue than fool."[17] He had a specious tongue and a lying heart and gained control over the Indians by pretending to have supernatural powers. Tecumseh, on the other hand, was a brave, talented and resourceful leader.

Harrison's attention was first directed to these Indians when he received news of the burning of Tetepachsit in 1806. He rebuked the Delawares and ordered them to drive the Prophet from their town, because he saw in this ugly incident evidence of a carefully laid plot to get rid of the old Indian chiefs who were favorable to the United States and to reorganize the tribe on the basis of another allegiance. He did not realize that it marked the first step in a more ambitious scheme for an Indian confederacy. When this policy was jeopardized by the older Indian chiefs, Tenskwatawa conceived the diabolical plan of putting them to death on the accusation of witchcraft. By 1809 the two brothers had gained a great deal of influence, if not an ascendancy, over the minds of the Delawares; the Kickapoo were already completely under their control. With Little Turtle and the Miami they had been less successful, and the Potawatomi chief, Winamac, opposed them, thereby marking himself for destruction.[18]

6.

Not long after the Fort Wayne Treaty of 1809 rumblings of discontent among the Indians became audible. It is said that the cession made by this treaty "amounted to a declaration of war between Tecumseh and Harrison." The Wyandot joined the Shawnee and the war spirit in all the tribes was so aroused that many warriors left their own tribes to join

Tecumseh. Among those sent by Harrison to investigate the conditions and temper of the Indians was John Conner. He and other scouts, Francis Vigo, Toussaint Dubois, William Prince, Joseph Barron, Michael Brouillette, and Pierre La Plante all made the same report of uneasiness and belligerency among the Indians.[19]

The sudden display of power by Tecumseh and his brother alarmed Harrison. It had been a source of satisfaction to him that a line of peaceful Delaware towns stretched along the banks of White River across the central part of the Indian country. He knew something of their history through his secretary of the territory, John Gibson, who had encountered them and the Conner family at Schoenbrunn, Ohio, as early as 1775. The Delawares during the first years of the Revolution had held aloof from the British. White Eyes, their noted chief, had fought on the side of the Americans. They were the last tribe to surrender their neutrality. Always their Moravian teachers had instilled in them the virtues of peace and a settled life. Harrison had noted with approval that Moravian missionaries had again settled among the Delawares in Indiana and that the requests of the latter to the government had been for agricultural implements, help in building rail fences,[20] and for teachers. The tribe was respected by all other tribes and wielded an influence out of proportion to its numbers. His trusted young scout, John Conner, with his brother William lived among them.

In view of these years of friendly relationship, Harrison was more distressed than he cared to admit when the upstart Shawnee brothers opened their campaign in the Delaware towns. To be sure, John Conner had assured him two years ago, after bringing him a letter from Wells which intimated that British influence was behind Tecumseh, that there was no immediate danger of hostilities, although the Chippewa, Ottawa, and some Potawatomi were disaffected. His suspicion of the Prophet was so aroused that he sent Conner with a message to the Shawnee in Ohio demanding that they send away Tenskwatawa and his Indians. He suggested that they might go to the Lakes where they could "hear the British more distinctly." Conner brought back the Prophet's categorical denial that he had sent for any Indians to come to him or that he had any dealings with the British.[21]

In the spring of 1808 Tenskwatawa left Greenville and settled with his band on the banks of the Wabash. From that time on John Conner was employed increasingly by Harrison as his emissary to the Prophet. Thievery was increasing under the encouragement of the treacherous and wily Shawnee, and Conner was sent to look for some stolen horses. While he was not very successful in recovering the stolen property, he was able to carry back to the governor news that the Prophet had in his town about thirty or forty Shawnee and about ninety warriors from the Potawatomi, Chippewa, Ottawa, and Winnebago.[22] The Prophet's messages were full of lies and hypocrisy which increased Harrison's suspicions of him. The Delawares likewise grew alarmed, and acting upon the advice of Conner made protests in person to the Shawnee leaders. They were silenced by the eloquence of Tecumseh, and even Harrison was half convinced by the Prophet's protestations of friendship during a visit to Vincennes in 1808.

7.

As time passed, however, the activities of the Shawnee leaders grew in scope and power. In fact each month brought news that the Prophet's teachings were only a hypocritical cloak hiding a well-organized conspiracy which was already under way. It also became clear that the British were furnishing them with ammunition.[23]

The outlook was black indeed, if Harrison could not find one tribe in which he could put his trust. It is evident that the Conner brothers exerted a strong influence to hold the Delawares neutral at this stage. In May, 1810, John Conner brought to the governor a Delaware chief who reported that the Delawares were sending a delegation to the Indian council to dissuade the other tribes from listening to the Prophet. This was heartening tidings. Back to the Delawares he sent Conner with a speech in which he pointed out that destruction of the tribes would be the only result of a revolt against the United States and that war would endanger even friendly tribes because of the "difficulty of discriminating friends from foes." He besought the chiefs to send fresh instructions to their representatives at the Indian council, remonstrating against war.[24] Thus did Harrison, before taking up the gage of battle, endeavor to erect a bulwark of sentiment against the impending conflict.

A few months later, Tecumseh, who had not yet openly assumed leadership of his movement, appeared for the first time at Vincennes. This was the first time since the Treaty of Greenville that Harrison had seen him, and he now recognized him as the "Moses" of his family. Tecumseh, on this occasion, boldly advanced the doctrine set forth by Brant in 1786. Indian lands were held in common, and no single tribe had the right of alienation. Power was vested not in the chiefs, but in the warriors of all the tribes in council. It was a revolutionary theory and the British, recognizing its potency as an irritant between the Indians and Americans, encouraged its adoption. It was strongly supported by Matthew Elliot, who was still running true to form.[25] Tecumseh, who had by this time acquired the leadership once held by Pontiac and by the now aging Little Turtle, adopted the policy of his famous predecessors, which was to unite the Indians against the wrongful usurpation of the land by the whites.

8.

The year 1811 was a time of preparation on both sides for a conflict which now seemed inevitable. The spring and summer were full of minor incidents which served to fan the flames. An annoying policy of the Shawnee leaders was to ignore, if they did not actually encourage, depredations of bands of outlaw Indians whose passions they had aroused and whose actions they could not restrain without antagonizing them. Intimidation of the settlers, thefts, and murders became frequent. John Conner, who was in Vincennes in the spring of that year as a witness in the General Court, was again employed by Harrison to investigate these occurrences.[26]

Harrison, in an effort to secure a workable system of Indian supervision in the territory without giving William Wells too much authority, recommended to the secretary of war that there should be no principal agent for the Indians but that "Wells should be sub-agent for the Miamies and Eel River Tribes . . . [John] Shaw Sub-agent for the Pota-

watimies and Conner for the Delawares." It is evident that
Harrison had full confidence in the latter by this time.
Suspicion had been aroused against Conner earlier than this
because of his close association with Wells, but from now on
he ranked among Harrison's dependable scouts.[27] Men like
Conner were greatly needed by Harrison, and he had great
difficulty in finding them. There were many avenues by
which scouts and interpreters could profit at the expense of
the Indians and of the United States government. Temptations to use their understanding of the Indian languages, customs, and character to further their own ends or in repayment
for British gold were plentiful. The United States government was still new; Harrison must often have wondered if
steady loyalty had been generated in the breasts of those whose
earlier allegiance had been to some other nation—perhaps
France or England.

By August, 1811, Harrison had reached the conclusion
that an expedition would have to be made against the hostile
Indians if orderly government was to be maintained in the
territory. The settlers were fearful, the Indians restless, the
Prophet openly insolent. Tecumseh had undertaken a journey
to the southern tribes shortly after his visit to Harrison. There
remained no doubt that unless the Prophet and his band were
humiliated or dispersed very soon, defensive measures would
have to be maintained throughout the winter, a situation which
would "greatly distress the frontier."

Harrison still hoped that a display of military force would
be sufficient without resort to battle. At the time that he was
preparing his expedition against Prophet's Town he made one
last attempt at conciliation. He sent for the Delaware chiefs
to meet him on the march, for he wanted them and other
peaceably inclined chiefs to make a final effort to dissuade
the Prophet from the plan he and Tecumseh were rapidly con-
summating. John Conner probably bore this message; however that may be, he was with the Delaware chiefs when they
set out from their towns on October 6, 1811. William Conner
may have been with them also. When they were only a few
miles on their way to join Harrison, they were met by an
arrogant delegation from the Prophet, and a threatening demand that they join in a war on the United States. The Dela-

ware chiefs listened without reply, but their actions were eloquent. Quietly they designated four of their number to accompany John Conner to meet Harrison as they had promised, while those remaining set out on the trail to Prophet's Town to face the leader and try to persuade him to give up his plan. They scorned to discuss the matter with intermediaries. The sincerity of the Delawares is quite apparent in this incident.

When Conner reached Harrison, he declared that the Delawares now believed that the Prophet was ready to make an attack and that his followers were sure of victory. The governor, still hopeful of peace, decided to await the result of the visit of the Delaware chiefs at Fort Harrison, the new post in process of construction on the Wabash. Three weeks later the Delaware chiefs arrived from Prophet's Town with a story of insults and contemptuous treatment from the Indians at that place, and tales of fanatic zeal finding expression in fantastic rites and dances. Still anxious to avoid a conflict, the governor sent another delegation, composed this time of Miami and Potawatomi, to make certain demands on the Prophet, but this delegation did not return.[28] Harrison now faced arbitrament by the sword.

9.

The army began its march from Fort Harrison to Prophet's Town under the greatest apprehension, for it was rumored that the Indians greatly outnumbered the soldiers. Harrison constantly hoped that he might be met by the delegation he had sent to the Prophet. When the army arrived on November sixth within five or six miles of the town, the interpreters, among whom was John Conner, were placed with the advance guards to see what could be done by parley, but the only answers they received were insulting gestures.[29] Harrison delayed action as long as he could, still hoping his delegation would appear bearing good news. The Indians attacked the sleeping camp of soldiers at four thirty o'clock on the morning of November seventh.

The Battle of Tippecanoe was fought about seven months before war with Great Britain was declared. Harrison hoped that an effective victory over the Indians would bring them to their senses and show the futility of revolting against the

United States. But he had miscalculated the depth of the Indian resentment to the land policy, the strength of the Indian leadership, and the determination of Great Britain to make use of both of these elements to further her own cause. The battle, victory for the United States though it was, instead of closing a chapter in Indian warfare, really opened the War of 1812 in the western country. Depredations and murders by the Indians increased. As Harrison feared, it became very difficult to prevent suspicion from falling upon innocent and friendly tribes. The hostile Indians seemed to delight in raids in the vicinity of the neutral Delawares and Miami in order to implicate them and thus force them into the conflict. There was a series of death-dealing forays in April, 1812, among which was one upon the Driftwood Fork of White River.[30]

The situation of the settlers became critical. Families abandoned their homes. Such great distress and alarm prevailed in the eastern and southern parts of the territory that it looked as though these sections might be depopulated. The Delawares were accused of complicity in these murders, but Harrison, who was fully aware of the strategic importance of keeping them friendly, recommended to those settlements which the Delawares had frequented "as much forbearance as possible towards that tribe," because they had "ever performed with punctuality and good faith their engagements with the United States, and as yet" there was "not the least reason to doubt their fidelity." It was also certain "that if they should be forced to join the other tribes in war, from their intimate knowledge of the settlements they would be able to do more mischief than any other tribe."[31]

As another measure to protect the Delawares and keep them friendly and loyal, Harrison sent a special messenger, Major Davis Floyd, to suggest that they remove to friends on the Mississippi or join the loyal Shawnee living on the Auglaize River in Ohio. Soon after Floyd's departure on this mission a Delaware Indian brought letters to Harrison from John Conner and Captain Hendrick, assuring him that the Delawares had no hand in the late murders. A speech from the Delaware chiefs also protested their innocence of any participation in these crimes. Recalling the "uncommon faithfulness" of this tribe, Harrison's anxiety deepened, for the evidence was strong against them and the settlers were greatly outraged.[32]

A letter which throws some light upon the situation was written to Harrison on May 6, 1812, by Colonel James Noble, an important political and military figure in the territory. He had received a letter from John Conner enclosing a speech by the Delaware chiefs at White River in which they reported that a hostile party of Potawatomi had passed the lower town of the Delawares in the direction of the settlements. Noble described the alarm of the settlers in the Whitewater region, many of whom were leaving the territory precipitately. To "quiet the minds of the people" who remained, Noble had stationed two detachments of rangers of fifteen men each at blockhouses on the West Fork of Whitewater. In his letter to Harrison, Noble said: "Upon the receipt of Conner's letter I wrote him, advising the Dellawares to keep clear of our settlements. They might be injured through mistake, and at the same time observed that confidence was placed in them by you sir."[33] The whole situation had by this time become so involved that Harrison, writing of these happenings to the secretary of war a week later, confessed that he was "perfectly at a loss as to the orders proper to be given in the present state of the country."[34]

The situation was likewise perplexing to John Conner. To maintain the neutral attitude of the Delaware nation was no easy task when other tribes were either on the warpath or about to take it because of the wrongs they believed had been done them by the alien white race. The Delawares, however, for the most part remained inoffensive, although a few joined the Miami at their Mississinewa towns. It is notable that at an important Indian council held on the Mississinewa River, May 15, 1812, at which Tecumseh defended himself against the charge that he and his brother had instigated the attacks on the white settlements, the Delaware spokesman interrupted him: "We have not met at this place to listen to such words. The red people have been killing the whites, the just resentment of the latter is raised against the former . . . . there is no time for us to tell each other you have done this, and you have done that; if there was, we would tell the prophet that both the red and white people had felt the bad effect of his counsels.

Let us all join our hearts and hands together, and proclaim peace through the land of the red people."[35]

While John Conner was interceding for one group of Delawares, his brother William was exercising a steadying influence in another direction. A significant incident took place either before or after the large Indian council referred to above. On this occasion Tecumseh was holding a council with the Delaware Indians at the mouth of Fall Creek near the present site of Indianapolis when young Captain Zachary Taylor reached there with a company of three hundred men and prepared to encamp. When William Conner, who was with the Delawares, heard of the proximity of the troops, he sent word to Captain Taylor to put the creek between his camp and the Indians. Taylor complied, and doubtless took other precautions which Conner's message may have intimated were necessary. This was perhaps Tecumseh's last chance to appeal to the Delawares alone. He recognized his opportunity and used every resource of his oratory to arouse them to a frenzy of anger against the Americans. Had it not been for the calm, wise, persuasiveness of William Conner and Chief Anderson, the incident might have had a tragic sequel. The Delawares, however, swayed by their trusted leaders, dispersed and returned to their villages.[36]

About the first of June, Floyd, Harrison's messenger to the Delawares, returned from the Delaware towns with the report that this tribe was "entirely to be depended upon," which confirmed the assurances John Conner had given Harrison the previous April. After the expedition against the Miami towns on the Mississinewa in December, 1812, the Delawares moved to Ohio, near the town of Piqua. Here they were under the protection of the United States government.[37] Any responsibility for their welfare and for their neutrality was thus lifted from the shoulders of John Conner.

Governor Harrison had not realized that the series of treaties which he had so ably negotiated would precipitate war in the western country. When the conflict seemed inevitable, he tried by every means in his power to avert it or postpone it. When all means short of war failed, he endeavored to keep neutral as many tribes as possible. In the end only the Delawares could be thus accounted, but this he considered an im-

portant achievement. A strong factor in accomplishing this
was the influence and the work of John Conner and his brother
William, both of whom served as scouts and interpreters for
Harrison.

CHAPTER VI

THE WAR OF 1812 IN THE OHIO VALLEY

ON JUNE 18, 1812, war between Great Britain and the United States was declared. The officially proclaimed purpose of this war was to redress the wrongs charged against Great Britain in violating the rights of the United States and its citizens on the high seas. The administration at Washington planned the invasion of Canada. It was the purpose, as appears from the debates in Congress, not only to invade but to conquer and annex Canada.[1]

In the Ohio Valley internal Indian conflicts had retarded both the increase in population and the growth of white settlements. This condition was more extensive and intensive in Indiana than in Ohio or Kentucky. For the settlers the issue was to evict the hostile Indians and to make the frontier safe. For the British the dispute involved territory and retention of control of the important fur trade. As the Canadian fur traders were aggressive and powerful,[2] it became the policy of the British to acquire the friendship of the Indians and enlist them as allies. It seems that these clashing interests could only be resolvable now by war.

Tecumseh at once went to Malden in Canada to join the British. His opportunity had come to rehabilitate the Indian confederacy which had been almost shattered by the Battle of Tippecanoe. All the tribes, save the Miami and Delawares, rallied to his standard.[3] Events disastrous for the United States followed swiftly. In July and August forts Mackinac, Dearborn (Chicago), and Detroit were surrendered to the British. American authority on the Lakes had vanished, and the American military boundaries in the Ohio Valley were thrown back to the Maumee and Wabash rivers, precariously held by Fort Wayne and Fort Harrison, respectively.[4]

These disasters stunned the Americans in the Ohio Valley. The Indians, led by Tecumseh, were now firmly attached to the British cause, and the Ohio Valley was exposed to attacks of combined British and Indian forces. The horrors of Indian warfare were again upon the settlers. Fighting Indians was

(68)

like fighting demons. They were almost as elusive and quite as fiendish. Kentucky and Ohio, which had emerged into statehood with able governors, began active preparations to prosecute the war with renewed vigor, for the burden of defending the borders of the Ohio Valley fell upon them.

2.

In 1812 Indiana was a territory with seven organized counties. The militia at this time showed a strength of between four and five thousand men. Several companies of rangers— made up from the militia—were sworn into the service of the United States, and Lieutenant Colonel William Hargrove was given command. The service of these troops was confined to the territory, and Hargrove was instructed to protect the settlers against Indian outrages as far as possible. In spite of these measures, a succession of small raids kept the borders in a state of dread.[5]

In August, 1812, before news of Hull's surrender was received, Kentucky gave Harrison a commission as major general of militia, in full command of an expedition to reinforce Detroit. Federal management of war in the West was unsatisfactory. The secretary of war was incompetent. Harrison and Brigadier General James Winchester both sought command of the regular forces in the Northwest, and were kept on tenterhooks by uncertainty concerning the final decision at Washington.[6]

Harrison, meanwhile, went on with his preparations for a movement on Detroit. In reducing his program to military essentials, he had to cut off its political excrescences. This was not so difficult, as the war party was now somewhat sobered. But while Detroit was his main objective, it was also necessary to watch carefully the movements and temper of the Indians in the Ohio, Indiana, and Illinois country. Attacks on the rear or flank of the army might prove disastrous. Nor was it conceivable that while the main campaign was being carried on, the settlements should be left unprotected. Harrison, therefore, had two immediate objects: first to relieve Detroit, and second to protect the settlements. He expected the militia and Hargrove's rangers to take care of the latter, leaving him free to plan his Detroit campaign. In the achievement of these purposes, the Conners had a part—John in Indiana, keeping an eye on the Indians there, and William with the attacking forces.

News that Detroit had surrendered reached Harrison late in August, and immediately afterward he learned that Fort Wayne was besieged by two hundred British regulars and a thousand Indians commanded by Colonel Matthew Elliot. Harrison's immediate concern was Fort Wayne. With some twenty-two hundred men he marched to its relief, reaching the fort on September 12. A week later he was relieved by General Winchester, temporarily victor in the struggle for command of the northwestern army. Harrison returned to Ohio, intending to organize a force to be used against the Prophet, but new instructions from Washington led him to take up again his plan for an expedition against Detroit. On September 24 he received word that command of the northwestern army had been placed in his hands. He took command with the rank of brigadier general in the regular army.[7]

Shortly after Harrison's arrival at St. Mary's, Ohio, he ordered Colonel William Jennings to open a road from St. Mary's to Fort Defiance by the way of the present town of Ottawa, a distance of about seventy miles. He also directed him to build a blockhouse midway between the two places. St. Mary's was the principal depot for army provisions, and at Fort Defiance provisions were also to be accumulated. One item of the instructions relates particularly to the Conners: "Some of the friendly Indians will be employed as guides, and Mr. William Conner will attend you and act as interpreter."[8] This is the first known written record of the activities of William Conner since 1802. For ten years he had been living on the banks of White River a life indistinguishable from the Indians except for his trading operations with his brother. How he first came to the attention of Harrison is not known, but undoubtedly the governor knew of him through John, for the relation between the two brothers was close. William seems to have been the less adventurous of the two brothers, less disturbed by events, more settled and reserved, with perhaps something of Indian stolidity. Harrison believed in his trustworthiness or he would not have chosen him as interpreter and leader of this band of friendly Indians. They were in all probability

Delaware friends and neighbors of William Conner, used to dealing with him at his post.[9]

3.

The month of September (1812), was full of unrest in Indiana Territory. While Harrison was preparing to relieve Fort Wayne, there occurred at Pigeon Roost settlement in Scott County one of the most dastardly Indian outrages in the history of the territory. It was incited by the Prophet. In one hour's time, one man, five women, and sixteen children were murdered and the cabins in which they met their deaths were burned. Some of the Delawares were suspected of being in the number of these raiders, most of whom were Shawnee.[10] Simultaneously a body of Winnebago, Kickapoo, Shawnee, Potawatomi, and a few Miami attacked Fort Harrison but were repulsed by a small garrison under the command of Captain Zachary Taylor.[11]

The Miami were now wavering in their neutrality. The success of the Americans in raising the siege of Fort Wayne, and rumors that General Hopkins of Kentucky was to lead an expedition into their territory, sent them hastening to St. Mary's in October, 1812, to beg peace from Harrison. As the latter had considerable evidence against them, they finally threw themselves upon the mercy of the president.[12] About this time, at least during that month, Harrison sent William Conner to the Mississinewa towns to watch the Miami. Conner listened to their discussions as to whether they should join the United States or Great Britain, and seeing the influence of Tecumseh swing the balance in favor of the British, went no further into the Indian country. John Johnston, Shawnee agent at Piqua, wrote to Harrison that it was "fortunate that Mr. Conner did not proceed farther than Massassineway, thereby leaving Gen. Hopkins at liberty to proceed up the Wabash."[13] This comment is enigmatical but thereby hangs an unusual tale of a good plan telescoped into a bad performance and ruined.

General Samuel Hopkins, honorably distinguished in the War of the Revolution, with an army of two thousand mounted Kentucky riflemen, started for the country lying on the borders of the Wabash River and the vicinity of the Illinois River to destroy the villages of the Kickapoo and other hostile Indians. After crossing the former river and making four or five days march beyond, the officers mutinied and the forces returned to Fort Harrison, where the army disbanded and returned home with the general following. He then organized another army of three regiments of Kentucky infantry to attack the rebuilt Prophet's Town. Small companies of regulars, rangers, and scouts accompanied them. The army reached its destination on November 19, destroyed the town, and returned to Fort Harrison. On the way back a detachment fell into an ambuscade with severe casualties.[14] Such were the inglorious ends of glorious beginnings that General Hopkins sheathed his sword and quit the service. The only military result from these two expeditions was greater encouragement to the Indians. William Conner learned of the fiasco from them.

The Indian unrest was increasing. John Conner brought word from the Delaware towns in Indiana to Piqua on October 10 that the Miami were urging the Delawares to join them in the war against the United States. They were active propagandists, sending nine messages to the Delawares in eighteen days, but the Delawares stood firm. In a letter of October 23, John Johnston reported to Harrison that he had sent John Conner to White River to watch the Delawares, to "keep them straight," to collect news and bring it to him. William Conner had been assigned to conduct some Delawares past Greenville, which had been the rendezvous of Tecumseh and the Prophet in 1808 and where there was evidently still some hostile Indian influence. Apparently in response to a request for a competent guide or agent, Johnston promised to send William Conner to Harrison as soon as he returned from Greenville, recommending him as better suited to Harrison's purpose than his brother John.[15]

It had now become imperative for Harrison to destroy the Miami towns on the Mississinewa as they were in a strategic situation for receiving provisions and assistance during the war and for the assembling of hostile tribes. The Miami had participated in the attack upon Fort Harrison and the siege of Fort Wayne in September of that year. Their warriors had also been involved in several of the murders of the settlers.

It is probable that William Conner joined Harrison at Franklinton, Ohio, now the site of Columbus, about October 25, 1812. A month later Harrison designated him as a guide for Lieutenant Colonel John B. Campbell's expedition to the Mississinewa, for he knew Conner was well acquainted with the country through which the expedition would pass. Harrison also suggested that John Conner, who was on the Whitewater in Indiana Territory, could easily be summoned, for Campbell could not be too well supplied with guides. John Conner did not accompany the expedition, but William was with the force which reached the Mississinewa on the seventeenth of December. On that day the troops killed eight warriors, took forty-two prisoners, and destroyed four villages. In this short skirmish Conner came close to death when his horse was shot down while he stood behind it. Before daylight next morning, about four o'clock, Conner was standing in front of the fire outside the Colonel's tent. As the commanding officer was inquiring how far it was to the Indian village, a bullet knocked a burning coal of fire from the log. Conner reached for his rifle and remarked that they did not need to go to the town to find the Indians. They were present. The battle had indeed begun. After a short and furious encounter the Miami retreated. Including the skirmish the day before, at least thirty-eight warriors were killed and more than forty prisoners were taken. The American loss was ten killed and forty-eight wounded.

Conner and the other scouts rendered such good service when the battle was at its height that they were cited for valor and good conduct. When Colonel Campbell learned from one of the prisoners that Tecumseh with six hundred warriors was but eighteen miles below him, he thought it prudent to return to headquarters, and they began the difficult march back.[16] The result of this battle was to break up the headquarters of the Miami in Indiana and place this tribe definitely in the ranks of the enemy.

4.

Harrison's army at the beginning of 1813 nominally consisted of ten thousand men, but the effective force was much less, probably six thousand three hundred infantry.[17] It was composed of untrained settlers, frontiersmen, brave but brooking no restraint, ignorant (some of his officers were unable to write their reports), and sometimes mutinous. The term of enlistment was short, which occasioned a rapidly changing personnel. Officers as well as men lacked a sense of serious responsibility. Kentucky volunteers were the best soldiers, but they would enlist only if allowed to serve on horseback, although infantry was badly needed. Roads were of the poorest. Provisions were often delayed. The rations were sometimes one half or none at all or of the poorest quality. Diseases of all kinds decimated the army, and graft honeycombed all the operations from the quartermaster's department even to the appointment of surgeons. The Indians were an uncertain quantity, not excepting those who professed loyalty. Much confusion existed because of the weak, vacillating war administration at Washington. In addition to the instability of the army and the deplorable conditions attending its transportation and supply, the difficulty of crossing the Black Swamp lay between Harrison and Detroit. This dreaded obstacle, stretching between Sandusky and Maumee rivers just below Lake Erie, was impassable unless sufficiently frozen to bear the weight of an army and its equipment.[18] The vast quagmire had filled the Moravian captives with terror during their journeyings in 1781.

In spite of these discouragements, Harrison had not, at the beginning of 1813, definitely given up the plan of an advance against Malden. The left wing of the army, under Winchester, began its advance toward the Rapids of the Miami (Maumee) on the last day of December, expecting to be met there by the central and right divisions. Winchester arrived on January 10 and encamped. Led on by appeals for protection from the inhabitants of Frenchtown, a village on the River Raisin about half way between the rapids and Detroit near the site of the present Monroe, Michigan, he dispatched a part of his forces to that point. This detachment was attacked the day after its arrival but succeeded in driving off the British. Winchester joined the detachment with reinforcements, but two days later, on January 22, 1813, the British fell upon the Americans in force and inflicted a disastrous defeat. Most of the American prisoners were massacred by the Indians, with the acquiescence of the British. The western people were shocked, indignant, and deeply stirred.

Harrison had by this time moved forward to the rapids, but poor transportation and inadequate supplies had combined to prevent his arrival in time to forestall the fiasco of the River Raisin. Harrison now had no doubt as to his course. Winchester had failed because his attack was premature and he lacked reinforcements. Harrison's military instincts told him that the campaign was not advisable at a time when the army would be far away—two hundred miles—from the base of supplies. He saw now that no attack could be successfully maintained until the Americans gained control of Lake Erie. Why heed the prodding of excited and uninformed critics and venture where disaster would likely await his army as it had Hull's and Winchester's? It was unfortunate that this winter campaign had been planned but it would make matters worse to attempt it under existing conditions. He repeatedly advised the War Department as to his conclusions. A long correspondence ensued, with the result that Harrison was left to his plans while the government took steps to regain control of Lake Erie. Fort Meigs was constructed at the rapids and Harrison went into winter quarters, intending to undertake a new advance in February.[19]

The policy of the British in the wars of the Revolution and of 1812 was to employ Indians, "very excellent surgeons," according to Captain Elliot,[20] and very helpful in devastating the settlements in the lost northwestern territory. The British command winked at their barbarous atrocities. This policy was not wholly approved in England but nevertheless it prevailed. Harrison was loath to incorporate the Indians in his army, for he knew and feared the horrors of their warfare. Besides he had a poor opinion of their dependableness. In the spring of 1813, however, apprehending British invasion, he began to enlist them by employing a band of thirty friendly Indians as scouts or spies. William Conner was with them. Later about two hundred Delawares and the same number of Wyandot, Seneca, and Mingo joined his army and rendered satisfactory service. Some of them remained with the army until the conclusion of the war in the Northwest. This employment proved to be helpful to the situation in Ohio and

Indiana, a tinder box in which the slightest provocation on the part of either Indians or whites would start a conflagration. Temporarily the settlers were satisfied as to Indian loyalty, and border friction was lessened.[21]

Encouraged by the results at River Raisin, the British and the Indians attacked Fort Meigs, on the safety of which depended the success of Harrison's campaign to retake Detroit. With nearly one thousand regulars and militia and twelve hundred Indians led by Tecumseh, gunboats on the river and artillery on land, General Proctor kept up heavy fire during the first eight days of May, but to no avail. The fort was staunchly built and withstood the assault. Some of the Americans who had been sent across the river to attack a British battery were taken prisoner. A number were tomahawked, but it is said that Tecumseh, proclaiming it a "disgrace to kill a defenseless prisoner," saved many from torture and death. The siege was a failure and Proctor retreated. The Indians—half of them from the Wabash—dispersed. This was the second battle in which William Conner had participated.[22] Another one was to follow which would be decisive in the northwestern territory.

5.

Shortly after Proctor's defeat at Fort Meigs there were rumors of a second invasion of Ohio by the British. Harrison had, during the year, collected military and artillery stores at Upper Sandusky. Unfortunately, they were unfortified and only eight hundred raw recruits were there to defend them. Fort Stephenson stood on the bank of the Sandusky, nine miles above its mouth at Sandusky Bay. It was exposed to the attacks of British gunboats sent up the river from Lake Erie. Harrison's headquarters were at Seneca, ten miles south of Fort Stephenson and about equally distant from Fort Meigs.

Harrison's chief concern now was the safety of his military supplies at Upper Sandusky. Should Proctor attack Fort Stephenson, which was nothing more than "an untenable stockade," it would probably fall, and Fort Seneca would be the next object of assault. In that event he would need all his resources and reinforcements to turn Proctor down the river to Lake Erie. Victorious, Proctor would proceed up the river and seize the supply depot at Upper Sandusky. Harrison had an alarming report that the woods around Camp Meigs were swarming with Indians, while Tecumseh was reported to be in command of two thousand of them somewhere between Fort Meigs and Fort Stephenson.

Would these savage hordes unite with Proctor's army as it passed out of the Bay of Sandusky and proceeded up the river? These were questions occurring and recurring to Harrison's mind, so much that he anticipated that these things might happen. Harrison's critics frequently said he took too much counsel of his fears. It was a tense moment. At such a time the human mind may become confused as to values and make mistakes in choice. That was what happened to Harrison.

At a conference with his staff officers, among whom was General Lewis Cass, who had joined him at Seneca in July, it was decided that Fort Stephenson should be abandoned. Accordingly, at ten o'clock on the night of July 29, he sent William Conner and two Indians from Seneca with a written order to Major George Croghan (a nephew of George Rogers Clark) to abandon and burn the fort and repair to Seneca. Conner lost his way. The unfamiliar trail was difficult to follow in the darkness. Hostile Indians were roaming through the wilderness and he may have had to abandon the trail at times to avoid them. He had been a prisoner of the Wyandot here, but he was a lad then and thirty-two years had elapsed.

The message was intended to be delivered that night, but Conner did not reach the fort until ten o'clock the next morning. When Croghan received the order he decided that it was more hazardous to retreat than to remain at the fort, and he sent a message by Conner saying, "we have determined to maintain this place, and by heavens we can." The reply was worded in such vehement fashion because Croghan expected Conner to be captured and his message to fall into the hands of the Indians. But Conner delivered the reply to Harrison on the same day, and the latter immediately sent Colonel Samuel Wells with a squadron to relieve Croghan of his command on account of his act of disobedience. The squadron was attacked by Indians and while there were casualties on both sides, Colonel Wells reached the fort and took charge. Croghan returned with the squadron and after he had explained the situation to Harrison, was allowed to return to his command. On the afternoon of August 1, the British appeared with the gunboats in the river. Proctor's force consisted of 500 regulars and more than 700 Indians. Colonel Elliot, who accompanied Proctor, demanded surrender of the fort to prevent the dreadful slaughter that would follow resistance. The doughty youngster in command refused to comply, whereupon the British opened a furious fusilade. Croghan fought stoutly back with his 160 men and one piece of artillery. Proctor's position was difficult. The fort was withstanding the assault, and its defenders showed no signs of yielding. His Indian allies were discontented with the delay. Proctor was afraid to remain with Harrison only nine miles away and he did not want to leave without accomplishing some advantageous result. On the afternoon of the second, the 41st Regiment was picked by Proctor to make a vigorous assault under cover of smoke against the northwest angle of the fort. After two hours' fighting with disastrous results, the British retired, and at three o'clock in the morning of August 3, Proctor and his surviving troops re-embarked for Malden.

Small and apparently inconsequential happenings sometimes change the flow of important events. If William Conner had not been delayed a few hours this page of history would be written differently. Croghan, according to his own statement, would have abandoned the fort as ordered, had Conner arrived during the night of July 29. With that result Harrison would have fallen back to Upper Sandusky and the decisive engagement with the British in this invasion probably would have occurred there.

As it happened, a very important victory was incredibly achieved by a youth of twenty-one. For his part in this affair Harrison was subjected to criticism which threatened to impair his military position. The American people could not understand his reasons for failing to go to the assistance of Croghan in his hazardous position, as he had an effective command and was within hearing of the guns, only ten miles away.[23]

6.

Early in 1813 the Navy Department had begun operations on Lake Erie. Oliver H. Perry, a capable young officer, was in charge of them. During the summer Harrison kept in touch with Perry and supplied some men for the fleet. When Harrison, conscious of the growing criticism of his inactivity, was at Seneca in September, considering the best movement of the army, he received Perry's famous dispatch of the tenth that Lake Erie was again under American control. Harrison's campaign was now directed to the recovery of Detroit and the invasion of Canada.[24]

Events moved rapidly from this time on. Harrison mobilized his troops which embarked for Canada on September 20 under the protection of Perry's fleet. The Battle of the Thames ensued on October 5. The American forces actually engaged in the battle were estimated by Dawson and McAfee at 2,500 to 2,700, of which 120 were regulars and 30 were Indians. The British forces were estimated at 2,000 to 2,400, of which 1,500 were Indians and about 800 were regulars. The Indians in the American army were attached to Colonel George Paull's company and ten or twelve of them in charge of Conner were assigned to a position for the purpose of seizing the enemy's artillery at the opportune moment.[25]

The spectacular feature of the battle and the decisive maneuver was the frontal charge of Colonel Richard M. Johnson's regiment of mounted Kentucky rangers, part of which rode roughshod through the enemy's battle lines, shooting to the right and to the left and capturing or killing most of the British regulars, while the other section drove the Indians out of the underbrush on the left and put them to flight. General Proctor fled and escaped. Tecumseh was slain. The Kentuckians claimed the honor of the victory.

Controversy as to who won the battle, Harrison or Johnson, finally became political. It seems a factual statement that the maneuver was suggested by Johnson, subordinate officer, and was approved by Harrison, the highest commanding officer, who ordered its execution.[26]

7.

A question that occasionally revives even to this day is, Who killed Tecumseh? It has never been and probably never will be satisfactorily answered. It was Conner's opinion that no one would ever know who fired the gun that killed him.

Reverberating through the years it has called forth many answers. Several writers have claimed the distinction for Colonel Richard M. Johnson. It was considered by the Kentuckians of sufficient importance in 1837 to entitle Colonel Johnson to election as vice-president of the United States. Johnson, himself, avoided this claim, but his friends urged it. William Conner thought that Colonel Whitley, a distinguished veteran of former Indian wars, was more likely deserving of the honor. The fatal shot was from a small-bore rifle such as the frontiersmen usually carried, and Whitley's body was found a few feet away from Tecumseh's, with a rifle of that type. The soldiers generally believed that the fatal shot was his. Colonel Johnson was mounted and armed with horse pistols, which would have produced a different wound. This was the ballistic evidence as Conner knew it.

There are also many conflicting accounts of the identification of Tecumseh's body on the battlefield. It is said the Kentuckians "first recognized it and had cut long strips of skin from the thighs to keep . . . for razor straps in memory of the river Raisin." This brutal detail did not have any political value so the politicians did not make use of it.[27] William Conner is said to have inspected the body and confirmed the identification made by some of the Indians. He had known Tecumseh for many years, and for six years they had been neighbors on White River.

Nine days after his victory, Harrison called the chiefs of the Potawatomi, Miami, Wea, Chippewa, Wyandot, and Ottawa to Detroit. He required of them a suspension of hostilities; if there were any murders or depredations committed by any of them upon the citizens of the United States all signatory tribes were to unite in punishing the offenders. Hostages must be given, and all prisoners were to be delivered at Fort Wayne or some other post. William Conner and five others acted as interpreters. The Indians began to realize their mistake in allying themselves to the British now that the heavy hand of the United States was laid upon them.

For nine years after the Fort Wayne Treaty of 1809 no Indian treaties of any importance concerned lands in Indiana. The Battle of the Thames broke the power and ended the aspirations of the northwestern Indians. Their only great leader was dead and his followers dispersed. There was no one to succeed him. The Prophet was as useless as a bad fuse which had failed to ignite the bomb.

The only treaty the Indians had ever regarded as binding upon them was Wayne's treaty of 1795 at Greenville. It was therefore fitting that after nineteen years of sanguinary struggle the compact between the Indians and the United States should take place at Greenville on July 22, 1814. It was called the treaty of peace and friendship. The Indians, disappointed and humiliated by the British defeat, realized that they must now make peace with the United States. The treaty was signed by the chiefs for the Wyandot, Delawares, Seneca, Shawnee, Ottawa, Miami, Potawatomi, and Kickapoo. They agreed to aid the United States in any war with Great Britain or with hostile Indian tribes. The council opened on July 8, 1814, and continued to July 23. General Harrison presided. William and John Conner were present and signed the treaty as witnesses. It gave peace to the Wyandot, the Delawares, the Shawnee, the Seneca, and to the Miami nation. Indulgence was granted to certain bands of the Potawatomi, the Ottawa, and the Kickapoo which during the troublesome period had been virtually outlaws. The boundary lines between the lands of the United States and the Indian nations to whom peace was granted (except as to the Seneca) were confirmed as they had existed prior to the War of 1812.[28]

Other treaties were held beginning in June, 1816, and extending as late as 1840, by the terms of which portions of the territory comprising the present state of Indiana were relinquished by the Indians.

In all there were thirteen Indian treaties negotiated and executed with tribes in Indiana and Ohio in which William and John Conner acted as interpreters or witnesses, sometimes separately and sometimes jointly.[29] Until the close of the War of 1812 the negotiations of the treaties and their execution were attended with the bitter and fierce opposition of the Indians. After that event the negotiations were not so difficult. In 1818 the Delawares, by treaty, agreed to move west of the Mississippi. By 1834 the long hostility of the Potawatomi to the United States was ended. In 1840 the Miami ceded their remaining lands and agreed to join the other tribes in the West. The efforts to extinguish Indian titles had been incredibly difficult. What the result would have been without Harrison's skill in the first negotiations, no one can tell.

8.

The War of 1812 was a military blunder, promoted by politicians, which almost wrecked the Union. Nevertheless, whatever may be the opinion of the futility and wastefulness of both men and money and the wicked corruption of this war, the fact remains that for Indiana it was of vital importance.[30]

Notwithstanding Harrison's success in the Northwest, the fortunes of the Ohio Valley were determined by the results of the war in the East and by the treaty of peace following its conclusion. In the negotiations for that treaty at Ghent in August, 1814,[31] the British commissioners made two demands which, if they had been agreed to by the American commissioners, would not only have nullified the result of Harrison's victory but would have radically changed the map of the Northwest. One of these demands—*sine qua non*—was for a barrier country between the United States and Canada to be permanently owned and occupied by Indians as an independent nation. This proposal embraced an area beyond the Greenville (1795) line in Ohio, Indiana, Illinois, and Michigan in which perhaps one hundred thousand Americans were settled. The other was that the United States was not to have any naval force on the Great Lakes nor to maintain any forts on their shores, while the British were allowed both.

The American commissioners stubbornly opposed these demands, which were so preposterous as to threaten an end to negotiations. They were unconsciously aided by the swirling course of English internal affairs and foreign relations. The British commissioners referred the decision to the British cabinet which, thoroughly perplexed, submitted it to England's military authority, the Duke of Wellington. It is interesting to recall that the subsequent victor of Waterloo advised the British cabinet that under the circumstances of the war England was not entitled to demand any territory from the United States —truly a British concept. So far as the British demand was concerned the status of the Northwest was determined by the word of this man who in a few months was to solve the problems of Europe by his sword. Before the treaty was finally completed, the unanimity of the American commissioners was threatened by a stiff-necked controversy between Adams and Clay. It is said that "in this delicate situation only the authority and skill of Albert Gallatin saved the treaty."[32]

After five months of controversy the treaty—*status ante bellum*—was finally signed on December 24, 1814. The Northwest remained a part of the United States. Two other results important to this section were achieved which are not referred to in the treaty. The power of the Indian in the Northwest was broken. The English fur trade would henceforth be confined to the boundaries of Canada.

By the terms of the Treaty of Greenville (1795) Indiana was almost wholly an Indian reservation. Before and during the War of 1812 the Indian tribes in Indiana were largely controlled by the leadership of Tecumseh. The excepted tribe was the Delawares. The Miami, influenced by the Delawares, stood out against the blandishments of Tecumseh for a time but finally yielded. The position of the Delawares was difficult. The memory of the Gnadenhütten massacre of 1781 hung over them as a dark, foreboding cloud of American faithlessness which they were not allowed to forget. Their lands were again being taken away from them. Extermination seemed to face them by these two methods. As a tribe, in Indiana and Ohio however, they remained neutral. Some of their warriors were, doubtless, in British ranks, but as a group they steadfastly refused to open war upon the Americans. Harrison realized and appreciated their situation and the great importance of their attitude to the Americans. William and John Conner were trusted counselors of this tribe both in the consummation of the treaties negotiated by Harrison in Indiana and in the maintenance of their neutrality in the Indian troubles in Indiana before and in the War of 1812. It may be fair to assume that a source of this peaceful attitude of the Delawares may be found in the Moravian mission towns in Ohio where David Zeisberger had grimly held his Indian community neutral during the early years of the Revolution. In the War of 1812, influenced by the Conner brothers who had shared this background, the tribe maintained its neutrality to the end.

CHAPTER VII

John Conner, Founder of Connersville and State Builder

IF AN airplane could have flown low over the prairies, the forests, and the rivers of Indiana in 1813, this area would have presented the appearance of one huge armed camp made up of many small units. All settlements, even those of only three or four houses, had their fortified blockhouses. Larger communities had forts to accommodate a greater number of families. Stockades surrounded the forts that were garrisoned and within these enclosures were kept the horses of the mounted rangers. The trails and crude roads were sentineled by single militiamen, stationed at high points to survey the surrounding country for the Indian enemy. There were in what is the present state of Indiana only two forts of any importance for the protection of this territory—Fort Wayne on the north and Fort Harrison on the Wabash. A series of forts in the eastern part of Ohio and a few in Kentucky along the Ohio River were of more value but not adequate. Due to continued petty Indian raids, however, blockhouses were to be found by this year in every section that contained white settlers—even those on the well-protected eastern border.

The three counties of Wayne, Franklin, and Dearborn constituted the eastern group of the seven organized counties in the Indiana Territory of this period. They were united by the Whitewater River. Its two forks, known as the East and West forks, rise in what was then Wayne County (now Randolph) and come together in Franklin County just below the town of Brookville. The river flows on southward through the northeast corner of Dearborn County and joins the Miami River a short distance above its mouth, the center of which determines the boundary between Ohio and Indiana. This section was commonly known in the early days as the Whitewater Valley, or, sometimes, simply as the Whitewater.

On November 25, 1812, Harrison wrote from Ohio that "John Conner is on White Water in the Indiana Territory and may be easily sent for." In what capacity he was there in these troublous times, it is not so easy to determine. He had been sent by Harrison in October to watch the Delawares and report their movements, but by the end of November the tribe had begun to move at Harrison's direction from its towns on White River to the Shawnee towns on the Auglaize River in northern Ohio.[1] This exodus of the Delawares from Indiana, which was completed by June, 1813, deprived John Conner of his field for trading and any special duty in connection with the war.

Meantime the settlers in the Whitewater Valley had become apprehensive because of their close proximity to the Indian country. There had been no open hostility of any large group, but there were instances of theft, murder, and capture of individuals by Indians, singly or in small bands. Forts were garrisoned and houses fortified. In Wayne County, there were at least nine blockhouses, four with stockades, besides which about every fourth house near the Indian boundary was strengthened to be able to resist attacks. There was a proportionate number in Franklin and Dearborn counties. That there was a blockhouse near Conner's Trading Post on what was soon to be the site of Connersville, there is no doubt.[2] It seems inconceivable that a man who had rendered such good service to Harrison before and during the Battle of Tippecanoe was not assisting in this protection of the frontier. The military records are complicated by the presence of another John Conner who came to Franklin County in 1813, so that it is difficult to disentangle the two service records. It seems likely that the subject of this narrative was either the John Conner who was third corporal in the company of Captain James McGuire of the volunteer militia of Dearborn County from August 28, 1812, to February 27, 1813, or that he was the private John Conner who was enrolled in the company of militia from Wayne County under command of Enos Butler from October 13, 1812 to January 12, 1813. As the dates of duty overlap he could not have served in both. At any rate it may be assumed that he was serving in some capacity, most naturally in the blockhouse or fort near his post.[3]

2.

These forts and blockhouses bristled with importance in the year 1813. Circling above the sites of Indian towns and settlements, an air-pilot would have found no signs of occupancy. Many of the towns had been burned, the land laid waste, the crops left ungarnered. A sharp eye might occasionally discern a single Indian skulking through the forest, or a small band half hidden in the shadows of a river bank, or a half-starved group sneaking back to secure abandoned grain. These were few, however, and their spirits were broken. In the latter part of this year our pilot might have seen a thin dark file of Indians, the disbanded army of the Thames, making its way down from Detroit and Canada to deserted homes in Indiana. It was a weary, sullen, and disheartened group. Betrayed and embittered, the Indians realized that their return meant only the beginning of another trek westward.

Lest this observer of the air catch the contagion of their discouragement, let him turn southward and observe the pioneers from Ohio, Pennsylvania, New York, Virginia, Kentucky, and North Carolina who have heard of the defeat of the Indians and with high hopes and courage are forming another line which enters Indiana from the south and east. They are coming with their wives and children, their baggage and their cattle, in wagons and on foot, on horseback across mountains and plains; on rafts down the Ohio. There are native Americans and European immigrants, for the most part substantial people, sober, industrious, kindly, and democratic. Some are Quakers, and practically all, even those from the southern states, are opposed to slavery.[4] In March, 1812, there were not 35,000 inhabitants in what is now Indiana. By the close of 1815 there were 63,897. Through the Whitewater Valley immigrants came pouring into Indiana from the east and south.

Situated since 1808 on the Whitewater River, only five miles east of the western boundary of the Twelve Mile Purchase and less than a mile from the southern boundary of Wayne County, John Conner watched this tide of immigration, moving slowly at first, gradually gaining until interrupted by the war, and then increasing again. His trading post near Cedar Grove had been one of the first white settlements in Franklin County; in his new location he was one of the first white settlers of the region later organized as Fayette County. For several years Conner had been investing the money he had acquired from his fur trade and from his father's estate in various tracts of land in Franklin County. By March, 1813, he owned a farm of 320 acres near Cedar Grove which included the site of his old trading post and mill; 160 acres on West Fork of Whitewater in Laurel Township, besides parts of sections in or near the present site of Connersville.[5] His Indian wife had died. Their two sons, James and John, were probably with their father at this time. James died while still a youth and John left Indiana in 1820.[6]

With the chief tie that bound him to his Indian life gone, and with an increasing number of white settlers occupying land adjacent to his, it was natural that Conner should identify himself completely with his own people. His thoughts turned to marriage and to the daughter of Jabez Winship, his old neighbor at Cedar Grove. On March 13, 1813, John Conner and Lavina Winship were married. She was a young woman of twenty-five and he thirteen years older.[7] He took her back to his trading post in the northern part of Franklin County and began the reorientation of his life. His Indian trade was no longer lucrative, and as a sawmill was an obvious need of the new settlers, he built one near his post.

3.

It was in the year of his marriage that he conceived the idea of platting a town in this vicinity. At least eleven lots were contracted for purchase during the year, nine of which had some improvements on them in the way of buildings or fences.[8] For several years it existed only in his mind and in a rough drawing on paper. "The most of the land which comprises the present site of the town was then a dense forest," wrote a contemporary describing its appearance in 1816. "A small tract of land had been laid off by John Conner into town lots which lay along the river bank, on Water street and along Main (now Eastern) street, and a few log-cabins had been erected." Conner's granddaughter tells an incident illustrative of the modest beginnings of the town. John Conner, she says, was "building his cabin, which as yet had neither roof nor floor, when an emigrant wagon drew up and stopped, and the new-comer asked to be directed to Connersville. My Grandfather, standing in the door, laughed heartily and said, 'My friend, you are right in the heart of the town.' "[9]

Conner's post and dwelling—probably a two-roomed log cabin—was situated in what is now the middle of Eastern Avenue between Eighth and Ninth streets, outside the original plat of the town. As a protection against the Indians, a heavy wall had been erected around the cabin, with a gate that fastened from the inside. The log blockhouse which was on the rear of Block No. 8 fronted what is now an alley but what was originally the old Whitewater Trail. The original town consisted of two main streets running north and south, Main and Water streets, and it was only two blocks wide and five blocks long.

In the summer of 1816 Conner built a gristmill near his sawmill. Here he employed George Shirts, who came with his family from Cincinnati to Indiana after serving in the War of 1812 as soldier, scout, and messenger. Shirts was a miller by trade, and he superintended Conner's mill besides assisting in the dressing and packing of furs at the trading post.[10] The Indian trade became active again for a few years after the Delawares returned from Ohio prior to their departure from Indiana in 1820.

In such an embryo town did Lavina Conner begin housekeeping. It was sixty miles from Cincinnati, the nearest community of any size, accessible by barge or flatboat when the weather was good, otherwise only by the narrow trail through the woods. The essential commodities had to be hauled in wagons over almost impassable roads which seemed more like paths. "Three notches" on the trees indicated a public highway. The "blazed" tree led only to a settler's cabin.

This cabin was of rough log construction. A large one was eighteen feet by twenty-two feet with a fireplace in one end and the entrance in the opposite end. A window about two feet square was closed with a shutter which had wooden hinges like those of the door extending across its width. The sides of the structure were of round logs, the cracks between filled with small pieces of soft wood driven in from the inside, and the outside well coated with clay mortar. Clapboards laid on ribs of log supplied the roof. The puncheon floor was a construction of split logs. The outside chimney frame was made of split pieces of log finished with small split sticks laid in clay mortar mixed with cut straw. Unless stone could be procured, the chimney back, jambs, and hearth were made of well-tempered clay which was thoroughly beaten. Small openings in the cabin were covered with greased paper. Handmade furniture of the simplest kind met the bare necessities. Beds were frequently made upon the floor. Meat, corn meal, and dried beans were the staple articles of diet in the winter. There was neither tea, nor coffee, nor sugar. Maple sugar and molasses which could be obtained in abundance from the sugar maple trees took the place of cane sugar. A beverage was made by pouring boiling water over a toasted corn dodger sweetened with maple sugar.[11]

Yet under conditions like these the community grew and prospered. On December 4, 1815, there were 1,430 voters in Franklin County and the total population was 7,370—larger than any other county except Knox.[12] Although John Conner was among the earliest settlers he was elected to no office until 1816, when he became a member of the state Senate. Men were here, however, whose names were to be written large across the history of the state, and from whom John Conner was learning many things—John Test, James and Noah Noble, Stephen C. Stevens, Isaac Wilson, Oliver H. Smith, and many others. Franklin County was an anteroom to the state, a training ground for new citizens. Many came and settled here until they got their bearings in the new environment, made scouting parties further inland for more desirable locations, and eventually removed to the point of their selection. The nucleus of the first settlers in Hamilton County came from Connersville. The Conner brothers had selected their locations wisely. People, not goods, were now in the shuttle of their trail.[13]

4.

Indiana emerged into statehood in compliance with an enabling act by Congress granting authority for formation of a constitution and state government. On June 29, 1816, the Constitution—providing for a General Assembly of two branches, a Senate and House of Representatives—was adopted. The first session of the Assembly convened at Corydon on November 4, 1816. The formal and final admission of the state into the Union took place December 11, 1816. John Conner was the first senator elected from Franklin County.

An English traveler who came to Indiana in this period gives a sharp pen picture of this part of the state and its people. "It is seldom that a view of 200 yards in extent, can be caught in Indiana. . . . It is a long time before an English eye becomes accustomed to their [the trees] size and grandeur. The live poplar, or tulip-bearing tree, of which canoes are made, the sycamore, the walnut, and the white oak, grow to a prodigious size." He describes his own traveling apparel and equipment and it is evident he has adopted these from the natives—broadbrimmed straw hat, long trousers and moccasins; shot pouch and powder horn slung from the belt; rifle at his back in a sling, tomahawk in a holster at his saddle bow; a pair of saddle bags stuffed with shirts and gingerbread; boat cloak and Scotch tent buckled behind on the saddle. Game was not so plentiful, as he writes, for on one morning he hunted without success, missed some ducks, saw a large herd of deer, killed nothing but a paroquet.[14]

Through a country like this and dressed probably in some such fashion came the legislators to Corydon, capital since 1813. Over traces on horseback, or down the rivers in canoes, they found their way. John Conner had one of the longest routes traversed by any of them. He came on horseback down the familiar Whitewater Trail and found his way across country by old Indian trails or buffalo traces to Jeffersonville and thence to Corydon.[15] Notwithstanding the difficulties and perils of the journey, the full quota of members reached the little inland village for the opening session. The town had been selected because it was away from the rivers, out of the line of many Indian trails and thus protected by its very isolation. It was a community of less than one hundred buildings—rude cabins or houses of hewn logs. The courthouse in which the legislature met was a two-story structure, forty feet square, of gray limestone. From the center of the roof arose an imposing hexagonal belfry surmounted by a steeple roof topped by an iron shaft bearing a large ball. There was one room on the main floor and two on the second floor. The arched entrance was on the west side. The west half of the room was floored with flagstones, and separated by a railing from the east half, where the House of Representatives met. A slightly raised floor of wide wooden planks covered this section. There was a large fireplace in each end. In the northwest corner a stairway with a landing led to the upper floor, and a creaky door on the landing gave a semblance of privacy. One room was reserved for the use of the Senate, and one for the meetings of the Supreme Court. The building as a whole was severely simple—expressive of the lives of the people. It dominated the town, the masterpiece of their fellow citizen, Dennis Pennington, whom they affectionately called "Uncle Dennis." Another prominent citizen of Corydon was John Tipton, and for a few months Isaac Blackford made the little town his home. Tipton and Davis Floyd, who had but recently moved to Corydon, were well known to Conner.[16]

The little town was overcrowded when the legislature convened. Supplies from Louisville were often delayed due to the condition of the roads and streams, so that board as well as lodging sometimes left much to be desired. The plain simple people of this frontier community shared what they had with the legislators, and all, inured to privation, made the best of conditions which they could not change. In this village where the way of living was of necessity informal, and in this miniature courthouse which was informal too, it is likely that all the legislators were soon well acquainted. There was a fine democracy in those days. The talents of the native backwoodsmen were respected by men of more learning, and while the former jokingly referred to Senator James Beggs as "Mr. Syntax," they were undoubtedly grateful for his help in framing the difficult parts of a bill.

Although this was the first session of a legislature after Indiana became a state, it was not the first law-making body, for the territorial assembly had preceded it, and still earlier the governor and judges had exercised certain legislative functions. They had laid the foundation of legislation, and their acts were still in force until superseded by legislation of the General Assembly. A comparison of subjects upon which legislation had been passed from 1800 to 1815 with subjects acted upon after organization of the state, shows that much of the latter was but an elaboration of the former, a change in detail or substitution in whole or in part. The subject of county boundaries and of the forming of new counties was to occupy legislators in Indiana for many years to come. In 1816

there were fifteen counties. New ones were added at every
session for the next twenty years.

5.

Ten men composed the Senate, a body small enough to act
as a committee of the whole upon most questions. This number seems small to modern eyes, but to James Beggs, who had
been a member of seven of the eleven sessions of the old
territorial assembly and had presided over four sessions of a
Legislative Council composed of only five members, this new
group, twice the size of the former one, must have seemed
imposing.

Dennis Pennington, Ezra Ferris, William Prince, John
Paul, William Polke, and the presiding officer, Christopher
Harrison—all had gained experience in the territorial legisla-
ture. Baird, Ferris, Pennington, Polke, De Pauw, and Daniel
Grass had been members of the Constitutional Convention.
Many senators had military as well as legislative experience.
Prince had been with Aaron Burr in his southwestern expedi-
tion and had served at times as an intermediary for Harrison
with the Indians. John Paul was a veteran of George Rogers
Clark's campaign. Both of them as well as De Pauw and Grass
had been officers in the army or militia during the recent war.
There was a physician-minister among them, Ezra Ferris,
who, with Christopher Harrison, probably had the best formal
education of any of them. There were founders of towns,
De Pauw of Salem, Paul of Madison, Grass of Rockport, and
Conner of Connersville. De Pauw was the son of a Frenchman who came to this country with Lafayette and served with
him in the War of the Revolution. The members of this first
Senate were elected to serve for three years which all did with
the exception of Prince, who resigned during the first session
and was succeeded by Isaac Montgomery; and Grass, whose
place was taken in the third session by Ratliff Boon.

In the House were men who afterward became prominent
in the history of Indiana—Isaac Blackford, who, the next
year, was to become a judge of the Indiana Supreme Court;
James Noble, who was shortly to be elected to the United States
Senate; Williamson Dunn, well-known jurist; and Samuel
Milroy, prominent in military and political affairs.

It was in such a group that John Conner was to serve his apprenticeship in statecraft. He who was completely at home in the councils of the Indians was now to match his wits with men of his own race. All had had experience as judges, administrative officers, or as legislators. John Conner had none.

The first three sessions of the legislature will be considered as a unit, for the men who composed them were the same, with few exceptions, and the measures were similar and overlapped from one session to the other. There was necessity for considerable legislation for the new state. The first bill which John Conner introduced, only a few weeks after the first session opened, was a bill for the incorporation and better regulation of the seat of justice of Franklin County, the town of Brookville.[17] This led to a general enactment instead of the cumbersome method of special enactments for each town. The act providing for this was the accepted recommendation of a committee of which Conner was a member. Another act issuing from a committee on which he served, related to county and township officers.[18]

County boundaries and the formation of new counties received much consideration. The bill for the formation of Fayette County had a troublesome career. The first petition for it was presented in the House early in the first session, but after committee action and two readings it was indefinitely postponed and did not reach the Senate. In the next session another bill was introduced in the House by James Snowden of Franklin County and in the Senate by John Conner almost simultaneously. The House bill was soon tabled but Conner had better luck. His bill passed the Senate by a vote of six to four—only to be again indefinitely postponed in the House. At the third session it was again brought up, this time in the House by Jonathan McCarty of Franklin, and after amendments and some delay it passed with a good margin of votes. Favorable action was quickly secured in the Senate on December 24, 1818, and it became a law. This measure was important to Conner, for the town he had platted was in the center of this county and the logical site for the county seat.[19]

He was to be affected by another act passed during this time. This related to the office of sheriff, providing that

when a new county was laid off, the governor should appoint
the first sheriff to act until the next general election. A bond
of five thousand dollars had to be furnished. Conner was
appointed first sheriff of Fayette County on December 30,
1818.[20]

Two acts relating to gristmills and millers were passed—
one in the first session relating to the payment of damages to
owners of land through which a millrace was cut. Conner
voted against this, doubtless for personal reasons. A second
act, passed January 29, 1818, was more detailed, including and
superseding the first.[21]

The subject of roads insistently demanded attention, for
the development of the state was largely dependent upon them.
Up to this time the roads had been chiefly old Indian trails
and buffalo traces. Trails which had been widened and the
roads that had been constructed were both of the rudest character, with only the largest trees removed and attempts made
to bridge streams and swampy places. Over the latter, logs or
poles were placed crosswise and covered with dirt. There was
great need not only for improvement of existing roads but for
more of them to link different parts of the state. To meet
these needs required increasing revenue, of which the state had
little. For more than half a century this question was to vex
legislators, for its importance could not be minimized.

An act for opening and repairing public roads was considered in the first session, both houses appointing committees for
this purpose. Conner was one of those who voted against the
Senate bill, which failed to pass. The House bill, which received favorable consideration by both bodies, was concerned
chiefly with regulations for establishment of roads by county
commissioners, road taxes, and related matters. In the following session another law, originating also in the House, was
passed, repealing all earlier laws on the subject. Its provisions
were mainly regulatory, and these were amended and altered
by an act of the session of 1818-1819, reported by a committee
of which Conner was a member. An important provision of
this act declared all roads public highways that had been in use
and worked by the public for a term of three years. This is
the first record of Conner's service on a road committee, but
not his last. It was a subject that always claimed his interest.[22]

Other important bills relating to crime and punishment, establishment of libraries, medical societies, public seminaries, the circuit and supreme courts, were passed in these early sessions. John Conner's interests were at first largely local, but he took an active part throughout and increasingly his mind was broadened.[23]

6.

At this time the Indians were in possession of the central and northern parts of Indiana, asserting title under the provisions of Article 4 of the Greenville Treaty of 1795. The Delawares claimed "all the lands lying on the streams running into White river, supposed to be one hundred miles square." The tribe then numbered eight hundred souls in this locality. In the summer of 1817 a council of Delawares attended by William Conner, interpreter, denounced the report that they had sold their lands on White River, and urged a kindred tribe to join them there and strengthen their settlement. They expected soon to have a population of at least two thousand, including Delawares and members of other tribes.[24]

The outer boundary of the organized counties coincided with the Indian treaty lines, the Twelve Mile Purchase of 1809 on the east, the Grouseland Treaty of 1805 on the southeast, and the Ten O'Clock Line of 1809 running northwest to the Illinois boundary. The country half encircled by this boundary was in possession of the Indians, barring easy communication between the east and west portions of the state, and blocking development northward. A natural result of this condition was the motion presented in the House of Representatives on December 24, 1817, "that a committee be appointed to enquire into the expediency or inexpediency of memorializing congress on the subject of obtaining by purchase or some otherwise, from the Indians, permission for the state of Indiana to lay out and open a public highway, from the town of Brookville . . . to Fort Harrison, on the Wabash." Stephen C. Stevens of Franklin County was the author of this motion and when it carried was made chairman of the committee to draw up the necessary resolutions. During the time when the resolutions were under consideration, Graham, of Jackson County, asked for a closed session of the House in which to introduce a subject requiring secrecy. This matter was also referred to a secret session of the Senate. A joint committee appointed for its consideration was made up of Conner, Beggs, and Polke, senators, and Sullivan, Graham, Daniel, Stevens, and Ferguson from the House.

It seems more than a coincidence that all the House members with the exception of Graham, were members of Stevens' committee in regard to the road from Brookville to Fort Harrison. No intimation, however, is given in either *House* or *Senate Journal* as to the subject that was discussed in the secret session. Conner reported for the committee and certain resolutions were adopted in both bodies. The veil of secrecy was not lifted until a year later and then only partially by the laconic statement in the *House Journal* that it was relative "to the extinguishment of Indian title to land." It also seems more than a coincidence that the day after the last secret sessions were held, the House moved to postpone consideration of Stevens' road from Brookville until the following December. Something was evidently expected to happen in the interim, and something did happen—whether precipitated or encouraged by this secret action of the General Assembly no one can say from the evidence at hand.[25]

A most important treaty with the Wyandot and other Indian tribes, at which William Conner was interpreter, had been held at Fort Meigs prior to the 1817-1818 session of the legislature. The Delawares from Indiana were represented by Chief Anderson, although very little territory in Indiana and none in this state claimed by the Delawares was considered in the negotiations. On September 29, 1817, the treaty was signed, but ratification was postponed because individual reservations were granted to Indians without the restrictions governing conveyance which had been considered advisable in other treaties. These terms aroused comment and criticism in the current press, for it was feared that they would lead to trouble in the eventual transfer of these lands to the whites. Indiana was interested because the terms of this treaty might serve as a precedent for impending treaties in this state. One year later, September 17, 1818, the same commissioners, accompanied this time by John instead of William Conner, signed a supplemental treaty at St. Mary's which brought the provisions as to Indian tenure in line with other treaties. Public anxiety was quieted and the main objectives of the negotiation had been secured.[26] John Conner had a part in the result.

A series of treaties were consummated at St. Mary's a month later involving the great central part of Indiana, including the territory through which Stevens had proposed building a road.[27] Before these were held, Jacob Whetzel, a forthright pioneer, had secured permission from Chief William Anderson to build a trace large enough for an ox team from Laurel, in Franklin County, to the mouth of Eel River at the present Worthington.[28] He progressed during the summer of 1818 as far west as the bluffs on White River at the site of Waverly, about halfway across the region which would have been opened by Stevens' road. The first settlers sometimes took matters in their own hands when legislative processes were slow.

7.

The political situation in Indiana at this time was undergoing a great change. Jonathan Jennings had been an important factor in its development since before the War of 1812. Harrison's influence was waning at that time, and if the war had not given him a fresh opportunity, his political star would have been eclipsed even then by the rising figure of Jennings. Harrison's removal to Ohio definitely eliminated him from state politics in Indiana, and control centered in the hands of three men who were supported by Whitewater Valley and the antislavery element in the state. The three leaders, James Noble, United States senator, William Hendricks, congressman, and Governor Jonathan Jennings had been in the saddle since 1816. Jennings was unsurpassed as an aggressive and adroit politician, the master spirit of the triumvirate. He came into power on the slavery issue, skillfully defeating the Virginia and Kentucky coterie in Indiana—friends of Harrison and supporters of negro slavery. He was the prototype of later vociferous politicians, upholding the rights of the common man with special privileges to none.

Since Harrison, the successful treaty maker, was no longer living in the state, his natural successor as negotiator with the Indians was the bold but subtle man who was now governor. In April, 1818, Jennings was appointed federal commissioner to treat with the Indians for the cession of lands in central Indiana. There were difficulties in the way of accepting the appointment. Under the Indiana constitution, as he was well aware, his right to act in this capacity was open to challenge, for Article 4 provided that no person holding any office under the United States should exercise the office of governor.[29] The future of the state was involved, and Jennings was an opportunist. This negotiation was a matter he was confident that he could handle successfully with the help of the Conners, upon whom he could rely for expert interpreting and for support with the Indians. He did not hesitate long, if at all, before accepting the appointment in the face of certain bitter criticism.

Another incident which occurred about this time contributed fresh fuel to the flaming charges of Jennings' opponents that he flouted the laws and the Constitution. The territorial legislature of 1813-1814 had passed an act more effectually to prevent dueling, which required territorial officials and attorneys to take an oath that they had neither engaged in nor carried a challenge for any duel. The law was re-enacted by the first state legislature. In May, 1818, Jennings created an uproar in the opposition press by appointing as presiding judge of the first judicial circuit an attorney who had been disbarred from practice for failure to take the required oath. There can be no defense of this action. It was bold, unscrupulous, and defiant, and according to his opponents, entirely characteristic of Jennings. The end was what mattered to him, not the means. His action was deeply resented. Vituperative words rolled from tongue to tongue in a veritable hymn of hate. The columns of the *Western Sun* and the *Dearborn Gazette* were crowded with indignant criticism of his acceptance of the post of treaty commissioner, and of his court appointment. Gallant knights of the pen disguised as "Regulus," "Brutus," "An Observer," and "Man of the Moon" were quick to make this the occasion for renewed tilts against him.[30] These ebullitions were peculiarly characteristic of the times.

When he returned from the successful negotiation of four Indian treaties by the terms of which the Indian title to all of central Indiana was extinguished, he found Lieutenant Governor Christopher Harrison in his chair, not only discharging the duties of chief executive but claiming under the constitution that Jennings had vacated his office by accepting the federal appointment. Jennings angrily threw his commission in the fire and ignored the pretensions of his lieutenant governor. The General Assembly of 1818-1819 opened in an air of much tenseness. The press noted that the members looked at each other with "scowling apprehension" instead of the "pleasing calm" of other sessions. The dilemma was a delicate one. Jennings had just completed a treaty with the Indians which would make possible the rapid development of the state, but in so doing he had violated the constitution, according to the interpretation of his enemies. They wanted to deprive him of his office and insisted upon a legislative inquiry. When it came to proving the commission, however, they found themselves without the necessary evidence at hand. The document itself was gone, and there was no one to swear to its exact form or content. John Conner was among those whose deposition was taken, and his is typical of the others. He stated that he was at the council with the Indians at St. Mary's; that he understood that Governor Cass, Governor Jennings, and Judge Benjamin B. Parke were United States commissioners; that an instrument purporting "to give authority under the United States" was read by Governor Cass, but that if it had a seal he did not see it. This sort of evidence fell short of proving the commission, and the legislature by a narrow margin sustained Jennings. Both William and John Conner supported Jennings during the treaty negotiations and in this proceeding.[31]

8.

A short time after the passage of the bill for the organization of Fayette County, John Conner asked for a leave of absence for the remainder of the legislative session, a matter of only a few days. No doubt his anxiety to return home was related to the formation of the new county. Commissioners to locate the seat of justice had been named in the act, and he wished to present the claims of his town for this honor. The commissioners met at the house of John McCormick, one mile north of Connersville and not far from John Conner's, on the third Monday in February, 1819, and the next day chose the site for the county buildings.

As the first sheriff of the county, John Conner filed the list of grand jurors with the circuit court. The first case was one against the sheriff for trespass, to which he pleaded guilty. A jail seems to have been the first necessity of a new county and to provide for one was the function of the sheriff. The contract for this building was let in March, 1819, to Conner's friend and neighbor, Jonathan John, for the sum of $764. By the following August, the jail was completed, a log structure 30 by 16 feet containing three rooms. It was located about the site of the present town hall.[32]

Connersville was a rapidly growing community. Arthur Dickson (or Dixon), one of the first to enter land in the township, was interested in mercantile business and was associated with the firms known as Jacobs, Dickson and Test; Jacobs and Dickson; Conner and Dickson, and Dickson and Conner until his death in 1823.[33] Even before the town became a county seat it gave evidence of its cultural ambitions by organizing the Connersville Library Association (May 21, 1818). The deep interest of the pioneers in this enterprise is established by their subscription for fifty shares of stock at five dollars each. Thirty-four subscribers were present at the first meeting. Conner was elected one of the directors.[34]

His interests were widening. By this time, in addition to his mills and lands near the town of Connersville, he had business interests of all kinds in the town itself, and had acquired more land in and near the town. Prior to 1819 it is said that he was the "guiding power of the settlement."[35] So busy was Conner's sawmill in these days that one of the early settlers who arrived in 1818 and needed lumber to erect a dwelling for his family, found the mill taxed beyond its capacity and was obliged to adopt Conner's suggestion of using the mill himself on moonlit evenings. The gristmill had a similar run of trade, men coming on horseback from a distance of forty or fifty miles and camping near by while they awaited their turn.[36]

It was in these years that John Conner was interpreter for the Indian treaties of 1817 and 1818. In the latter year he was appointed by the legislature one of the commissioners to select the county seat of the new county of Ripley.[37] Two years later he assisted in selecting the site of the state capital. In this period of prosperity Conner erected a frame house of some pretensions near the site of his mill.[38] On May 27, 1820, his son, William Winship Conner, was born in Connersville. He was named for his father's beloved brother and he carried the maiden name of his mother.[39]

9.

After a lapse of two years, John Conner was again elected state senator from Fayette and Union counties to serve in the legislative session of 1821-1822. When he arrived at Corydon on November 28 he found a different group from the one of which he had been a member. There were now sixteen senators instead of ten. Only three of the old number were members, Patrick Baird, Ratliff Boon, and Daniel Grass, and Grass did not attend the session. Boon was lieutenant governor and presiding officer. None of the members was outstanding in public affairs.

The subject of roads to which Conner had given consideration in his earlier legislative years was again highly important. Indeed the time of the members of this General Assembly was about equally divided between the discussion of roads and county boundaries. The three per cent fund, which was first used in 1819-1820 for road purposes, had proved a great boon, solving the revenue problem temporarily, at least. Twenty-five roads had been authorized at that session and a supplemental act on roads passed in the following session provided for the marking of several of them. In the present session (1821-1822) Conner served on the Committee on State Roads. To this committee were referred fourteen petitions and motions for establishing and changing roads. In addition, a House bill locating certain roads was referred to this committee. Before they could make a report, Conner and two other members of the committee were added to a committee for consideration of a bill appropriating $100,000 of the three per cent fund to the opening of certain roads therein specified. This bill passed the Senate on December 18, 1821, Conner voting for it; it later passed the House. Two other acts on roads were passed at this session, one favored by Conner and one not.[40]

The matter of improving the navigability of the rivers in Indiana was closely related to the question of opening roads. Conner was not so sympathetic to this matter, however, opposing a movement toward the examination of the falls on the East and West forks of White River in Martin and Daviess counties preparatory to the improvement of navigation of the river in that region.[41]

Under the Constitution of 1816 impeachment of civil officers was begun in the House of Representatives and tried in the Senate. Two such cases were heard at this session. Conner was present at both trials, which were lengthy, tedious, and expensive, considering the fact that only minor officers such as a justice of the peace and county clerk were involved. During succeeding years many attempts were made to get rid of this troublesome provision, none of which was successful before the adoption of the Constitution of 1851.

There was a clash between the House and Senate as to the method of voting at general elections. The Constitution had stipulated the ballot, with the provision that if the legislature of 1821 deemed it expedient it could change to viva voce procedure; the decision made then was to be unalterable. The House, by a slender majority, favored the change. The Senate upheld the ballot system by an 8 to 7 vote, Conner voting for its retention. His vote was thus one of the decisive ones in a matter of considerable importance.[42] As in a game of battledore and shuttlecock the proposal was driven back and forth between the two branches until finally through this indecisiveness the ballot was retained. It seems incredible that the House proponents could so disregard the trend of the times. The American colonies had abandoned the viva voce, and at this time the states generally had adopted the ballot. Those that had not, did so later. The viva-voce system was glaringly inadequate and unsound. This was also the judgment of the Constitutional Convention in 1851.

CHAPTER VIII

The Conners at the Treaties of St. Mary's—Departure of the Delawares

ALMOST two-thirds of the domain of the young state of Indiana was in possession of Indian nations in 1818. Their ownership was recognized by the United States government, and within this area Indiana could exercise only very limited jurisdiction. In fact, if the state desired to build a road or canal in that region, permission to do so had to be secured from the tribal owners. As stated in Chapter VII, the legislature in 1817 considered the advisability of testing the Indian attitude toward further cessions by seeking permission to build a road from Brookville to Fort Harrison, but dropped the project for the time being. The capital was located in the southern part of the state and it was impossible to plan for its removal to a proper location near the center until the Indian title had been extinguished. As the white settlers were increasing, there was a growing demand for an actual statehood conforming to the boundaries set forth in the Enabling Act. The Indian titles were a barrier to that end.

2.

The last great assemblage of Indians in Ohio was at St. Mary's in the fall of 1818. St. Mary's was a tiny settlement of not more than six or eight families living in blockhouses erected during the War of 1812. It was of some importance as a military post at that time. The pristine wilderness was gone, for the trees had been cut for military reasons in 1812. Harrison had had temporary headquarters there in September of that year, and had ordered a road built to Fort Defiance. William Conner was the interpreter on this project, as previously mentioned, and was thus familiar with this region. The village, originally known as Girty's Town, had an unsavory name. Though James Girty had ceased his trading operations here before the War of 1812, he had been succeeded by another Irish trader of no better reputation—Charles Murray, who at this time languished in jail on the charge of murder. His family, however, maintained a boarding house here in which the treaty officials were lodged. Anticipating that there would be a large gathering of people, other families had moved in to have a part in what promised to be a harvest festival.

The Indians began to congregate during the latter part of August and encamped along the west bank of St. Mary's River. Near by were boarding houses for the aides of the commissioners, barracks for soldiers, and stands for the traders. The place took on the appearance of a carnival or fair. The displays of goods and furs; the ever moving throngs of Indians; the wrestling and jumping matches, foot and pony races and gambling devices; the maneuvers of troops attracted and held the attention of both whites and Indians. One article, not on display, was whisky, surreptitiously circulated. Food was plentiful, for the government furnished staple necessities as well as cattle and hogs in droves. The Indian hunters provided game.

The United States commissioners, Lewis Cass, Jonathan Jennings, and Benjamin Parke, were accompanied by the governor of Ohio and their secretaries, interpreters, and agents. A troop of Kentucky cavalry served as their escort. The setting for this event, so momentous to the citizens of the new state, seems bizarre to modern eyes, but it was consonant with the times. By day the rays of the sun strove unavailingly to dispel the autumnal haze. At night the campfires, shattering the heavy curtain of darkness by their radiating flares, revealed restless groups of taciturn Indians and communicative whites. The chatter of traders, the dignified demeanor of the commissioners and governors, the trappings of the cavalry troops, and the grim, dark figures of the Indians were picturesque features of the occasion.[1]

3.

The serious business of the assemblage was first taken up in council on September 20. Besides the three commissioners there were present twenty-two others, including John and William Conner, who signed one or another of the treaties as witnesses for the United States. The Potawatomi had thirty-four chiefs and warriors present; the Wea, seven; the Delawares, eighteen, including Chief Anderson, father-in-law of William

Conner; the Miami, sixteen, of whom Chief Richardville was one. All of these subsequently were signatories of the treaties. The whites were outnumbered in the council by more than three to one. Besides these Indian participants there were also in the camps chief men from the Wyandot, Seneca, Shawnee, and Ottawa tribes which had just concluded a treaty for other lands—an undetermined number who had no direct interest in the subject matter of the proposed treaties but who felt, perhaps, that the proceedings might have an indirect bearing on their own lives.

The extinguishment of Indian titles in central Indiana was difficult to accomplish for several reasons. It will be recalled that by the Treaty of Greenville ownership of all the lands within the present limits of Indiana (with certain exceptions) was vested in the Indians. Jennings, reporting to John C. Calhoun, secretary of war, on October 28, makes this comment:[2] "The claims of the several tribes of Indians, with whom the negociation was had, were so interwoven by treaty and tradition, especially to the lands they have lately ceded to the U. States, within this state, that the object of the Government was rendered thereby the more difficult to accomplish. The clanish jealousies and suspicions which exist among them, particularly on such occasions, induced us to negociate a seperate treaty with each of the tribes concerned."

The claims for individual and village reservations presented another set of complexities mentioned by Jennings. There was, also, the necessity of combating the influence of some of the white traders residing among or trading with the Indians. The interests of this group were adverse to the United States, and they had advised the Indians, especially the Miami, to place high values on their lands and to hold out for large annuities as a condition of cession. The Indians, adept in the arts of intrigue and duplicity, followed this advice only too readily.

Still another obstacle to rapid negotiation plagued the commissioners. The Miami were asserting exclusive ownership of "the country between White River and the Ohio." In 1804 the United States agreed to consider the Delawares the sole owners of this land on the strength of a grant from the Miami to the Delawares, but the Miami denied that they had conceded anything more than the right of occupancy. At the Fort

Wayne Treaty of 1809, where John Conner acted as interpreter of the Delawares, the Miami conceded to them an equal
right with themselves in the disposal of this land. In addition,
the Miami claimed the same rights over the land held by the
Wea. This situation was further complicated by the attitude
of John Baptiste Richardville, chief of the Miami. He was a
half-breed, sagacious, possessing as much knowledge of the
value of the land as the whites. He later became, so it is said,
the richest Indian of his time in North America.[3]

After wrangling until October 2, the Potawatomi and Wea
signed separate treaties ceding their title to the land with minor
reservations. The next day the Delawares, by treaty, relinquished all their claim to land in Indiana with some reservations. The Miami were refusing to sign. The United States
had to have the assent of Richardville; otherwise the proceedings would fail. On October 3, Jennings was in so much doubt
as to the outcome that he deemed it advisable to inform the
lieutenant governor that his absence might be prolonged.[4]
Richardville was demanding reservations for himself and members of his tribe which were greatly out of proportion to those
provided in the other treaties. In the meantime, William Conner, who had learned that reservations would be made to other
individuals situated like himself, told the commissioners that
he ought to have the land he occupied set off to him, and John
Conner, to whom the Delawares were indebted, requested payment of these debts. Jennings dissuaded them from present-
ing their respective claims, assuring them that adjustment
would be made by the government later. With this understanding the two brothers withdrew their applications and zealously exerted their influence to secure the execution of the
treaties. Chief Anderson of the Delawares, who was opposed
to the treaty, probably signed with great reluctance, hoping
that it would fail of ratification. The Conners, at the proceedings of St. Mary's Treaty, could have prevented any purchase of land on White River and perhaps any cessions of lands
whatever, as was attested by both Jennings and Cass some years
later, in written statements to James Noble, United States
senator from Indiana.[5]

Liberal concessions had to be made to the Miami and particularly to Richardville. The commissioners deplored the

undesirability of some of the provisions upon which the stubborn Miami insisted, but gave way rather than lose the benefits that would accrue from securing title to the great central section of Indiana. On October 6 the final treaty of the series was signed.[6]

By the terms of the treaty with the Delawares, the United States bound itself to provide and guarantee to them land, and the peaceful possession thereof, west of the Mississippi; to pay them full value for the improvements ceded; to furnish horses and pirogues to transport them; to pay a perpetual annuity of $4,000 in silver in addition to that provided for by former treaties.[7] Individual grants to the amount of sixteen hundred acres in Indiana were made to certain Delawares, and the sum of $13,312.25 was agreed to be paid to claimants named by the Delaware nation.

Concerted opposition by the Indians to the execution of these treaties was effectually weakened by the outcome of the War of 1812. Had the Indians refused to sign them, it is merely a conjecture what would have happened. Supposedly at that time there were seven thousand Indians in the state. In the northern and central parts they could roam at will and, if so disposed, brutally ravage the unprotected settlements. This was a contingency that the United States government earnestly wished to avoid.

4.

After a lapse of several months during which no word came to him from anyone in authority concerning the matter of his claim, William Conner decided to file a petition in the United States Senate for a prescription of six hundred and forty acres. The Committee on Public Lands made its report on March 13, 1820. It found that petitioner had resided at the Delaware towns situated in a country lately belonging to the Delawares and ceded by them at St. Mary's in October, 1818; that petitioner had made considerable improvements on the land where he wished to remain to raise his half-breed family. It further appeared to the committee from a certificate of Jonathan Jennings, governor of Indiana, that petitioner contemplated asking a reservation of this land similar to others granted by the treaties, but was dissuaded from so doing lest applications for reservations should become so numerous as to prejudice negotiations for the treaties. The governor stated that Conner was as much entitled to a reservation as many for whom provision was made. The committee were of the opinion that the petition ought to be granted as prayed for and reported a bill giving him pre-emption right upon payment of the government price for the land. Further action on the bill was indefinitely postponed on April 12.[8]

In 1822 Noble again presented Conner's petition. A new bill was introduced and passed without amendment. What came out of the Congressional gristmill on May 7, 1822, was an act authorizing a patent, without payment, to Conner and his Indian wife during their natural lives jointly and to the survivor of them during the natural life of such survivor and then to their children in fee simple as tenants in common. This title was of no value to Conner. He could not build upon the land or sell it. Without giving up hope of eventually securing the pre-emption he had asked for, he took the precaution of entering the land at the Brookville Land Office, lest it be sold and he be left without remedy.[9] A patent was not taken out until 1830. The entry was for 648.28 acres adjacent to or adjoining on the north, west, and southwest, the cabin which was his home and trading post. This cabin and later his brick house, were on other lands which he entered and for which he received government patents in 1823.

William Conner was not without friends in this emergency. General James Noble was one of the United States senators from Indiana of whose talents and character any state would have been proud. With John Conner he had been a member from the Whitewater region in the first legislature in 1816. Jonathan Jennings, another old friend, was now in Washington as a member of the House of Representatives. General Lewis Cass, a sturdy, patriotic figure who had first known Conner at Fort Seneca during the War of 1812, had become governor of Michigan Territory. Sometime in 1822 after the act of May 7 became a law or after William Conner had made the land entry at Brookville on August 31 of that year, William's claim was taken up with Noble, Cass, and Jennings, and the two last named were reminded of the promise they had made at the treaties of St. Mary's.

William Conner

Conner's friends did their best to further his claim. In 1823, Noble presented two petitions on his behalf, offering with the second, the evidence of Jonathan Jennings and Lewis Cass that Conner had been influential in obtaining the St. Mary's cessions. In the next two sessions, John Test and Noble brought the claim before the House and Senate respectively. When Noble again presented Conner's memorial, in the session of 1827-1828, it was accompanied by the petition of "sundry" Delaware Indians (presumably Conner's Indian wife Mekinges and five of their children) interested in the section of land granted to Conner, praying that he be authorized to dispose of the land in such a way as to make their interest available. On January 29, Senate Bill 77, granting Conner the right of pre-emption, was introduced. The bill passed the Senate but was tabled in the House.[10]

One more attempt was made to secure the passage of an act that would establish Conner's title to his lands at the Delaware towns. John Conner, as agent for William, filed a petition in the Senate showing that the grant of 1822 was of little use either to William or his wife Mekinges, for the latter had removed to the West "in spite of his persuasions that she should remain." Accompanying this petition was a memorial from Mekinges and her children, Jack, Nancy, Harry, James, and William (Eliza did not join for some reason), authorizing a release of their interests under the act of May 7, 1822, upon payment of the government price of the land to their friend William Marshall for their benefit. William Anderson, chief of the Delawares, and four Delaware captains, all residing in Missouri, joined in the memorial, and it was properly witnessed by the United States Indian agent, John Campbell. The letters of Cass and Jennings, before mentioned, were also submitted as proof of the understanding with the Conners at St. Mary's. A bill drawn to meet the needs of both petitioners was introduced by Noble on December 9, 1828. It vested title in Conner on payment of the government price of the land, $810, this sum to be applied to satisfy the claims of Mekinges and her children under the act of May 7, 1822. On the fifth of January the Senate Committee on the Judiciary made an adverse report, holding that however just and reasonable the prayer of the petitioner might be, it would not be proper for Congress to pass an act repealing the law of 1822, and thus attempting to divest Conner's wife and children of the rights granted them by that act. The bill was tabled the next day, and on March 3, Conner was given leave to withdraw his petition and papers.[11] Conner was now at the end of the road as far as the government was concerned.

Defeated in his efforts to obtain sole title by government action, William Conner began negotiations through James M. Ray and John D. Stephenson to procure deeds from his Indian family for the several parcels of land comprising the 648-acre tract. Since the children were still minors, the process was a protracted one. Beginning in 1830, a series of deeds was executed through a long and tedious period, the last one not being obtained until 1855. The title thus remained undetermined for about twenty-five years. The procedure was prolonged by the attitude of the General Land Office at Washington, which refused approval to conveyances unless it was shown that the consideration was fair and the grantor capable of managing money. To this there could be no objection, but it did entail incessant delays.

Conner, meanwhile, had had actual possession of the land since some time prior to the treaties of St. Mary's. Several persons had covetous eyes upon this desirable tract, among them, William G. and George W. Ewing, of the family of rich fur traders at Fort Wayne. As late as 1852 they were maneuvering to get their fingers into this pie, but the fact that Conner had been in possession for so many years made them afraid that the purchase of any reversionary interest would be too much like "buying a law suit and a hard one," so they dropped the matter.[12] In May, 1855, Conner received a deed for the interest of William Conner, Jr., his Indian son, which was the last one outstanding. This was just about three months prior to his death. No doubt a heavy sigh of relief escaped his lips when at the end of more than a third of a century, he became the sole owner in fee simple of the land that should have been granted to him at St. Mary's.

5.

It is an anomaly in the relationship between the Conner brothers and the Delawares that, although the Conners were interpreters and witnesses in thirteen treaties, including ten by which the Delaware Indians relinquished all their interest in the greater part of the present state of Indiana, the tribe does not appear to have lost a whit of respect and confidence in them. The Indians might well have expected the Conners to back their opposition to cessions of land, both as friends and as traders who depended upon Indians living in their neighborhood. It is not apparent that the Conners used their influence against cessions in any of the treaties. It is indubitable that at St. Mary's they effectively supported the proposals of the government. If the Delawares had any misgivings about the Conners they showed no signs. The reason for this is an interesting subject for inquiry.

The facts seem to be that the Conner men possessed a type of leadership that was acceptable to the Indian mind. They met the Delawares on a basis of absolute equality. For years their lives had been identified with the life of this tribe in a most intimate, sympathetic, and friendly fashion. They had been tested by the Indian standards and had not been found wanting. They were courageous in the midst of danger, they were impervious to physical discomforts, they respected the Indian customs and entered into them, they knew when to be silent and when to speak. The wisdom of their counsel had been proved more than once. They had been a significant economic factor in the lives of the Delawares, for with other traders they had provided a market for furs and in return had supplied articles necessary to the personal comfort and satisfaction of the Indians. They had influenced this peaceful tribe against participation in war. They had defended them when the impulsive action of one of their number might have involved the whole tribe. It is probably true that they charged the Indians high prices for their merchandise, and undoubtedly they exchanged whisky for their furs. That was the custom of all Indian traders. Currency was little used as a medium of exchange. Goods, trinkets, and liquor met this need. They gave no credits.

One of the evils of the trade was a frequent cheating of the Indians by unscrupulous traders. The ill feeling on the part of the victims sometimes led to frightful reprisals, and reacted against the government in its treaty negotiations. It was not confined to small traders. The big men in the traffic were sometimes guilty of intrigue and design to overreach the Indian. The influence of men in high political stations was sometimes improperly sought to secure sales of goods or allowances of claims or reservations in treaties. The light of publicity flared on two prominent citizens, Colonel John Tipton, Indian agent, and John Ewing, senator from Knox County, who, in 1829, indulged in criminations and recriminations of conduct at two Indian treaties in 1826, as elsewhere related. The Conners had a long-sustained reputation among their uncivilized customers for fair dealing.

6.

To return to the year 1818—the year of the treaties of St. Mary's—William Conner, with his Indian wife, Mekinges, and his six half-blood children, was living in the log cabin he had built sixteen years before. The Delaware language was used entirely in his household.[13] His trading post was maintained in the same cabin and around it were grouped a few portable Indian lodges. Nothing was left of the Indian village of the days before the War of 1812 except a few huts and the charred remains of log houses. About four miles south of his post some Delawares had re-established themselves at the spot formerly known as Lower Delaware Town. Chief Anderson had returned to Wapeminskink. Except for a French trader known as Bruett, married to a white captive, who lived on the west side of the river near Lower Delaware Town, the nearest white settler in this lonely region was sixty miles away.

Two hundred and fifty acres of level land consisting of several small, beautiful prairies lay irregularly on each side of the river. The soil was unusually fertile. Beyond were dense forests, dark and shadowy, unbroken except by Indian trails. Through these tangled woods ranged bears, elk, deer, and panthers. The touch of civilization here had been so light as to leave but little impress. By force of circumstances, William Conner had up to this time been set apart from his own race, mingling his life and activities solely with a people whose instincts and habits were little touched by civilizing influences. During these years he regarded the Delawares as the best of the Indian tribes and often spoke of himself as a Delaware.[14]

The following year was to mark a change in all these conditions. William Conner had remained a son of the wilderness while his brother John, with whose life his own was so closely intertwined, had been making new contacts with people of his own race. By this time John had been married to Lavina Winship for six years, and she had borne him children. He had become a landowner, a man of means and influence, the founder of Connersville, an experienced legislator. William was aware of the changes that had come to his brother, for they were always in close and intimate touch both in their business and personal relations. They had met recently at the St. Mary's treaties. Both knew that it was only a question of time until the Indians of all tribes would leave the state—perhaps in their own lifetime. John was quick to make his adjustment to the changing times. William was deliberate and did not so easily change his moorings. He clung to the Indian life he loved, but now it was receding.

Events soon pointed the way for him. On a trip to Connersville he became acquainted with John Finch and his large family of children and stepchildren. They had been in Connersville for about two years, and Finch now seemed interested in the White River country. Finch had brought his family from New York, accompanied by his brother Solomon and family. After a short time at North Bend, Ohio, the home of General Harrison, where Solomon was employed, they came to Connersville. Elizabeth Chapman, Finch's young stepdaughter, by whom even at this time William Conner was attracted, retained in after years her vivid childhood memory of the tall, commanding figure and bright, piercing eyes of General William Henry Harrison as he rode through the town on horseback, resplendent in his uniform.[15] In his inner consciousness William Conner knew that when the Delaware tribe left Indiana, which it had agreed to do not later than 1821, Mekinges and the children would go with it. All his future plans had to be made with reference to that contingency. Perhaps it was just as well that his family should go, for it was plain that the Aryan stock would soon predominate in the settlement. The ways of the two races were forever apart.[16] There was a mutually resentful racial feeling, a relic of the recent war, that boded ill for their intermixture. William

Marshall with his Indian wife might go with the Delawares, but the pull of his white blood was too strong in Conner. While the Conners had lived with the Indians all of their lives, no Indian blood flowed in their veins.

7.

Another factor was soon to strengthen his inclination to remain in Indiana. In the spring of 1819 a group of Connersville families decided to move to the prairie which lay south of the present site of Noblesville and two or three miles north of William Conner's Post.[17] The site selected was beautifully located on the western edge of the prairie around which the river curved in the form of a horseshoe. This was a part of the land which had been secured from the Indians at the treaties of St. Mary's. Anxious to have first choice of the land, these enterprising settlers from Connersville proposed to pre-empt it by settlement. George Shirts arrived first with his family. He was at this time employed by William Conner "dressing and packing furs for him and transporting them on packhorses to Connersville." He had probably been here since the previous fall but he did not bring his family until spring. They settled temporarily on Conner's land. Shortly after, Charles Lacy arrived without his family. In April of the same year came a larger group composed of Solomon Finch, his wife, Sarah, his daughters, Rebecca, Mary, and Alma, and his sons, James and Augustus; Israel Finch; Aaron Finch and Amasa Chapman, respectively son and stepson of John Finch, who did not come himself until later; William Bush and his two sons, John and Jared; and James Willison. Amasa Chapman was a brother of Elizabeth Chapman mentioned above. He entertained the party with his flute on their tedious journey, on one occasion when they passed an Indian village playing an accompaniment to the dance of a squaw and her papoose. After a long, cold, wearisome journey they arrived at the junction of Stoney Creek and White River. Here they secured a canoe and ferried across. They chose a ridge across the prairie for the place of settlement. Bush settled south of the Finches, and Willison finally chose a spot on the bluff at the mouth of Stoney Creek. In July the families of William Bush, James Willison, and Israel Finch arrived, and a month later came John Finch (brother of Solomon) and the rest of his family.

These pioneers came on horseback, with their possessions and small children in wagons drawn by ox teams. The domestic animals were driven on foot. Their way led through the present site of New Castle, through Andersontown, which was then nothing but a half-destroyed Indian village to which the Indians had returned, thence to White River. It was the trail long familiar to the Conners by which they came, and so rude was it still that some one of the number had to go ahead and remove logs and brush before the cavalcade could proceed. It took about nineteen days to make the trip. The first party of settlers had built rude cabins for their families so that they were all housed by the time the second party arrived. The one in which Solomon Finch was living had been built mostly by Aaron Finch, who was skilled in this work, so it was turned over to Aaron's father, John Finch, and Solomon built another one southwest of the first—not more than 150 yards distant. The arable land had been planted with corn and vegetables, but insects were numerous and troublesome; vagrant wolves and wildcats killed the domestic animals. The grain food was limited to corn which there was no mill for grinding. Wild game could always be procured for meat, and the river abounded in bass and pike, but compared with their Connersville surroundings, conditions were inexpressibly hard. The transition from village life in Connersville to forest life on White River presented many difficulties.

In August the fatal ague and fever attacked the little settlement. George Shirts's wife was the first to die, then the gay Amasa and little George Finch, son of Solomon. Nearly everyone was sick. There was no doctor, and medicines were contrived from the native herbs. When they were unable to garner the crops they had planted, hunger, as well as sickness, threatened them. Conner's corncrib was never empty, for his prairie land was productive and he was a good farmer. In this extremity, as in others when food was scarce, he sold his corn to those who needed it for their families at less than the retail price, and if they had neither money nor barter he sold on credit, or gave them the needed corn.[18] They pounded it in a handmade mortar, sifting the finest for bread and boiling the coarse remainder to eat with milk. This dish was called "samp," and was far from palatable.

Conner had experienced all the difficulties that the new settlers were now facing and undoubtedly he was helpful to them in a thousand ways—suggesting remedies for the fever, helping to construct rude coffins, instructing them about the soil and crops, assisting in the erection of their buildings, sharing with them his knowledge of the wild beasts, the haunts of game, and the best places to fish. Elizabeth Chapman was attracted to him and her admiration kindled as she saw this competent woodsman moving in their little circle unabashed by desperate illness, danger, or death.

During the following year, 1820, the settlers became more accustomed to their new environment. John Finch was a blacksmith, and it is natural that he should note the form taken by the curves of the river at the new settlement and christen it Horseshoe Prairie. With the blacksmithing outfit which he had brought with him—he was a gunsmith and wheelwright too—he was able to fashion most of the tools that the little community needed. He also made knives and bells that pleased the Indians. It was doubtless he who fashioned the tin grater which the settlers used when the corn was hard enough to grate. Crude as this was, it was an improvement on pounding the meal by the Indian method. George Shirts had become expert in dressing deerskins, and with his instruction the settlers were enabled to dress the skins for their moccasins and leather breeches. It was not long before Bush contrived to make a little hand mill with two good-sized stones to lessen the labor of providing the ever-necessary meal. In the winter, Israel and John Finch built a horse mill which met the requirements of this community until Isaac Wilson's mill was erected on Fall Creek in 1821. The settlers brought their own corn and the horses to grind it and paid six cents a bushel toll. Thus one of the essential industries was started.[19]

One of the group in after years recalled that it was not necessary to raise flax in these first years, for nettles were found in abundance on land near the watercourses, and it was soon discovered that the lint on them was as good as flax or hemp. They were cut, cured, combed, cleaned, and prepared for spinning and weaving just as flax would have been. Out of them were made summer clothing, towels, sheets, and bed-ticking. "They seemed to be something to us about like the manna was to the children of Israel. One little fellow was going to gather nettles enough to make him a pair of leather pants!"[20] In the summer of 1820 a school was opened and conducted by Sarah Finch. The pupils were all Finch children.

8.

Important news came to the little settlement in the spring of the year. On January 11, 1820, the General Assembly passed an act appointing commissioners to select a site for the permanent seat of government in Indiana. Congress, in the Enabling Act of 1816, had granted to the state four sections of land for a capital, to be located by the General Assembly on lands thereafter acquired from the Indians, before public sales had begun in the selected area. The New Purchase and the subsequent surveys of the central section of the state made it possible and desirable to carry out these provisions.[21] The commissioners were instructed to meet at the cabin of William Conner. John Conner was appointed from Fayette County as one of the ten commissioners; the others were George Hunt, Wayne County; Stephen Ludlow, Dearborn; John Gilliland, Switzerland; Joseph Bartholomew, Clark; John Tipton, Harrison; Jesse B. Durham, Jackson; Frederick Rapp, Posey; William Prince, Gibson; and Thomas Emmerson (the name is now spelled Emison), Knox. They were empowered to employ a clerk.

The proceedings of this group are sketched in a journal kept by John Tipton.[22] It gives a roughly drawn but vivid picture of the times. On the sixth day of the journey from Corydon, there arrived at William Conner's house Governor Jennings, who was present ex officio, and Tipton, together with Colonels Durham and Bartholomew, veterans of the Indian wars, who had joined them at Vallonia. The difficulties of travel in this period were great. What seemed to be a road more often proved to be a furrow of mud or rutty dust which diminished to a trace through the woods and was traversable only on horseback and sometimes only on foot. Taverns were infrequent and far apart. The nights were generally spent in blankets laid among weeds with sometimes an improvised

shelter of bark.   The silence of the night was pierced by the
hooting of owls or the howls of wolves.   These commissioners,
however, were traveling in the best style of their times.   They
rode on horses and carried their personal baggage in saddle-
bags, while a colored boy, Bill, followed with a pack horse
loaded with bacon, coffee, corn meal, and a tent.

Upon their arrival at William Conner's cabin, they found
Hunt, John Conner, Ludlow, Gilliland, and Emison waiting
for them.   Governor Jennings and General Tipton were among
Conner's guests.   Some of the others stayed with John Finch.
They waited until late in the evening for Rapp and Prince but
when they did not come were sworn in for their duties and
adjourned until the next day.   When they met under the trees
at Conner's place the next noon—his cabin was too small to
accommodate them all—Hunt was appointed chairman and
Benjamin I. Blythe, clerk.   They adopted formal rules pre-
cisely defining the manner and method of conducting meetings.
Rapp appeared that day and was sworn; Prince did not come
at all.   With no other business immediately before them, they
adjourned to meet at the mouth of Fall Creek the next day.
During the next four days they viewed the land at the con-
fluence of Fall Creek and White River (where the McCormick
family had recently built a cabin), and at the Bluffs on White
River near Waverly, where the cabin of Cyrus Whetzel was
located.   On May 27 they made their decision in favor of the
Fall Creek site.   Their report was not signed for ten days.
Although the township lines had been run, the surveys of the
section lines had not been completed, and the commissioners
were obliged to wait until this could be done.

Undoubtedly the fact that the junction of Fall Creek and
White River was the converging point of Indian trails from
Vincennes, from the falls of the Ohio, from Whitewater, from
the upper Delaware towns on White River and the Potawatomi
and Miami towns on the Wabash, had a strong influence upon
these men who realized that the roads of the settlers would
follow the trails for many years to come.   In addition, there
was a good fording place at this point for those seeking lands
farther west.   It may have been this fording place which first
attracted the Indians to it.   It is a noticeable fact that many
of the locations of large cities in this country were originally

the converging point of Indian trails or the former sites of Indian villages.[23]

One determinant in favor of the Fall Creek site was the fact that it had the best landing near the center of the state for boats coming up White River. After the surveys were completed the commissioners met at McCormick's cabin and signed their report. In less than two hours thereafter a boat landed here before their eyes and unloaded the household goods of two families moving to the mouth of Fall Creek. It seemed a good omen for their choice and Tipton jocularly mentioned in his Journal the landing of "the first boat . . . that ever was seen at the seat of government."

It was an advantage that the site was near the mouth of Fall Creek. Mills could be located on Fall Creek and thus town and mills would be on the same side of the river. Easy access to the base of grain supplies, easy methods of transportation, these were cogent reasons for locating the city from the standpoint of pioneers who had suffered untold privations for lack of them. It is a matter of regret that there was no one present to speak in favor of a healthful location. Perhaps those who favored the Bluffs had that consideration in mind, but the site was discarded because "the banks were too high to allow a convenient boat landing." Had anyone suggested that within twenty-seven years these reasons for the selection of this site would be obsolete, he would have been laughed to scorn. In less than fourteen years William Conner was actually interested in promoting a railroad to Indianapolis. In 1838 Tipton was advocating in the United States Senate a railroad grant in Indiana![24]

As more than a week elapsed between the time when the commissioners reached their decision and the completion of the surveys, there was plenty of time for other activities. Hunt and John•Conner went home, while the others returned to William Conner's house to spend the night. The fishing was good and Governor Jennings proved quite expert with the gig used in the canoe, an exciting method of catching fish. Judge Fabius M. Finch says that "the surface of the water as far as the eye could reach, [was] so literally covered with fish— about six inches below the surface—that they appeared to touch each other and in many instances did touch; and this of all

kinds of fish, from the monster muskalonge to the hated gar."
There was no chance of a failure to "catch."

Deer hunting in canoes at night by torchlight was the best
sport of all. As described by Judge Finch, there were two
persons in each canoe, one to paddle, the other to use the gun.
The guns and a torch were in the bow—the steersman in the
stern. As they approached a deer, tempted by the warm
weather to feed on the grass near the water, the gunner would
rock the boat and the deer would stand fascinated for a
moment by this strange apparition. The crack of the gun
broke the spell, and the hunter waited tensely to see whether he
had made a hit. There was also the popular Indian game of
moccasin, a favorite one with the Miami and Potawatomi. A
half dozen newly made moccasins were placed in a semicircle
on a flat surface. The operator would place his hand under
each moccasin, dexterously leaving a bullet under one of them.
Then the bets would be made as to which moccasin covered the
bullet.[25]

Jennings was courageous but he had enemies and he usually
carried some sort of a weapon as was quite common in those
days. On this occasion he had a silver-hilted dagger in a silver-
mounted scabbard, which he lost on Conner's farm, probably
when engaged in one of these pastimes. Later, one of the
little Finch boys found it and brought it to Conner for identification.[26]

The pleasant days passed quickly until the surveys were
completed. On the seventh of June the commissioners met
again at Fall Creek and signed their report. Only two locations had serious consideration—the present site and the
Bluffs, fifteen miles farther down the river. There have been
random statements from time to time to the effect that other
locations were discussed, such as the present site of Noblesville,
New Britton, Strawtown, and William Conner's land, but they
are only unsupported personal recollections. The land selected
amounted to 2,560 acres, four sections in township 15 north,
range 3 east. This choice was ratified by the legislature on
January 6, 1821. The name "Indianapolis" was given to the
new capital and notwithstanding the merriment, ridicule and
criticism it provoked, was adopted.[27]

Shortly after June 7 all the commissioners had departed

and the community settled down to a humdrum existence. This sojourn of the little group of men from different parts of the state had broken its monotony. It had been an honor to entertain the first governor of the state, a very human and a kindly person who entered into all the homely sports with skill and interest. Outstanding among the commissioners were rugged, outspoken John Tipton and the dignified and other-worldly Frederick Rapp. Several of the visitors had seen service in the War of 1812; all were pioneers in the counties from which they came. The settlers recalled how cordially they had all greeted the Conner brothers and with what simple dignity William Conner had moved among his guests. The outcome of their mission was of vital local interest, too, for the choice of a site less than twenty miles away would stimulate development in their own community. Already there had been several additions to the settlement—the Robert Duncans, the family of Charles Lacy, the Baxters, the Audricks, James Wilson, and Curtis Mallory. The last named was a school teacher. Eight other families had passed through the settlement to points beyond, nearer the site which had been selected for the capital. These were but the first of hundreds yet to come. There would be changes taking place almost over night, creeping upon them almost before they were aware. They were to be caught and carried on the swiftly flowing stream of a commonwealth in the making.

9.

William Conner's place did not receive much consideration from the commissioners; if it had, it would have been portentous for him, for he had as yet no title or even color of title to this land upon which he had lived for so many years. The United States was now the owner of it. If it had been selected, he would have had no choice but to give it up. All of his work of clearing, cultivation, and improvements would have gone for nothing. He knew now as a certainty that Mekinges and the children would leave for the West with the Delawares, in obedience to the tribal law that the Indian wife must stay with her people. In the hubbub of this last company of guests she had moved quietly about, attending to their needs and keeping the children out of the way. But her ways were not the ways of a white woman; her housekeeping was not like theirs; these differences he had noted first by contrast with his brother's home at Connersville, and later in the homes of the settlers on Horseshoe Prairie. There were other matters, however, to be considered.

In a mood of meditation he entered his cabin. There at the head of his bed was the trunk of silver dollars accumulated by years of trading, and near it lay his rifle. That was his wealth. It must be divided with his partner, Marshall, who planned to go with the Delawares. Marshall would look after Mekinges, but she and the children must be provided for. Sixty ponies should be hers. And one stipulation he must make. From time to time the children should come back to see him, which they did. If land came to him from the United States government he would pay them for their interest in it, notwithstanding the fact that they were going to a country where land would be given them by the government. As he stepped out of the cabin his eyes rested on the field across the river that had been cleared and was now under cultivation, his beloved prairie, the slowly moving river. This was his home. Here he was destined to remain. His thoughts turned to the settlement on Horseshoe Prairie. Upon the film of his vision appeared the trim, gracious figure of Elizabeth Chapman. How capable she had seemed in that household of little children in John Finch's home. With these reflections came the conclusion that his cabin was too old to serve much longer. Every year brought more travelers to his door and the number would increase with the coming of the state capital. His rough shack had been too small for his recent guests. He was sorry he could not have offered better lodgings to Governor Jennings. A new ambition stirred in the breast of William Conner. The opportunities and means for his metamorphosis were surely and steadily approaching.

10.

The Fourth of July was the great day of celebration among the pioneers, more widely observed than Christmas. It came at a time of year when there was a lull in the farm work and the weather was generally good, making it possible for them to get together from greater distances. Never before, however, had it been celebrated in this section, for the excellent reason that there was no one here except Conner and the Indians and the latter were scarcely in the mood! It was different now. The young people of the settlement were not to be denied the excitement of a picnic dinner with toasts to all the great Americans living and dead and other subjects of national and local interest. It cannot be that the new capital was overlooked on this occasion.

James G. Finch has described this first celebration :[28] "They drove forks in the ground, laid poles up on them and then covered it with brush with the leaves on. Under this shade they ate their dinners and drank their toasts with great glee and hilarity. At night they had a dance; there was no such thing as a fiddle in fifty miles of them so they had to depend entirely upon vocal music and frequently the musician was in the dance." Young Amasa Chapman, the flute player, was dead. This may have been William Conner's first celebration of the Fourth, but frequently thereafter his farm was the gathering place for the community on like occasions. Of course all the Finches were there; John Finch's family of six children under fourteen years and several older ones; Solomon Finch's family of five young people; Lacys, Bushes, and the Shirtses, the Mallorys, the Duncans. The Willisons and the Baxters may not have been present, for they were indulging in some petty feud with the Finches about this time—another phase of frontier life.[29] Were the Indians there as onlookers, Mekinges too, and her brood of six? If so, the affair must have appeared as strange to them as did their Indian dances and councils to white eyes.

II.

In late August or early September the Delaware Indians began collecting near William Conner's cabin preparatory to their departure to their new home in western Missouri. They probably came from their old settlements on White River. Chief Anderson was undoubtedly among them for at this point his daughter Mekinges would join him. The old chief felt bitterly about the St. Mary's treaties which had deprived them of the lands on which the Delawares had lived since about 1795. The Indians were a forlorn, dejected company—

weakened by diseases and drunkenness, poorly fed and clothed. Mekinges prepared to join them with her children, Jack (or John), Nancy, Harry (or Hamilton), James, William, and Eliza. Their ages are not known but they were all under eighteen and possibly under fourteen years old.

Conner set about the division of the proceeds of the trading post with his partner, Marshall. James G. Finch (son of Solomon) was only an eleven-year-old boy at the time, but he assisted at the division and related the story afterwards: "When they were dividing their money they would count out two large piles of silver dollars and have me turn my back, and one of them would point at a pile and say who shall have that?" The disinterested little boy would reply with one of their names and the matter was settled. At this time the property settlement did not include any real estate. Mekinges was given the promised sixty ponies.[30]

At last a sufficient number of Indians had assembled to start on their march. Mekinges and the Conner children mounted their ponies. The half-breed son of John Conner, his namesake, was among them. He had been staying with his uncle for some time. Perhaps his father was there to see him off. Marshall put his own family in readiness. The proud old chief took his place at the head of the procession and the trek westward began. William Conner gazed until they were lost to view and the last bit of dust raised by the ponies' feet had sunk to the ground. He reflected proudly that Mekinges was the best dressed of all the Indian women.[31] She and the children had been given half of his property. He did not own any real estate at that time, but later when the title to six hundred and forty acres was vested in him, his wife, and their children, he purchased their interest at what was known as the "Congress" price. They were also participants in the annuities granted at St. Mary's.

Their new lands in the West proved far more valuable than those they had left in Indiana. When they migrated they first went to western Missouri. Later they removed to Kansas and finally to Oklahoma. They and their descendants shared in the prosperity of that country with their white neighbors. Nancy Conner's grandson, Richard C. Adams, great-grandson of William Conner, became a leader of his people in the South-

west. As attorney for the Delaware Indians with the Cherokee
nation he industriously reminded the government of the
United States, in speeches and articles preserved in the Library
of Congress, of the loyalty and services of the Delawares in the
War of the Revolution and in the Civil War. In these
brochures, *passim,* is to be found the history of that tribe from
the time of the first white invaders to the present. He mentions a John Conner, a Delaware interpreter who was
commended by John R. Taylor, Indian agent in Texas in 1857,
as having rendered such important services that the state of
Texas made him a citizen and gave him a league of land.
Conner had devoted his best years in trying to make peace
with the wild and warlike tribes. He may have been a de-
scendant of William Conner. It is the family tradition that
John, the half-breed son of John Conner, at the time of his
death in the 1860's had a large farm with a red brick house
overlooking the Missouri River. Of two hundred and one
adult Delaware males it is said that one hundred and seventy
enlisted in the United States Army in the Civil War. Some
of the third generation of the Conner Delawares were perhaps
in this enlistment. Of the daughters, Eliza Conner became
Elizabeth Bullitt and was living as late as 1861. Nancy was
dead before 1852, leaving a daughter and a son. Descendants
of these half-breed children of William Conner have been
more or less engaged in the political, industrial, and agricultural life in the Southwest since the first decade of their
removal in 1820.[32]

CHAPTER IX

The Transformation of William Conner—The Founding of Noblesville

A CIVIL marriage occurred at the cabin of John Finch on Horeshoe Prairie on November 30, 1820. A glamour attaches to this wedding. The past year had been full of dramatic incidents for this little pioneer settlement—the coming of all the new families in the spring, the meeting of the commissioners to select the site of the capital, the first Fourth of July celebration, the assembling and departure of the first group of Delaware Indians, the shadow of death that had fallen upon several of the families, which seemed to be an accompaniment of every autumn—and now a wedding—one of the first in the New Purchase. It would have been a notable happening in a humdrum year; it was the crowning event of these crowded twelve months.

It was unusual because of the participants. The bridegroom was a dominating figure in the community. His adventurous past, his unusual relations with the Indians, his knowledge of the woods, his mature demeanor—all these were thrown in high relief by the fair young girl whom he had chosen. The great differences in their ages—about thirty years—caused some speculation as to the success of this venture; still more marked was the contrast in the environments from which they had come. So long had William Conner lived among the Indians that the contour and coloring of his face resembled theirs; his gait and bearing, his gestures and voice seemed more like theirs than the white settlers. Elizabeth Chapman seemed to be marrying a man more Indian than white. She had been born in New York—a state old compared to Indiana—in the month and year when her bridegroom was building his cabin on White River. He had lived the rough life of the wilderness, while she spent her childhood in a sheltered home protected by her mother and brother and later by the large family of her stepfather. She had had no intimate contact with the Indians and had not even been a member of a crude pioneer community until these last few years. She exhibited, however, a courage and a faith that commanded from the little company who watched her the same confidence engendered by the manly assurance and calmness of the groom.

In all of the New Purchase there was not a magistrate, for there were not yet enough settlers for the organization of a county. Fielding Hazelrigg, a justice of the peace from Connersville, was requested to perform the ceremony by virtue of a license issued by James M. Ray, a deputy clerk of that place and a long-time friend, who was accommodating enough to risk the penalties of the law in issuing a license outside his own county. John Conner and Benjamin I. Blythe rode up from Connersville with Hazelrigg to attend the wedding. Perhaps James M. Ray came too, and a young lawyer named William W. Wick, who had been almost a year in Connersville and a year later was to marry Laura Finch, a half-sister of the bride. All the settlers in the immediate vicinity were present as a matter of course. The Finches, the Bushes, the Duncans, and the Mallorys are named, but it is scarcely to be doubted that the guests also included the Shirtses and the Lacys. There were some unexpected guests—a band of friendly Indians who, out of respect and affection for William Conner, camped near John Finch's house for a day or two before the wedding and did not leave until the festivities were over. The merry company of pioneer men were clad in buckskin trousers and vests; the women wore homespun blue or brown flannel dresses, neatly made but not too closely fitting, with tucks or flounces at the bottom and a white ruffle around the neck, capped by a chintz or calico bonnet with a single bow of ribbon. Beyond this company was a circle of quiet, waiting red men, like the chorus of a Greek play.

Unfortunately John Finch was ill, but that in no way affected the lavish hospitality of his household. How all these guests were accommodated in his small two-room cabin cannot be imagined, nor how the ceremony could be seen by all. Perhaps one of those rare Indian summer days that sometimes occur in Indiana allowed the celebration to be held out of doors. Through the eyes of the imagination can be seen silhouetted in the wooden frame of the doorway the erect, bronzed woodsman, the bridegroom who is turning an entirely new page in the history of his eventful life. By his side is a slender, shy, young woman, endowed with all the womanly graces. Facing them stands the magistrate. Grouped around them are relatives, friends, and neighbors with eager, curious, expectant faces. The dusky border of Indians looks silently, steadily, at the central figures. It was a strange, incomprehensible sight to them. They had never seen a marriage of the whites before. Its ritual had for them no solemn import, but it excited their curiosity. What was the meaning of these questions and answers? To them a marriage was a matter of simple agreement —mutual consent expressed by the reception of presents; refusal indicated by the rejection of them. It was not only the novelty of this proceeding, however, that held them spellbound. It was the chief figure—William Conner. All that he had meant to them must now have recurred to them, his fairness, his justness, his honesty, and his kindliness. He had been the husband of the daughter of their chief and in the veins of their relatives, his blood was mingled with theirs. If they saw in this mysterious ceremony the end of long years of the closest association; that their ways would be no longer his, and his ways no longer theirs, their grim, immobile faces did not betray them.

The ceremony was followed by a substantial backwoods feast. Corn was the usual fare in this little community, but on this day there was an abundance of bread made from wheat secured from "over yonder in the White water." Fowls were furnished by Jean Baptiste who lived near the trading post; fine fish came from White River; roasted quail and pheasants and venison steaks were plentifully distributed on the tables; the sweets of the feast were wild plums and crab apples preserved in maple sugar, but the *pièce de résistance* was the concoction from the wheat flour. After the feast the Indians broke camp and silently slipping into the forest were soon veiled from view by its yellowish haze. There was no honeymoon or wedding trip. The bride and groom either forded or ferried across the river and rode horseback to Conner's cabin three miles away. Here Elizabeth Conner was installed as mistress of the combined dwelling and trading post which had been her husband's home for eighteen years.[1]

Elizabeth Chapman Conner

2.

The year following this event was marked by the advent of more families along this part of White River. There were now three settlements—the one of which William Conner's cabin was the center; the Horseshoe Prairie community, two and a half miles north of Conner's near the mouth of Stoney Creek; and Strawtown, about eight or nine miles farther north from Horseshoe Prairie. The last-named settlement was near the site of the old Indian town of Nanticoke, or Nancy Town. Its first white settler was John Shintaffer, an Indian trader. There were eight settlers there in 1820 and the following year added six more, some with their families and some without. The settlement at William Conner's, consisting of the Bushes, the Shirtses, and the Lacys had been increased by the Duncans and a man named Chapel Brown. Solomon Finch was employed by Conner during this year and had removed to his farm temporarily. It was probably while Finch was at Conner's that a distillery was built, and a horse mill, similar to the one on Horseshoe Prairie erected by the Finches. Andrew Wallace, who had charge of the government survey of the county, had been staying with Conner, and Josiah F. Polk, a young lawyer from the East, was also there. The colony at Horseshoe Prairie, also, was increased by several families. One newcomer was Allen Baxter, who sowed the first wheat in the county. News that the land would soon be offered for sale increased the interest of prospective homeseekers who wished to select their lands personally before buying.[2]

3.

A disturbing happening this year reminded the settlers that mere occupation of the land did not insure law and order. The trouble arose in the settlement at Strawtown, but it created great excitement in all three places. A Potawatomi Indian who came to John Shintaffer's trading post accused the trader of diluting the liquor he sold him with river water. The Indian was half drunk and easily overpowered by the trader, who angrily threw him into the midst of a heap of logs which he was burning. The Indian was in no condition to extricate himself and Shintaffer looked on at his horrible death. When news of this atrocity reached the tribe they were quick to act—

sending ten or eleven braves armed with tomahawks and knives
to Shintaffer's cabin. The near-by settlers, fearing that their
own homes might be in danger if Shintaffer were killed, rallied
to his support, though no one of them could have been in sympathy with his action. A pitched battle ensued and one of the
settlers, Benjamin Fisher, was killed. The Indians made a
hasty retreat, broke camp, and fled to Fort Wayne. It was
a horrible reminder to all in the vicinity that they were still
uncomfortably close to a highly inflammable tinderbox. The
incident shows Conner's post and his relations to the Indians in
striking contrast, for no such disgraceful incident was ever recorded of his establishment. For many years to come the set-
lers were to realize that while the Indians who passed their
homes and sometimes stopped, were outwardly friendly, it took
very little to stir their revengeful wrath against those who
wronged them.[3]

4.

Slowly, steadily, and peaceably the little community was
moving forward. Enough grain had been raised over and
above the needs of the settlement, so that some could be sent
down the river to other settlements or to a larger market. It
was in May or June of 1821 that a keelboat from Indianapolis
stopped at Conner's to take on grain raised the year before.
Other keel- and flatboats had passed them carrying pioneers
and their household goods to points beyond, but evidently this
was the first time such a boat had stopped for produce. It
was a new sight to all, and to the younger settlers it was a
thrilling one. The boats that had floated corn down the river
before were canoes made from big poplar logs, lashed two
and two to keep them from turning over. The keelboat (a
covered freight boat, having a keel but no sails) could be pulled
up the river "by tying a rope to a tree and pulling the boat up
to it; or by poling, that is by pushing the boat along with
poles."[4] Transportation was one of the most vexing problems
of the pioneers.

A negro who assisted in getting the crop ready for the
market was of great interest to these settlers who had come
from northern states and who were probably little more familiar with the negro than the Indian. No one knew where he

came from. He lived for a while with the Indians, then went
to work for William Conner. He denied that he had been a
slave, but a Kentuckian who came through the country late in
1820 claimed him, secured a writ, and packed him off, to the
commiseration and indignation of the entire settlement. It was
the first insight of the settlers into the evils of slavery.[5]

5.

The chief excitement of the year was the opening of the
sales of lands in the New Purchase at Brookville. No public
land could be sold until it had been offered at public sale.
Bought at private sale later it cost only $1.25 per acre. The
advantage of attending the public sale was that a choicer selection could be made even though the price was higher. The
settlers had made their selection in advance and had been sav-
ing money for purchase ever since they arrived. It was an
important day and while some secured their choice, others were
doomed to disappointment. By an unwritten law among the
pioneers, whoever selected a piece of land and improved it, was
allowed first chance at it. In this new country it was not possible to make extensive and permanent improvements in two
years. Rough cabins had been erected by some, though others
had used only abandoned Indian huts. Sufficient fencing had
been erected to enclose pasturage for a small amount of live
stock. The land had been cultivated to some extent but there
were fields near each settlement that had been cleared and cultivated by the Indians prior to this time and naturally they made
use of these. Little attempt had been made to clear the land of
forest trees, for this was too big an improvement to undertake
on unsold lands.

John Conner made up his mind to remove from Connersville to a site near his brother William, and incidentally much
nearer the capital of the state. He proposed to erect a sawmill, a gristmill, and a carding machine on the land at Horseshoe Prairie, which seemed ideally suited to his needs. He
entered it at Brookville, outbidding a man named Audrick, or
Andrick, one of the more recent arrivals from Virginia who
expected to buy this land and said he would pay the settlers
for their improvements. This Conner refused to do for the
reason that the development of the prairie which he had in

mind would increase the value of neighboring properties and more than repay the owners. At the time Conner's action was resented by some. A contemporary commented years later that "Conner had the longest pole and he got the persimmon." Audrick, however, soon lost his reputation in the community for reliability and integrity. Conner kept his word and shortly his water mill, constructed with much care, was "the admiration of two or three counties."[6]

There was a redistribution of settlers after the sale of the lands. Twelve or more families settled below William Conner's near the river and on both sides of it. As the Horseshoe Prairie had been bought by John Conner, the Finch families moved about four miles east of it and four miles south of the present site of Noblesville. Ten or more families joined them there and the community came to be known as the Finch settlement.

Meanwhile John Conner was going ahead with his plans for the development of Horseshoe Prairie and had secured the passage of an act in the legislature of 1822-1823, of which he was not a member, authorizing him to erect a dam for a grist- and sawmill across White River at the Horseshoe Bend, which was only half a mile from the newly planned county seat. The act provided that the dam should be so built as to allow boats to pass.[7] The legislators still cherished hopes for the navigation of White River. As soon as this authorization was given, Conner started work on his proposed improvements. With characteristic energy he brought his family from Connersville to temporary quarters in one of the log cabins that had been built on Horeshoe Prairie; he let the contract for the millrace and the dam, employed all the men who were willing to work, and brought from the East millwrights and carpenters for the skilled labor. The mill was completed in 1823. It ground wheat and corn sufficient for the requirements of the community. Later the sawmill was finished and a carding machine was installed. Prior to this time the women had carded their wool into rolls by the use of hand cards. These improvements were of great benefit to the community.

6.

Increasingly, William Conner realized that his cabin no

longer suited his station in this rapidly growing community. Many of his cherished recollections, however, clung about it. Here was the real beginning of his location as a trader. Here for eighteen years he had lived with the Indians at the head of an Indian family. One feature of the cabin paid tribute to his reputation as a hunter and a crack shot. Over the door he had put up two little forks made from the limb of a dogwood tree in which he had placed an old-fashioned long-range rifle; near it hung a calfskin pouch and with it a gun charger— all intended and used for hunting game birds and small animals. His hospitality was so cordial and well known that this display did not disturb his guests, but it made his cabin appear more like a hunter's lodge than a home.[8] The site of the new capital was drawing large numbers of settlers and travelers, and he realized that with the coming of a new order and a new people his present dwelling would be out of place. On January 4, 1823, his first child by Elizabeth Chapman was born. The little girl received the name of Lavina, which was already cherished in the family, for it was the name of John Conner's wife and her little daughter, who died while still a baby.

Shortly after this event William Conner began to plan the building of a larger home. He entered the land on which the new residence was to be built on April 20, 1823, and on August 7 of that year the government issued a patent for it. A pleasant spot on the upper east bank of White River south of the cabin site was chosen as the location of the two-story brick house which he completed in 1823. The walls were solid brick, very thick. The woodwork was yellow poplar. It is said that the brick used in the house was burned on the premises and that mechanics were brought from the East to make "the delicate mantels, stairways and glass-door cupboards. The lines are purely colonial, light and unusually delicate for this region." It was considered at the time as "remarkably handsome," "elegant"—one of the first brick houses in the New Purchase. Nathaniel Bolton, state librarian, in a lecture in 1853 before the Indiana Historical Society said that during 1823 he "spent many delightful evenings" at Conner's mansion. Enraptured by the view before him, he said: "I never beheld a more delightful scene than when I looked down from the second story of Mr. Conner's dwelling on a field of three hundred acres of waving corn, some two feet high, with fifteen or twenty merry plowmen scattered over it at work. It was doubly interesting, coming, as I did, out of nature's forest, only broken by the occasional cabins and small patches of cleared land of the early settlers."[9]

Notwithstanding the ravages of time, the use of the house by tenants of succeeding owners, the stripping of its fine belongings and the years of neglect, the house retained its dignity and air of distinction. Arising in the wilderness it resisted for 112 years all innovations. In 1935 the house and surrounding acres were purchased by a public-spirited citizen of Indianapolis, Mr. Eli Lilly, president of the Indiana Historical Society. With great care and fine discrimination the house has been restored to its original condition.

A center hall divides the house, disclosing at one end the broad sweep of the prairie farm and providing at the other the usual mode of entrance from the land which leads to the main road. On entering the yard the old well first meets the eye. A veranda which was not a part of the house in William Conner's time has been added to the other entrance for the sake of comfort. Spacious rooms with a fireplace in each, open from the hall, and from it a graceful stairway leads to the second floor, where there is a similar arrangement of rooms with a fireplace in each. The original plaster on all the rooms seemed to have been dipped in the blue dye kettle, for such was its color, but no such traditionally gloomy wall covering could darken this prairie home, which was open on all sides to the air and sunlight. Adjoining the dining room on the south side of the hall is an old-fashioned kitchen containing a spacious fireplace with an oven on one side. A staircase which had been closed for many years has been reopened and leads to a loft-like room above the kitchen.

Mrs. Lilly has been remarkably successful in refitting the entire house with furnishings of the period and memorabilia of the original owner. Two chief treasures have found a space on the walls of the dining room. These are the original portraits of William Conner and his wife Elizabeth Chapman Conner, painted by Jacob Cox, early Indiana portrait painter. The cupboards in this room are filled with the dishes and glassware of this period. South of the house there is a small building added by Mr. Lilly to house the large collection of original and photostatic material concerning William Conner. Here in permanent files easily accessible are the photostat copies of the treaties of which Conner served as interpreter. Upon the walls of this building hang samples of all the different fur skins in which he and his brother traded. Below this house, the old distillery has been faithfully restored in its original situation. Once more the Conner homestead takes its place as an historic landmark of central Indiana.

7.

Clear as though limned against the sky was the ambition of the builders of the new state to convert a wilderness, unsubordinated to human hands, into town and village centers of civilization. Application for the formation of a new county north of Marion County was made to the General Assembly of 1822-1823, and it is reasonable to suppose that the Conners had a hand in drawing up the petition and suggesting the boundaries. On January 8, 1823, after a reconsidered vote, the Assembly authorized the formation of a county to be called Hamilton.[10] Commissioners named in the act were directed to meet at the house of William Conner on the first Monday of May to investigate and to determine the site for the county seat. Until suitable accommodations could be had at "the seat of justice" the circuit court proceedings were likewise directed to be held there. By this fiat Conner's dwelling was made serviceable to public uses.

At this time the young and clever Josiah F. Polk, who had come out of the East in search of his fortune, was living at Conner's house. He was quick to take advantage of the opportunity afforded by the formation of a new county to purchase lands that might reasonably be chosen for the county seat. Conner was familiar with all the land in the vicinity and was well and favorably known. He may have been ambitious also to emulate his brother as the founder of a town. The two men, William Conner and Polk, bought about one hundred acres on the east bank of White River some four miles north of Conner's Trading Post and in January, 1823, platted a town there and called it Noblesville.[11] They offered generous inducements to secure the county seat, and at a four-day session in March, 1824, the commissioners accepted their proposals. The proprietors agreed to donate to the county the public square and one-half of all in-lots and fractional lots and other land with certain reservations for their own use. Part of the donation was to be used for county buildings and the remainder sold, the proceeds thereof to be used to erect buildings. Polk built the first dwelling house. With money realized from the sale of lots and by private subscription the first public building, a jail, was started that year. It was a safe conjecture in any new county that while courts and commissioners might manage in temporary quarters, a stout jail was an immediate necessity.

The administrative, judicial, and fiscal affairs of this small political subdivision were handled as in other counties by a sheriff, judges, clerk, recorder, treasurer, and commissioners, some at first appointed by the governor but thereafter chosen in general elections. The first session of the circuit court was held in William Conner's house in August, 1823. John Finch and William C. Blackmore qualified as associate judges; William W. Wick was presiding judge; John D. Stephenson, clerk, Robert L. Hannaman, recorder, William P. Warrick, sheriff, and William Conner, treasurer.

In those days whisky could only be sold by license. Continual violations of this regulation were followed by indictments and trials. There were cases of grand larceny, frequent cases of trespass, and petty civil actions. The first term of the court lasted two days, with pending cases held over to the succeeding term. At the April term in 1824 some probate matters were disposed of. This was the last term of court held at William Conner's house. The Board of County Commissioners, also, during the years 1823, 1824, and 1825, with the exception of one meeting, convened either in William or John Conner's house. In 1825 the legislature directed the clerk to keep his books and papers at John Conner's until a suitable room was prepared in the town of Noblesville. It was not until 1826 that a courthouse provided the accommodations that had till then been furnished by the Conners for a nominal rent, or quite free.

8.

A tradition has existed in the Conner family for many years that James Fenimore Cooper visited William Conner sometime after 1823 to secure information concerning the Delaware Indians for his *Leather-Stocking Tales*. The accounts of this visit, as given by Conner's living grandchildren, were handed down to them by their parents, sons of William Conner. There is no extant record in Cooper's family or elsewhere that he was ever in Indiana.[12] His Indians, however, were Delawares, and he wrote of the virtues and courage of that tribe. It is said that he derived his knowledge of them largely from Heckewelder's writings or, if from other sources, it was confirmed by them. It will be recalled that Heckewelder was one of the Moravian missionaries who was a captive of the British Indians in 1781, as was the child, William Conner. General Lewis Cass had had a great deal of experience with Indians on the battlefield, in treaty councils, and as Indian agent. He had a practical mind; and to him it seemed that none of the idealized Indians in Cooper's novels were "the fierce and crafty warriors that roam through our forests." He regarded Heckewelder, whom he had known in Ohio, as a "kindhearted, plain old man" whose knowledge of Indians was gained largely from the Moravian group, and was not therefore generally sound. He felt so strongly about Cooper's gilding of the Indian character that he took occasion to criticize it in a review of Heckewelder's *Indian Nations* published in the *North American Review*. Another relevant comment has been made to the effect that Cass's mind was "bent upon destroying the romantic conception of savage life." It is not probable that Cooper derived his information about the Delawares from Conner, but had he done so, he would have received the same impression that he had from Heckewelder, for Conner considered the Delawares the best of all the Indian tribes.[13]

A French-American lawyer and philologist, Peter S. Du Ponceau, living in Philadelphia, was corresponding secretary of the Historical and Literary Committee of the American Philosophical Society and subsequently its president. His interest was excited by a grammar of the Delaware language which had been prepared by David Zeisberger, and he began an investigation of the subject. A voluminous and learned discussion occurred in the exchange of letters during 1816 between Du Ponceau, Dr. Caspar Wistar, then president of the society, and Reverend John Heckewelder. The attention of scholars generally was drawn to it. Did the Delaware language have inflections, suffixes, and prefixes as did the English language? The controversy revolved about these points. When Cass learned of Du Ponceau's conclusion that the Delawares had a grammar language, he looked upon it as merely another phase of romanticism about the Indians. He applied to Secretary of War Calhoun, for leave to appoint a suitable person to pursue inquiries as to the customs and languages of the Indians, to which consent was given.

Charles C. Trowbridge, of Michigan, who had been entrusted by Cass with other important duties, was directed in December, 1823, to proceed to the residence of William Conner on White River in Indiana. Trowbridge found Conner "an intelligent gentleman and an excellent interpreter." He further records that "Connor's residence was eighteen miles from Indianapolis, which had just been declared the capital of the State, but was not yet occupied by the legislature. Its population was about three hundred. We reached it on horseback, by an Indian trail. There being little population and no roads, there was no market for farm products. Wheat was worth twenty-five cents a bushel and corn six to ten cents. The Indians supplied us all winter with turkeys at six cents each."

Trowbridge was fully aware of Cass's skeptical attitude. In 1874 in an account of his trip to Conner's residence he wrote: "The General thought it all a myth. He had seen the border Indians in war, at treaties, around the camp-fire or dancing the 'begging dance' and he could not comprehend what subsequent investigation has so fully confirmed in regard to the structure of the Indian language, differing widely in words and varied by harsh gutterals and soft labials but all obeying the law of inflection, suffix and postfix."

Trowbridge spent three months at Conner's residence (the present brick house) with "Capt. Pipe, an intelligent Delaware chief, and some of his staff, daily occupied in researches into the manners, customs and dialect of his tribe." Captain Pipe was probably the son or nephew of the Captain Pipe who had

been one of the leaders in the capture of the Conner family
and the Moravian Indians in 1781, and who died in 1794. An
Indian chief's name usually descended to his successor. Trowbridge further says: "the investigations with Captain Pipe revealed a marvellous system of regular verbal inflection, and
prepositional arrangement. Although I have not for many
years paid attention to the subject, I believe similar investigations into the dialects of other tribes have exhibited confirma-
tory evidence of Duponceau's views."

At this time, although William Conner was living detached
from the Indians, Trowbridge noted that he was held in high
esteem by them as a man of probity. Trowbridge recognized
that Conner not only possessed much knowledge himself, but
he greatly appreciated his aid in getting information from Indian chiefs in that vicinity. The Miami chiefs, Le Gris and
Richardville, were very helpful to him as to the history, traditions, and language of their tribe. The inquiry begun at Conner's house in December lasted until March, 1824, when Trowbridge returned to Detroit. His conclusion was that Du Ponceau
had only reached the threshold of his investigation whether
General Cass was convinced of his error or not. A large mass
of very important data was transmitted by Trowbridge to
Cass who referred it to the government at Washington.[14]
Zeisberger's Delaware grammar is said to survive and repose
under lock and key in the library of Harvard University.[15]

9.

The year before the studious, painstaking Trowbridge visited Conner, another whose personality was strongly in contrast
met Conner at a religious service in the neighborhood and was
invited to spend the night at his cabin. This was probably in
1822. Baynard R. Hall was the name of this itinerant teacher
and preacher. He came to Indiana from the East about 1820.
In 1823 he was elected president of Indiana Seminary, now
Indiana University. He remained in the state seven and a half
years and returning East he wrote in 1843 an account of his
experiences and observations under the pen name of Robert
Carlton. The narrative is so clouded with pseudonyms and
anonymities that to identify persons and places is perplexing.
Dates are not given but can be arrived at approximately by

addition and subtraction. In 1916 an unexpurgated edition was issued by the Princeton University Press. It offers a key to the book in which "Mr. Redwhite" is identified as John Conner. Hall says that Mr. Redwhite "lived in a cabin, or rather a dozen cabins," and that "he owned tracts of very valuable land presented to him by his red lady's tribe." She was reported to have "deserted her husband to live with her exiled people." This description fitted William Conner's situation and not John's. In fact, at that time the latter was living in Connersville.

Hall and Conner, according to this account, became very intimate friends because of their coincident opinion that the Indians "have had abundant provocations for most of their misdeeds." Hall's interest in Conner's young wife was aroused, as he thought she was a survivor of the Wyoming massacre in which her mother had perished. His sensibilities were deeply stirred by that tragedy, and he comments disapprovingly that "when she talked of Wyoming it was without emotion!—while I was repressing tears!" Applying the antidote of facts to Hall's hyperbole, the Wyoming tragedy occurred in 1778 and Elizabeth Conner was not born until 1802. In 1822 her mother was living on Horseshoe Prairie.

His narrative includes a description of the supper—of the elegant appointments, particularly the silver—the "superbly made" tea and coffee; choice rolls; "delicious butter rising in unctuous pyramids, fretted from base to apex into a kind of butyrial shell work:—this resting on silver and to be cut with silver." Steaks done on gridirons; warm breads and puddings; cakes and fruits—all were served from silver plates, mats and urns and "on cloth as white as—snow." He asks, "was ever such a contrast as between the untutored world around and the array, and splendour, and richness of our sumptuous banquet?" It does seem too incongruous. The Conners had opportunities in their visits to eastern cities to procure not only the personal and household articles that were necessary to their comfort but others which were, in their surroundings, really luxuries. They had the means and indulged their tastes, but the lavish display described by Hall was unlike them. He probably was again misled by imperfect memory or by the possession of a too vivid imagination.[16]

CHAPTER X

John Conner, Early Indianapolis Merchant

TWENTY miles south of the Conner settlements near Nobles-ville, the new capital of the state was in process of develop-ment. Three McCormick brothers, Samuel, John, and James had journeyed thither from Connersville in an ox-drawn covered wagon as early as February, 1820. Twelve employees accompanied them to help clear the way as they traversed the roadless forest. They stopped on the east side of White River, one quarter of a mile south of the mouth of Fall Creek. The land at this place was about thirty feet above the river with good soil covered with thickets and but little heavy timber. A small stream meandered in a semicircular fashion from the northeast to southwest, until it emptied into the river about a mile below McCormick's. It was called Pogue's Run for George Pogue, an early settler, who had a cabin on its south-east bank.

Several other families had settled in this vicinity before the site was selected for the state capital. Among these were Robert Barnhill's family and his son-in-law Jeremiah Corba-ley. John Barnhill, the eldest son, assisted in making a ford across White River at the shallows above Fall Creek. A plague of locusts or worms had deadened the heavy timber in several hundred acres, which expedited to some extent the clearing of space on which to raise crops. When the town plat was made by Alexander Ralston and laid out by surveyors appointed by him, many of these first cabins were ludicrously out of place in it. Some were in the center of squares, others in the middle of streets and avenues, and still others were on land reserved for public purposes. The early handicaps were many. Sick-ness and death swept the little town with unusual virulence and as in the Horseshoe Prairie settlement, scarcity of pro-visions followed. Grain was brought from Whitewater on horseback, from Indian villages, and from Conner's Prairie up the river. The steady stream of settlers attracted by the sale of lots in the new capital continued, and the population soon numbered five hundred.[1]

A new county named Marion was authorized by the legislature of 1821-1822, with jurisdiction extending over the territory in which lay Conner's Prairie and the future site of Noblesville. An appropriation was made for a courthouse which was designed to house the state legislature when the capital was moved. Fearful of delay in the matter of this removal the citizens of Indianapolis petitioned in the fall of 1822 for representation in the legislature. James Paxton of Indianapolis was elected representative from Marion and adjoining counties; James Gregory of Shelby County was elected senator from Marion, Shelby, and six other counties. These two men, with the aid of the Whitewater contingency in the legislature, succeeded in getting a bill passed which fixed the date when Indianapolis should actually become the seat of government of the state as January 10, 1825.[2]

The town had a new access of energy. There were only a few stores and John Conner saw his opportunity. He and Richard Tyner, an old Whitewater friend, formed a partnership in which Isaac N. Phipps was included. The firm name was Conner, Tyner, and Company. Alfred Harrison, another young man from the Whitewater region, was engaged as clerk. The store was opened in June, 1823, and, as was customary, every kind of merchandise was carried for which there was demand. This embraced dry goods of all sorts, cotton, silk, wool, and linen; personal articles such as combs, umbrellas, parasols, and shawls; cutlery, queensware, hardware, tinware, saddlery, schoolbooks, groceries, shoes, etc. It was customary to keep in stock whisky, the usual price for which was twenty-five cents a gallon, if bought by the barrel. Nowland, in his *Early Reminiscences of Indianapolis* describes a curious usage of merchants at that time which was undoubtedly practiced in the Conner store: "An empty whisky barrel was set up on end in front of the counter, with a hole in the upper head for the drainage of the glasses. On this barrel was set a half gallon bottle filled with whisky, a bowl of maple sugar, and a pitcher of water, and often in winter a tumbler of ground ginger. . . ."[3] The whisky was not aged in wood and the fiery stuff aroused the tempers of the customers. Animosities thus heightened provoked scuffles and brawls that were complacently accepted by the town's inhabitants as ordinary happenings, according to the chroniclers of those days.

Conner was an experienced trader and merchant. The Indian trading post at Cedar Grove was his first venture and it was frequented by pioneers as well as Indians. After Connersville was founded and there was no longer any need for an Indian trading post in that vicinity, he established a store in the town which was still in operation, in charge of his partner, Arthur Dickson. On the death of the latter this store was closed in November, 1823. Thereafter the Indianapolis store was his sole mercantile enterprise and in it he was deeply interested. His former contacts in Philadelphia served him in good stead and he made personal trips to the eastern city to replenish his stock. Before starting he frankly urged his customers through the newspaper columns to settle their accounts "as frequent settlements should take place for the purpose of remaining long friends." The added statement that "cash will not be refused" can be understood only when it is recalled that trade and barter were still the common mode of exchange and the currency had been so debased and discredited that indiscriminate acceptance of it was not general. Doubtless for the trip East it was necessary to take a chance on it.[4]

2.

While the little town was bending all its energies to deserve the title of capital an incident occurred which was a grim reminder that it was just emerging from the wilderness. In the spring of 1824 a small party of Indians encamped in Madison County at a point about equally distant from William Conner's place and Indianapolis. It consisted of two men, three women, and four children of the Shawnee and Miami tribes who had ventured this near the settlements only in pursuit of game. They had been successful in getting a large quantity of furs which excited the cupidity of a depraved and brutal white man by the name of Harper. He enlisted another trapper, Hudson, two white settlers, Sawyer and Bridges, and a youth, Bridges' son, in a plan to trick the Indians into a defenseless position and then murder them.

This crime caused the greatest excitement and alarm. It was a bloody sequel to the crime against Chief Logan's family

in 1774 and the slaughter of the peaceable Indians at Gnadenhütten in 1781. The swift retribution which had followed
these acts had been frozen in the memory of the whites. With
the removal of the state capital from Corydon to Indianapolis
soon to take place, was central Indiana now to be drawn into
the bloody shambles of an Indian uprising? The murderers
were quickly apprehended with the exception of Harper, the
ringleader, who escaped. When news of this outrage reached
Colonel John Johnston, Indian agent at Piqua, Ohio, and the
War Department at Washington, William Conner was asked
by Colonel Johnston to go with him to all of the Indian tribes
and give them assurance that the government would punish
the offenders. They succeeded in obtaining the promises of
the chiefs and warriors that before taking matters in their
own hands they would await the action of the government.
The fears of the settlers were allayed and the murderers
quickly brought to justice and executed, with the exception of
the youth who was theatrically pardoned by Governor Ray on
the scaffold.[5]

3.

It was in this tense spring and summer that John Conner
announced his candidacy for membership in the House of Representatives of the state Assembly from Marion, Hamilton,
Johnson, and Madison counties. Support for him was urged
by the newspapers because of his experience, influence, and
efficiency, but political rancor was as prevalent in those days
as in our own. There were rumblings of a rear attack on his
war record—there was a fondness for shooting darts from
under a cloak of anonymity. Anticipating these contingencies
Conner wrote to Harrison for a certificate as to his conduct
while acting under his orders. On July 8 Harrison replied and
after referring to the incriminations made against Conner
shortly after the Battle of Tippecanoe which he said had been
explained at the time, he added: "not a shadow of suspicion
ever crossed my mind as to the *fidelity* of Mr. Conner to the
United States, and I continued to employ him after this event
with as much confidence as before." The fact was that
Harrison had placed Colonel Hargrove's company, to which
Conner was probably attached, in a comparatively unimportant

position which was not pleasing to the company, although it complied with the order. This afforded Conner's political enemies the opportunity to raise the issue of his war record.

John Wyant, who was regarded as a boor, stepped out boldly in an open letter to the *Western Censor* with the charge that Conner had side-stepped the fighting at the Battle of Tippecanoe—asserting that in fact he had not even been there. An unidentified interrogator publicly asked, "Is not Mr. Conner an Indian chief at this moment?" It does not take much imagination to conjecture what effect this question would have had at this juncture if the insinuation contained in it had been believed. Caleb Harrison, a supporter of Conner, stated in reply to his enemies that he had seen Conner fighting faithfully in Colonel Hargrove's company and that he had heard him "cheering his comrades saying 'Hurra, boys, the Indians are whipped.'" "A Legal Voter" next came forward in Conner's defense, charging that the persons now opposing "an enterprising, patriotic and useful citizen," had themselves been plotters with Aaron Burr. The Burr charge was a favorite brick and when hurled was hard to dodge. The contest was bitter and brief. The election returns in August showed that Conner had carried Marion, Hamilton, and Johnson counties (Madison County votes were not received in time to be included in the election returns), that he had a majority over the combined vote of his four opponents, and had beaten his chief antagonist by a vote of almost two to one.[6]

4.

The presidential campaign of 1824 was also a bitter personal contest, enlivened by the participation of four candidates, John Quincy Adams, Andrew Jackson, Henry Clay, and William H. Crawford. General Harrison was an elector on the Clay ticket, and the Conners were political adherents of Clay and Harrison. The Federalist party was dead and the Whig party was not yet fully organized. The issues were drawn by men and not by parties.

The Fourth of July celebration for the citizens of Hamilton County was held at William Conner's. John Finch was chairman and Josiah K. Polk read the Declaration of Independence and delivered the oration. The toasts that were tendered and "were drank with entire unanimity" reveal a reverence for the government, an understanding of political leadership, a sympathy for a foreign nation in its struggle for independence, and a recognition of the country's place in world affairs which is amazing, considering the remoteness of the group from any center of intelligence or instruction other than the local newspaper, which had none of the modern facilities for news.

Toasts proposed on this day were as follows: "The day we celebrate"; "The Constitution of the United States"; "Agriculture, Manufactories and Henry Clay their supporter"; "Clay in the chair, Adams in the cabinet, and Jackson in the field"; "May the United States be the first to acknowledge the independence of the Greeks"; "James Monroe"; "May the United States ever maintain superior rank among the civilized nations of the world"; "The Commerce of the United States— May it extend to the remotest parts of the globe"; "The state of Indiana"; "May the nations of the earth dread the Navy of the United States"; "The States of South America"; "De Witt Clinton"; "The American Fair." After "The memory of George Washington," William Conner proposed "Gen. Wm. Henry Harrison—the first talent of Ohio, and the neglected friend of his country." Other toasts were "Ninian Edwards"; "Henry Clay, the friend of internal improvement—may he be our next President"; "Henry Clay—Patrick Henry returned"; "May the flag of every tyrant fall before the eagle of liberty."

At the conclusion of the meeting, at the request of John Conner a vote was taken for president of the United States. Eighty persons voted; sixty-eight for Clay, eight for Adams, and four for Jackson. The power of Clay as an orator, his magnetic personality, and his undoubted loyalty to his country captured and held the admiration of these frontier people. He was living in a neighboring state from whence many Indianans had come and his earnest promotion of the War of 1812 which had freed the people of this section from the menace of Indian raids had won for him their unquestioning loyalty.[7]

5.

The capital city, selected in 1820, platted in 1821, and in the intervening years prepared for its objective by an earnest and enthusiastic citizenry, still presented in 1825 the appearance of a dense grove of tall forest trees, sugar, walnut, ash, honey locust, elm, hackberry, buckeye, mulberry, and beech. The thickets were so dense along Washington and cross streets that it was easy to miss the way and become lost. A thinning in certain places indicated that there buildings had been erected, but only one building by its height competed with these giants of the forest. This was the newly erected courthouse. The cupola and dome, belfry, spire, and vane rose nearly a hundred feet into the air and caught the sunlight through the topmost branches of the highest trees. A square building of brick made in the town, it was an imposing structure for the village, and like the one at Corydon shed an air of dignity on its surroundings. It stood in the center of the present courthouse square with its arched entrance fronting on Washington Street. A solid fence of oak and walnut enclosed the city pound in the northeast corner of the square which was balanced by the two-story rough-hewn log jail in the northwest corner. A well with a long graceful sweep completed the appurtenances of what might be called the first civic center. The high arching trees softened whatever of harsh ugliness these roughly wrought structures might have disclosed in an open, barren place. Washington Street had been cleared of trees to the river, though it scarcely presented the appearance of a road, so cluttered was it with stumps and unremoved debris around or over which the traffic had to move. There was traffic even in this early day. Down this street, which was to be a part of the National Road, came the tide of emigrants from the East in covered wagons with their children and their chattels. "Scarcely a day passes," records the *Gazette* of November 4, 1823, "but our streets are filled with the vehicles of removal.—While many are settling and making rapid improvements in our county and those adjacent, others are passing on to cultivate the rich prairies of the Wabash river and its tributary streams."[8]

Taverns were scattered along its length to accommodate travelers and legislators. The town was developing; the transient visitors were increasing. Thomas Chinn's Travellers' Hall was the farthest east; then came Major Carter's Tavern, which had just been erected opposite the courthouse and was embellished with a large new sign. Washington Hall, a partnership affair of Henderson and Blake, stood in the center of the block between Pennsylvania and Meridian streets on the south side of Washington. Near by was the post office, to which the panting horses of the mail stage drew up while the driver blew a mighty blast on his horn to announce his arrival. Close by was perhaps the best known inn of them all—the Widow Nowland's boarding house. Across the street John Hawkins conducted a tavern built of trees cut on the site. Down by the river bank where Asael Dunning was in charge of the ferry were two more inns, one managed by McGeorge and the other by McCormick. The latter had a cluster of little shacks around his cabin for the convenience of travelers who reached the river too late to make a crossing before nightfall. This was Indianapolis' first tourist camp.

A grove of forest trees on a little mound filled the circle which Ralston platted as the center of the town. From the outside corners of its four surrounding blocks radiated avenues to the outermost limits of the town. Yet from the very beginning Washington Street held first place in business activity. On it were the general stores, among them John Conner's, nearly opposite Washington Hall, and the little shops of tailors, hatters, shoemakers, clock repairers, tinkers, and cabinetmakers. An enterprising colored man, nicknamed "Fancy Tom," who had been a favorite barber of the legislators at Corydon, had moved his shop to Indianapolis along with the more important paraphernalia of the state. Jerry Collins' Whisky Shop fronted the street with the magistrate's house conveniently in the rear. This seeming mesalliance perhaps provided a desirable restraint.

Two shops which were important, even vital, to the life of this early community but which would have no place on a Main Street of today were the blacksmith shop and the spinning wheel factory. Scattered among these mercantile and industrial establishments were the printing offices of the two newspapers, the schoolhouse, the offices and the residences of prominent citizens such as Calvin Fletcher, the first lawyer, Dr. Samuel G. Mitchell, the first physician, Obed Foote, and Bethuel F. Morris, the town's agent. A two-story brick building had been erected opposite the statehouse square to serve as the residence of the state treasurer, Samuel Merrill, and accommodate his office and the office of auditor. While it is evident that most of the activity of the town centered in Washington Street, there were dwellings and shops both north and south. The most important building on the north was the First Presbyterian Church, which had just been completed on the west side of Pennsylvania Street between Market and Ohio. The capital of the state was at this time a small, sprawling, frontier community built among the trees with less than eight hundred inhabitants, about one-third of whom were children of school age.[9]

As Conner made periodical trips to the cities of Washington, Baltimore, and Philadelphia from 1802 to 1825, first as Indian interpreter and later more often for business reasons, he came to have an understanding of their growth, character, and physical appearance. Inevitable comparison of their conditions and those of Indianapolis must have entered his mind. Their locations were accessible to more people. Baltimore and Philadelphia had emerged into substantial commercial centers, but this result had required many years. Washington was still in the chrysalis stage but its evolvement gave promise of beauty. As he looked upon the raw conditions of the six-year-old Indiana capital, he knew that the realization of his hopes for its good future must be long deferred. Here it was in a wilderness without adequate communication or transportation to the widely separated small communities. Part of the state was yet Indian owned and controlled. The more settled areas regarded the new capital as an upstart and lent their efforts to the building up of other towns. The citizens of Indianapolis were annually shaken and demoralized by malarial chills and fevers. Lot payments were defaulted—so much so that the legislature had to come to the relief of embarrassed owners. Building a city here would be, inevitably, a long and difficult process—too long a time for him to invest in it. He decided against the purchase of any lots in Indianapolis, even though he had opened a store there.[10] The coming of the railroads and telegraph to solve the transportation and communication problem and furnish a sound basis of prosperity, was something he could not foresee.

6.

On January 10, 1825, the ninth General Assembly con vened in the courthouse at Indianapolis.   The entrance ha was spacious, containing the stairway which led to the senat chamber, a room 40¼ feet by 25 feet.   There were two othe large rooms on this floor, besides a small one which was dupli cated below.   The Hall of Representatives, on the first floo opposite the entrance, was 40½ feet square—larger in area than the entire building in which the Assembly had met in Corydon.   It was the most pretentious room in the building, with a gallery across the south and two large fireplaces.   The furnishings were severely simple but adequate.   Every member had his own table with a drawer that could be locked, and his own painted Windsor chair.[11]

John Conner was a member of the first session in the first state capital at Corydon.   He was now to serve in the first session in this second capital.   He saw many familiar faces. There were senators with whom he had served at Corydon— Dennis Pennington, Daniel Grass, Isaac Montgomery, John Gray, and James Gregory.   Other senators had been, in former sessions, members of the House when he was in the Senate, among them William Graham, Samuel Milroy, James B. Ray, and John H. Thompson.   William Graham had been in every session since the first, either in the upper or the lower house. This was the only term that John Conner served in the House of Representatives, but many of his fellow members were old timers in that body, notably David Maxwell, Stephen C. Stevens, and Thomas Hendricks.   There were thirty-five members in the House, by far the largest legislative group of which Conner had been a member.   Stevens was elected speaker and Conner was appointed on the committee to notify Gov- ernor Hendricks of the organization of the House.   A con- temporary editorial comment on the Assembly runs as fol- lows: "the representatives of the state of Indiana, who com- posed the ninth session, were men, (with two or three trifling exceptions) of sound mind—independent and liberal—just and tenacious of their rights—intelligent, and honest to their constituents.

"From such men we have nothing to fear—even those who

have visited the lobby, under an impression that the legislative
body would appear caparisoned in all the blandishments of
aboriginal simplicity—with buckskin hunting shirts, red
leggings and moccasons, have since acknowledged that even the
General Assemblies of New York and Pennsylvania are not
before them in correctness of deportment, appearance, & respectability of talents."[12]   Certainly no man had made longer
strides from "the blandishments of aboriginal simplicity" than
John Conner.   It may be questioned whether this ratio of improvement in legislators in Indiana from 1816 to 1825 has
since been maintained.

Conner was a member of three of the six standing committees.   One of these was the Ways and Means Committee;
another, the Committee on Military Affairs.   His membership
on the latter committee demonstrates how lightly regarded
were the aspersions made against his military record during
the campaign.   He was also on the important Committee on
Roads.[13]   Transportation was the big problem.   Petitions,
remonstrances, and resolutions fell upon the members of this
committee like autumn leaves.   The farmer needed good roads
to get his produce to town.   Shipments of goods in demand by
every community could not be made unless roads were provided.   Water transportation—rivers first, later canals—was
first considered when distance was involved, but a network of
roads must connect communities with these watercourses.   The
House was so overwhelmed by the deluge of communications
on the subject that it instructed the committee "to inquire as to
the radical defects existing in our road system, and to devise,
if possible, means by which the General Assembly" might "be
relieved from the extraordinary burden of legislating thereon;
with leave to report a bill or otherwise."[14]   Conner was deeply
interested in the subject and stood firmly against any reduction
of taxes for road purposes.

By an act passed on February 10, the Assembly provided
for a road to be built from Indianapolis to Fort Wayne.   The
commissioners appointed to lay out this road were James Blake
of Marion County, William Conner of Hamilton County, and
William Suttenfield of Allen County.   This was familiar
ground to both Conner men.   It was along the old Indian trail
from White River to Fort Wayne that they had sent their pony

trains laden with furs, twenty-five years before. This trail served the commissioners in good stead and when the road was laid out it followed very closely the path that the Indians had selected and the Conners used. According to a current comment, it presented "the most permanent bed, for either a natural or artificial road."[15] This road, however, like all other roads of this period, required constant attention. Lack of money, knowledge, and materials to build permanent roads were the causes of despair on this matter.

The only motion of importance offered by John Conner at this session was that a committee be appointed to examine the obstructions to navigation of the West Fork of White River. Later, the scope of this committee was enlarged to include an examination of the East Fork, and Conner was made chairman. This was another subject upon which both Conner men were well informed. William had lived upon this river for a quarter of a century and both of them knew all its peculiarities, its falls or rapids, its drifts and bars. It is doubtful if John Conner was surprised when Alexander Ralston reported that the river could only be made navigable for three months of the year. To open the river for low-water transportation from Conner's mill to Indianapolis would cost, at his estimate, from two to three hundred dollars. Acting upon his report, the legislature at the following session passed a law "to improve the navigation of East and West Forks of White River" as far as Randolph County. Hope did not die for the accomplishment of this much desired goal until 1831 when the steamboat "General Hanna" went aground. As late as 1866, however, another and last attempt was made by the "Governor Morton" which ended disastrously.[16]

Buried deep in the records of the early legislatures is evidence of their interest in and appreciation of public libraries. Two important acts were passed at this session—one for the incorporation of county libraries and one an act to establish a State Library. Indiana did not have to wait for the genius of Andrew Carnegie to stimulate interest in library work. A bill for the incorporation of medical societies for the purpose of regulating the practice of physic and surgery was also passed, with Conner's vote recorded in favor of it.

Resolutions touching the subject of slavery are intimations

of the conflict that in a little more than a quarter of a century was to rend the nation. Conner was opposed to slavery as were the Whitewater politicians.[17]

7.

Another resolution in a happier vein related to preparations for the visit of General Lafayette to Indiana, an event which would, in a visible way, connect this new commonwealth with the glorious history of the Revolution. General Lafayette, on invitation of Congress, was making his second and last visit to the United States. The General Assembly of Indiana appointed a committee "to take into consideration the propriety of . . . expressing their sentiments in reference to Major-general Lafayette." This committee consisted of six senators and twelve representatives, John Conner being one of the latter. On January 28 the committee made its report. The preamble recited the pre-eminent services and sacrifices of Lafayette in behalf of the American people, and the popular gratitude and respect for his character. It set forth the "peculiar satisfaction" of the General Assembly that it was his intention to visit the western section of the United States, and their "inexpressible pleasure" in offering him hospitality. The resolutions adopted provided that the governor be requested to transmit to Lafayette a copy of the resolutions with an invitation to visit the state, at the seat of government or such town on the Ohio River as the general might designate; and that the governor, together with such officers and citizens as might find it convenient to attend at the point selected, receive him with the honors due an illustrious guest. They were glowing resolutions reflecting the admiration and gratitude of the members of the legislature.

The general accepted the invitation and appointed Jeffersonville as the place for the visit. A committee of arrangements was selected. A disconcerting incident led to Lafayette's landing on Indiana soil earlier than was anticipated, in a visit as uncomfortable as it was informal. While proceeding up the Ohio River to Louisville, his boat struck a snag and sank. He was rescued from this wreck and spent the night on the shore near the present site of Cannelton. Early the next morning he left on another boat for Louisville. On May 12, 1825, at eleven o'clock in the morning he arrived at Jeffersonville for the scheduled visit, to be greeted by deafening salvos of artillery, by vociferous salutations from the citizens, and by the bombastic address of Governor Ray, whose fervid language must have staggered the visitor. In response, Lafayette expressed with emotion his gratitude for this enthusiastic welcome. A sumptuous dinner followed and numerous toasts were offered. At six o'clock he returned to Louisville. No guest more illustrious had ever set foot on Indiana soil.[18]

8.

The lands lying east of the Tippecanoe River and north of the Wabash were still owned by the Potawatomi and Miami in 1825. John Tipton, now Indian agent at Fort Wayne, wanted to see this area opened for white settlers, at least as far north as the Eel River. When he discovered in a request from some of the Miami chiefs for permission to visit Washington, an indication that the time might be ripe for another treaty, he promptly forwarded the request to the Indian Office. Ordinarily the government allowed such deputations only when the purpose of the visit had been approved, and it then assumed the expenses of the journey. In this case, however, the chiefs refused to confide their object to anyone but the president. After some correspondence, it was arranged that the head chief and another chief of the Miami might come to Washington, accompanied by such officer as they might select, with the understanding that their expenses would be paid only if the purpose of the trip commended itself to the president.[19]

The party selected included Le Gris,[20] head chief of the Miami, Tipton, Indian agent, and John Conner, interpreter. Le Gris was probably the son or nephew of the influential Miami Chief Na-ka-kwan-ga, nicknamed Le Gris by the French, a brother-in-law of the great Little Turtle, and signer of Wayne's treaty of 1795. His village, now known as Lagro, lay on the north side of the Wabash near its junction with the Salamonie.

On January 3, 1826, Tipton and Le Gris left Fort Wayne on horses; they were met by Conner at Piqua and the three journeyed eastward, encountering the usual vicissitudes of travel of that time. Unfortunately, Conner fell ill. Tipton records that he was "very sick," especially at Hagerstown, Maryland, where after stopping for the night they "hired a hack." They arrived at Washington on the nineteenth, and remained for about three weeks at the Indian Queen Hotel which charged them the sum of $101.31¼ for their keep. Conner was too sick to leave the hotel during at least two of the days while they were there. With heavy rains followed by a "violent snow storm" which covered the ground to a depth of twenty-three inches, and then a falling temperature and "very cold" weather, Conner's activities were necessarily curtailed. His illness was so aggravated by one of the colds that were prevalent in Washington that he required the services of a physician. Nevertheless he performed his duties as interpreter. His dynamic energy often carried him to his objective at the expense of his physical welfare.

Tipton was very busy. First, he did some shopping, buying a coat, vest, and hat for himself and a vest for the chief. He then visited the House of Representatives, stopped at the War Office several times, and once called on Governor Cass, who was also in Washington. On the twenty-seventh he went to the War Office again, evidently accompanied by the chief, for his journal records that "Lagrow made his speech." No doubt its theme was the sale of the Miami lands above the Wabash. James Noble wrote to Cass that he was "for accomplishing the important object," and again, urging proper compensation to Conner for the trip. This was subsequently arranged. At the suggestion of Senator Noble, Conner visited the War Department on February 3, taking Le Gris with him. Noble thought they should see the president if possible, and recommended that presents be made to Le Gris. Conner was very anxious to go home. At the conclusion of their stay— the day and evening before their departure—Tipton and the chief called on President Adams and Tipton attended Mrs. Adams' levee. The next day they took a stage for Baltimore, and from there to Wheeling where they boarded a steamboat, the "Pennsylvania." Its machinery broke down as it was ready to start. Tipton and Le Gris disembarked, leaving Conner and the trunks aboard. Traveling horseback they reached home on February 24. There is no record as to how or when Conner returned but it was probably by boat to Cincinnati.

The physical and mental exertions of this trip had taxed his strength to the utmost.[21]

The sequel of this visit came later in the year when on October 23, the Miami entered into a treaty with Lewis Cass, James B. Ray, and John Tipton, United States commissioners, whereby they ceded to the United States all their lands "north and west of the Wabash and the Miami rivers." William Conner was one of the interpreters. Le Gris received three sections at his home and one in Portage Prairie as reserves. It was also stipulated in the treaty that a house should be built for him. This was done in 1828 and here he lived comfortably until his death in 1831.[22]

John Conner did not live to see the treaty concluded. He had been in poor health for some time, but he was still under fifty-two years of age, and did not apprehend a sudden close to his vigorous life. On April 11, 1826, he advertised a new carding machine in the *Indianapolis Gazette* and invited inquiries at his store. When the notice appeared a week later, he lay at the point of death. Realizing a few days before that he was very ill, he had called in Dr. Livingston Dunlap, known in the community as a capable physician. On the seventeenth a will seemed advisable. Nothwithstanding his suffering Conner was rational. With composure he dictated the necessary provisions and the will was drawn and executed on that day with Dr. Dunlap and James Blake, another outstanding citizen, as witnesses. On the nineteenth, about two o'clock in the morning, he expired at his Indianapolis hotel, the Washington Hall.

The services were conducted according to the Masonic ritual. A scholarly and eccentric Presbyterian minister, Reverend George Bush, preached "an interesting and appropriate Funeral Sermon." A large procession was formed at Washington Hall at two o'clock in the afternoon of the nineteenth and the burial occurred that evening. When the cemetery was abandoned some years ago and some of the bodies removed, that of John Conner, one of the first placed there, had already mingled with the soil of the city which he had a part in making the capital of Indiana. His death deprived the new state and the newer capital of one of their most efficient supporters. The value of his public services was well recognized by contemporary newspapers. In private life he was "extensively useful." His frequent aid to immigrants and the indigent or distressed was widely known in the community. The loss by his death was generally and openly deplored. Another commentator said he had the "well merited confidence of his fellow citizens."[23] He possessed marked qualities of leadership, and the penetrating and broad understanding of his true relations to people and things, tangible and intangible, which is so essential to success. To these he added a persistent energy and courage.

Of course there was no photography in Indiana at this period. The only portrait of John Conner was by an unremembered artist. It hung in the home of his son, William Winship Conner, and unluckily was destroyed by fire. A composite description of his personal appearance as gleaned from his descendants tells us that he was tall and very erect, with head and body well poised, a physique slender and not rugged; that he had strong features, steel-blue eyes, steady, alert, and penetrating; a wide mouth with slightly compressed upper lip; and a square, firm jaw, the whole countenance exhibiting firmness and boldness. One who knew him said that he "was one of Nature's strong men. . . . When dressed in their [Indian] costume, and painted, it was difficult to distinguish him from a real savage."[24] It is a family tradition that John as well as William, had a strong sense of humor. If they sometimes laughed at ridiculous and embarrassing incidents involving others, there was no malice in the laughter.[25]

CHAPTER XI

WILLIAM CONNER, MAN OF AFFAIRS—CLOSING YEARS

THE CLOSE bond existing between the two brothers, William and John Conner, was severed by the death of the latter. The lives of these two had run in parallel lines for nearly half a century, in childhood environment, Indian trade, marriage, land ventures, treaty-making, town development, politics, and friends. Their relationship to their other brothers was always friendly but never as close. James, the oldest, and Henry, the youngest, had remained in Detroit, married wives of the Catholic faith, and become identified with that church.[1] William and John had felt the influence of the Moravian teachers more strongly and it set their bias toward Protestantism rather than Catholicism. The activities of all four brothers as Indian interpreters and as landowners in Michigan constituted common bonds which continued to bring about occasional meetings.

Both John and William Conner were members of the Masonic Order at an early day. Indeed, it is said that John was the "first man to bring Masonic membership into Eastern Indiana." He joined the Brookville Harmony Lodge in 1817. Masonry was under suspicion in the Whitewater region—so much so in fact that Luther Hinman was expelled from the Little Cedar Baptist Church in 1814 for being a Mason and failing to disclose the fact to his brethren. John Conner's interest in Masonry was not disturbed by this incident. In September, 1820, he made a horseback trip with Hervey Bates and John Sample to Jeffersonville to request a dispensation for a lodge at Connersville. The new unit was named Warren in recognition of the Revolutionary services of General Joseph Warren. In 1824 John transferred his membership to the more conveniently located Center Lodge of Indianapolis, of which William was now a member. Later William assisted in procuring a charter for Noblesville, which was granted in 1828. By 1830, the opposition to Masonry became so active throughout the country as to arrest the growth of the Noblesville lodge. Both of the Conners, however, remained faithful Masons to the end of their lives.[2]

The death of John laid the responsibility for his affairs and family upon William. The extent of this charge is revealed by the many matters mentioned in his will. The new house which had been contemplated was not to be completed, but there were provisions for keeping the present dwelling in a tenantable condition. The carding machine which he had just purchased was to be sold, together with enough personal property to supply funds for closing his estate. He desired that his mercantile establishment at Indianapolis be continued as long as it was "advantageous and lucrative," and that his farm and mill near Noblesville be rented or managed by his executors. He directed that his sons (his youngest son, Henry John, was now a babe) should be "well and safely educated," and recommended that upon their arrival at a fit age they be bound out to "suitable mercantile houses of which the proprietor is of correct morals and deportment." There was a marked difference in the aptitudes of the Conner brothers. William was a lover of land for its productiveness, as was his father. John's interest was primarily commercial—platting lands into lots or into sites for mills. He was a merchant and manufacturer. His will discloses this as a ruling trait. The inventory of his estate also confirms the impression that he was not a real farmer, for there were few farm animals in proportion to his acreage. The most valuable item was fur skins, mute evidence of his fur trade. A small number of serious books, biography, geography, and history, were listed, indicating a taste for good reading.[3]

In compliance with the will, William Conner continued the store his brother had established in Indianapolis. Alfred Harrison, who had worked in the store for a few months when it was first established, had recently entered into a partnership agreement with John Conner which William continued. Harrison carried on the active management of the store for the next few years under the firm name of Conner and Harrison. During the summer of 1832 a co-partnership was entered into with Alexander W. Russell, but it was dissolved in September of that year. The firm of Conner and Harrison continued until August 7, 1833.[4]

The first location of the Conner store was on the north side of Washington Street east of the alley between Meridian

and Pennsylvania streets.   This property was rented from
1823 to 1827.   In the fall of the latter year, William Conner
and Alfred Harrison purchased property on the northwest corner of Washington and Pennsylvania streets and conducted
the store there.   A year later Conner bought the lot on the
northeast corner of the same streets, erected a brick building,
and removed the store to that location.   When Conner and
Harrison dissolved partnership, the new firm of A. W. Russell
and Company moved into the building theretofore occupied
by the former.

The mills of John Conner in Hamilton County, including
wool carding, were managed by William Conner and Sennet
Fallis and were kept rented, at least until 1840.   The mills
(gristmill, sawmill, and distillery) he owned in Fayette County
and his two farms there, one the mill farm north of Connersville and the other south of that town, together with two town
lots, were not placed on sale until 1830.[5]

It was not so easy to carry out Conner's provisions concerning his sons.   At the time of John's death William had
only two children, Lavina and Richard, but the next year another son was born and named John Fayette.   These two sons
and three more who were born before 1836 had to be educated
as well as his two nephews.   Recognizing this potent need William Conner became interested in the educational facilities of
the new state of Indiana.

2.

Article 9 of the Constitution of 1816 dwells loftily on the
virtue and necessity of "knowledge and learning generally
diffused, through a community."   It made it the legislative
duty to provide for a general system of education free and
open to everyone.   The gradation was from the common
schools to the county seminaries and to a state university.[6]
The system broke down for two reasons—lack of funds and
competent teachers.   Thoughtful citizens and parents were
rightfully concerned about the education of their children in a
period when, according to an Indiana historian, the teacher
"was not uncommonly the laughing stock of the neighborhood."[7]

On November 7, 1831, a group of representative men met,

with Governor-elect Noah Noble in the chair, to consider what should be done to improve educational conditions. A convention of the members of the General Assembly, the officials of the state, and the friends of education throughout the state was recommended to be held in Indianapolis the third Monday in December of that year. There were some well-known names in the list of this group: David Wallace, Stephen C. Stevens, Ratliff Boon, Samuel Merrill, Calvin Fletcher, John Law, William W. Wick, Oliver H. Smith, John Wishard, Isaac Coe, John Tipton, Jesse L. Holman, all of whom were conspicuous leaders in political, judicial, or other fields. Conscious of the inadequacy of his own education, and therefore keenly aware of the importance of this cause, William Conner must have been a sympathetic and helpful member of this gathering.[8] The proposed movement had excellent support, but it faced the hurdle of meager resources in the state and counties. Serious as the situation was, it did not daunt these earnest men.

A group describing itself as the Association for the Improvement of Common Schools in Indiana met at Madison on September 3 and 4, 1833, with Senator William Hendricks in the chair. In the midst of heavy duties and responsibilities he was still an active friend of education. From the work of this association came the first organized plans for common schools. Among the vice-presidents were Judges Jesse L. Holman, Stephen C. Stevens, M. C. Eggleston, and Benjamin Parke. Dr. Andrew Wylie was there. The corresponding secretary was the Reverend J. U. Parson. He read the first annual report, which disclosed an appalling number of illiterates, and teachers who were dissipated, profane, or immoral. The committee appointed to nominate members to the association recommended that eleven be chosen from different parts of the state. Among them were Governor Noble and James M. Ray from Indianapolis, James Whitcomb of Bloomington, afterward governor and United States senator, and William Conner of Hamilton County. These and other movements to make the common schools more efficient jogged along until 1852 without much result beyond making the people school conscious. During that time private schools and seminaries metered education to those who could and would pay, with very good results.[9]

One indication of the type of pioneers in Indiana was the

penchant for serious books manifested by early laws for the establishment and maintenance of county libraries. Books were rare treasures, but they found their way into the Conner homes. Judge Finch says that in his boyhood he found the first novel he ever read, the *Scottish Chiefs,* in William Conner's library. Burns's and Shakespeare's works and other classics were also there. Fortunately they were in strong leather bindings, stout enough to withstand the wear of reading and rereading by the family and their friends. One who had lived in the William Conner home in 1835 afterwards said, "it was one of the blunders of my life when I left him. He had a great many books and read a great deal, and I had free access to them, which was a great treat to me, as I had not been used to before I went there, for books were scarce there in those days." The fondness of the Conners for good books was inborn. In view of their limited schooling it cannot be explained in any other way.[10]

On December 11, 1830, the Indiana Historical Society was organized for the purpose of "collecting and preserving the materials for a comprehensive and accurate history" of the country. Of the seven men selected to draft a constitution, two were or became governors and three were, or became, judges of the Indiana Supreme Court. William Conner was among the signers of that instrument.[11] He must have noted approvingly that one of the subjects listed for study was the history of Indian tribes within the state.

3.

Conner still saw occasional service as an interpreter. In the autumn of 1826 he was called, with his brothers James and Henry, of Michigan, to assist Commissioners Lewis Cass, of Michigan, and Governor James B. Ray and John Tipton, of Indiana, at a treaty with the Potawatomi. The negotiations, concluded on October 16 near the junction of the Mississinewa with the Wabash, resulted in the cession to the United States of an irregular slice of territory north of the Wabash and east of the Tippecanoe River, and a block in the northwest corner of the state. In addition, the tribe granted land for a road one hundred feet wide from Lake Michigan to the Wabash, and thence south through Indianapolis to a convenient point on the Ohio River. Several state senators and representatives were in attendance, probably as advisors on this article of the treaty.[12]

It was a curious paradox that when Indiana became a state there remained within her borders alien nations, owning and controlling the lands they occupied. These the state had no power to condemn or appropriate for public use, nor could it build roads or canals without the consent of the owners. The state of Indiana used the treaty grant to build and maintain a road from Lake Michigan to Madison, known as the Michigan Road. Originally the width was only forty feet, but after about fifty years it was increased by ten feet. Owners of adjacent land had by this time erected fences and buildings which extended into and upon the one hundred feet of the treaty right of way. In 1933 the Indiana State Highway Commission ordered fences moved back fifty feet on each side from the center line of the road, and the Appellate Court, in a case in which a landowner objected to this order, held that the treaty was still in force.[13]

Six days after the covenant with the Potawatomi, the same commissioners, also in the presence of a legislative group, made a treaty agreement with the Miami. William Conner, serving again as one of the interpreters, must have felt a special eagerness for its successful conclusion, for it was on business preliminary to this negotiation that his brother John made his last overtaxing journey to Washington. Besides ceding their lands "north and west of the Wabash and Miami rivers," the Miami conceded the right to open a canal or road through lands still reserved to them. Behind the request for this authorization lay the desire for construction of a canal from Lake Erie to the Wabash.

Trade with the Indians was flourishing at this time not primarily because of the furs they brought for barter, but because the annuities they received from the government gave them cash which they were imprudent in spending. Many were the traders who attended these gatherings to collect undeserved profits from the sale of horses and all kinds of goods. There was no lack of corrupt and unfair dealing on their part, and it was not unusual for the full amount of an annuity to be pledged before it was made over to the Indians.[14]

An aftermath of the Potawatomi treaty came three years later during the legislative session of 1829-1830, in a newspaper quarrel between John Tipton and John Ewing, a state senator from Knox County who had attended the negotiations as a witness. At this session William Conner was serving his first term, as representative from Hamilton, Madison, Hancock, and Henry counties, and all the country north of these counties not attached elsewhere.[15]

Tipton was general agent for the Potawatomi and Miami in northern Indiana. He had been appointed to this position by President Monroe in 1823, and maintained the agency at Fort Wayne until the spring of 1828. At that time, because of the influx of settlers to the northern part of the state, the Indians were removed to Eel River and the Wabash. To be nearer them and also because of his interest in land speculation, Tipton recommended the removal of the agency to the mouth of Eel River, the present site of Logansport. He was a promoter and enthusiastic supporter of the Wabash and Erie Canal project. Of a forceful and combative nature, Tipton was deeply stirred by a difference with Ewing concerning the sale of canal lands, fearful that Ewing had put his pet scheme in jeopardy. Recalling certain happenings at the treaty with the Potawatomi that reflected no credit on Ewing, he exposed them to public view with withering scorn. This aroused all the ire of the little Irishman, who was a past master in the use of invective. He called upon Tipton to retract and when no reply was forthcoming called upon other citizens who attended the treaty to vindicate him. Letters from Governor Ray, James Gregory, and William Conner all appeared in the *Indiana Journal*. Ray and Gregory gave Ewing almost unequivocal endorsement, but Conner's letter was milder and more measured. In part he wrote: "I know your anxiety in regard to the result of the treaty—and that you were sanguine as to means of its accomplishment, in part of which my long experience of the Indian character would not allow me to confide." Perhaps here is an inkling as to the source of irritation between Ewing and Tipton. The latter was as experienced as Conner in Indian ways, and the easy nonchalance and optimism of Ewing and Ray had annoyed both Tipton and Conner and perhaps endangered the conclusion of the treaty. Tipton wrote a final excoriating letter and the incident closed. It was typical of the times. Duels were now fought with the pen and not the sword.[16]

4.

Party alignments came into vogue in Indiana in the Jackson-Adams campaign of 1828. The parties were the Jacksonian Democrats and the National or Jeffersonian Republicans. Until then there were no party lines. Strong political leaders in different sections of the state commanded the votes on local issues, but these by no means followed national party lines. The Jennings group to which the Conners belonged was the dominating one. William Conner had had his first essay in politics in 1822. His friend, James M. Ray, living at this time in Indianapolis, was a candidate for clerk of Marion County on the "Whitewater" or "In Yander" ticket. The candidate of the "Old Kaintuck" opposition party was Morris Morris, a substantial citizen, also from Indianapolis. The race was a warm one. Conner campaigned for his friend in that part of Marion County which afterwards became Hamilton County. Ray received 217 votes out of 336 cast. A universal election custom was the free dispensation of whisky in cups, buckets, and jugs by friends of the candidates to all voters who wanted it. Holloway says that on this occasion "every voter was brought out, and pretty nearly every one was taken back drunk." This demoralizing custom prevailed for years.

William Conner's initial experience was successful but not edifying. He had no doubt heard much about the game from his brother, and in late years, his own home had been in the line of travel of many politicians on their way to and from the seat of state government. He was active in the organization of Hamilton County and had had ample opportunity to observe political methods at meetings of various county groups in his home. The treaties that he had attended had been open fields for politicians of all description. All that he had seen and heard strengthened his natural dislike for the subject. He used to remark "that there was too much 'log rolling' about legislation for him." This was a homely backwoods expression reminiscent of the days when the settlers helped each other to roll logs which had been cut in the forest to the site of a new cabin under construction. The significance is plain as applied to legislation where men combined to further each other's private interests to the detriment of the public welfare. The phrase has remained current in Indiana and, sad to say, is still applicable to certain political practices.[17]

However, even at this early date politics had an irresistible pull, especially for men of influence and leadership. Conner's legislative service opened at the time when party alignments were being made and when the subject of canals was of engrossing interest. The state of New York had made a spectacular success of a canal from Lake Erie to Albany. Indiana was eager to follow suit, and the land in the northern part of the state was admirably adapted to the scheme by reason of the network of rivers, lakes, and small streams along which the Indians had established regular routes for portages. A means of transportation that could be used at all times of the year was most important to the development of the state. Adequate roads seemed a long way off, and the idea of railroads had not yet seized the legislative imagination. The suggestion made in 1818 that a water route from Lake Erie to the Ohio and thence to the Mississippi could perhaps be achieved by a short canal connecting the St. Mary's River and the Little River, and thus opening navigation from the Maumee to the Wabash River near Huntington, gave way to a more ambitious scheme for the construction of a Wabash and Erie Canal. This project, with the increasing and satisfactory use of river steamboats, seemed practicable. Once the idea had become lodged in the public mind there seemed no end to its possible extensions. The connecting of all the navigable rivers, and all those that could be made so, in a vast statewide system of canals seemed desirable and feasible to William Conner, who was familiar with the trails and streams of Indiana from an early date. Probably no single enterprise of the state ever promised so much.[18]

The route of the Michigan Road was also under consideration at this session. The line of way selected by commissioners appointed in 1828 was the subject of much contention. Conner was very desirous that this road should pass through Noblesville. He was a die-hard on this point and when defeated on one proposition would come back with another. In the end he failed, for the route adopted lay through South Bend, Logansport, Indianapolis, Greensburg, and Madison.[19]

It was obvious that the Marion County courthouse would soon be inadequate for meetings of the General Assembly. Only four years before it had seemed luxurious in comparison with the courthouse at Corydon, but now, with the rapid development of the state in such immediate prospect, the legislators were beginning to feel crowded, and it was certainly none too soon to begin planning for a new statehouse. The first bill relating to this building passed the House at this session but was indefinitely postponed in the Senate. An act "to provide for the commencement of a State House" was approved February 10, 1831.[20]

Conner was not a member of the next legislative session. He was prominently identified, however, with the organization of the National Republican Party in Indiana, afterwards fused with the Whigs. When a convention was held in Indianapolis on November 7 and 8, 1831, Conner was a delegate from Hamilton County. This year marked the adoption of national political conventions for nominating presidential candidates. Besides a Protectionist convention at New York and a Free-trade convention at Philadelphia, attended by delegates from twelve and fifteen states respectively, three conventions were held in 1831-1832 at which presidential candidates were nominated. First was the assembly of the Antimasons at Baltimore, late in September, 1831. It was followed three months later by a convention of the National Republicans supporting Clay, and in May, 1832, a Democratic national convention nominated Van Buren. The Indiana convention held prior to the national one endorsed a protective tariff, liberal encouragement of internal improvements, and Henry Clay for president. William Conner, for all his dislike of politics, thus had a part in initiating the National Republican Party in Indiana.[21]

He was again in the legislature in the session of 1831-1832. Another subject, railroads, now claimed equal interest with canals. There had been those throughout the country who had scouted the practicability of railroads, especially in comparison with canals, but the successful completion of thirteen miles of railroad by the Baltimore and Ohio Company from Baltimore to Ellicott's Mills in May, 1830, had silenced most of the critics. Governor Ray was an ardent advocate of railroads and had urged their advantages over canals as early as 1827. It was not until this session, however, that the first railroad legislation in Indiana was enacted. Eight acts for the incorporation of as many roads were passed. A law supplemental to a previous act on the Wabash and Erie Canal was also enacted.[22]

5.

A few months after the General Assembly was adjourned, there occurred the last Indian outbreak to affect Indiana. Fear of the Indians was deep seated in the heart of every pioneer settler—fear and hate. For the most part the tribes living in Indiana since the War of 1812 had been peaceful. Northern Indiana had large reservations of Potawatomi and Miami. All other tribes had departed for the West. By the terms of a treaty made in 1804 with the Sauk and Foxes, Governor Harrison had secured a large cession of land east of the Mississippi and between the Illinois and Wisconsin rivers, with a provision allowing the Indians the privilege of living and hunting there until it was sold by the United States government. Long before the government sales, however, squatters took possession of the land, to the indignation of the Indians. Finally the incensed Indians were persuaded to agree to cross the Mississippi and never return. Black Hawk was a chief of the Sauk, and his native village was at the junction of Rock River and the Mississippi. His tribe had cultivated these fertile Illinois lands for half a century and when he heard that white settlers had taken his fields and plowed up the graves of his ancestors, he came back with 386 warriors, some old men, women, and children. Part of the latter group he left at the site of their old village. With his small band he pushed north along Rock River and camped. The Illinois governor lost no time in sending a large force of militia to discover his location. The Indians in the course of their advance surprised this force of white men and approached with a flag of truce, but when their messengers were killed by members of the militia obviously under influence of liquor, the Indians returned with murder in their hearts and hands. The militia fled and Black Hawk's War opened, spreading terror among the settlers, who had no way of estimating the number of Indians engaged in this murderous fray. Actually, it was only one hundred and fifty, but fleeing settlers and militiamen exaggerated the number. Many of the former living in Illinois sought refuge in Indiana and as the Indians there had been restless a general uprising was feared.

The militia of the Indiana counties bordering on Illinois made immediate preparations for defense and requested the governor of the state to call out the state militia. At once Governor Noble summoned the militia of Marion, Johnson, and Hendricks counties to meet in Indianapolis. The call was for one hundred and fifty men of the Fortieth Regiment belonging to Marion County and as many from the regiments of the adjoining counties. Two hundred and fifty men responded—each man furnishing his own horse, arms, and equipment. Colonel A. W. Russell, who had become a partner of the firm of Conner and Harrison only a few days before, was placed in command of the troops, and William Conner, mentioned by a local newspaper as "not only familiar with the geography of the country, but well acquainted with the Indian character," accompanied them as guide. He was considered "capable if any man was" to lead them through the trackless wilderness to Chicago. The troops assembled at the southeast corner of the present Washington and West streets, marching through a lane of tearful wives and mothers. From a horn of vast size came forth "the most doleful noise that ever reached the ears of man." They left Indianapolis on June 10, 1832, and arrived in Chicago to find the war practically over—at least their services were not required, for Federal troops were on the way. The Indianans returned by way of South Bend, where they were victimized in a way quite as painful, if less deadly, than Indian warfare or the cholera which broke out at Fort Dearborn a few weeks later. A South Bend newspaper bestowed upon them the derisive soubriquet of "The Bloody 300," which made them mad enough to fight ten times as many Indians as they had hoped to see. They reached home in time for the Fourth of July celebration, and had their wounded vanity soothed by a public dinner given in testimony to their valorous deeds. Their return proved to have been more justifiable than their going.[23]

6.

More and more Indianapolis was becoming the center of William Conner's activity, in business, political, and social lines. In an old hotel register which strange chance has preserved, there is a record of William Conner as a guest on March 14, 1834. The hostelry was the Union Inn, a two-story building on the south side of Washington Street, opposite the courthouse, kept by John Elder and Joseph Mathers. It was the custom of the time for those who registered to write some comment under the head of "Remarks." One guest noted that "March came in like a Lion To viz—freezing snowing & blowing," while Conner wrote hopefully a few days later, "Tolerable bad Roads but will be good soon."[24] Whether his optimistic note was occasioned by his confidence in more settled weather which would soon follow on the heels of spring, or whether it sprang from a faith that better roads were in the making, can only be conjectured. Toward the goal of good highways he and his brother had worked zealously, and while to men of later generations the roads which he called good would seem abominable, yet compared to the forest trail of Conner's earliest days they were indeed admirable, and still better means of transportation were on the way.

All had not gone smoothly, however, with the eight railroads that had been incorporated by the legislature of 1831-1832. The problem of financing them was greater than had been supposed. Surveys had been made on four of them, but nothing more. Ten days after Conner's visit to Indianapolis, noted in the Union Inn register, he was again in the town to attend the first railroad meeting held here to secure subscriptions for the contemplated Lawrenceburg and Indianapolis Railroad by way of Greensburg and Shelbyville. It was a public meeting largely attended. Committees were appointed to secure subscriptions in each township of Marion County and in the adjoining counties of Hamilton, Hendricks, and Morgan. Conner was appointed to the committee for Hamilton County. The first railroad track in Indiana was laid for this line—a mile and a quarter at Shelbyville—on which a horse-drawn car was operated for exhibition purposes.[25] It never became a part of that company's permanent right of way.

The subject of canals was one that had beset legislators since the first session of the General Assembly. John Conner had favored the canal proposed at that time, planned to skirt the falls of the Ohio at Louisville.[26] An act providing for such a canal had passed the territorial Assembly as early as 1805, but the undertaking collapsed when Aaron Burr's expedition failed. Burr's interest in the canal probably foredoomed it to failure. The second attempt in 1816 met with no better success but for different reasons. Capital could not be raised locally. The third attempt in 1818 met more serious reverses, considered by some authorities as efforts at sabotage on the part of Kentuckians who were jealous of Indiana's activity in this enterprise. Before Indiana could gather her resources for a renewed attack on this problem, Pennsylvania, Ohio, Virginia, and Kentucky joined forces to build the canal on the Kentucky side. This was the finishing blow to Indiana's efforts, and from that time (1824) until 1829 the canal question in this state simmered but did not boil.

The canal era in Indiana, chiefly in the 1830's, was characterized by stupendous errors of judgment and waste of money. In the end, it failed in its objects and flattened the state financially. By the session of 1834-1835 the members believed that the time had arrived when a general system of internal improvements should be devised. A bill was introduced for this purpose, but was overloaded with amendments of the "log-rolling" variety, and was finally tabled. It is said that it checkered the whole state with imaginary canals and roads.

There were such insistent demands in all parts of the state for cheaper transit facilities that the improvement act of January 27, 1836, was far too ambitious for the resources of the state. It carried a huge appropriation of $13,000,000, about one-sixth of the state's wealth, for the construction of canals, railroads, and macadamized roads.[27] Conner was not in the legislature at this time, but so strong was his faith in canals that he and John D. Stephenson bought eighty acres of land on which they laid out the present town of Alexandria. In their advertisements they pointed out that the proposed Central Canal would be very advantageous to the town.[28] The legislators saw no inconsistency in providing for both canals and railroads for the reason that the railroads would be feeders to the canals. It did not work out that way in the end, for the railroads supplanted the canals.

Conner returned to the House in the session of 1836-1837, after an absence of nearly five years.[29] There were now one hundred members in the House of Representatives. The new statehouse had been built not a whit too soon. It was by far the most imposing building which had ever housed the legislature and the first one devoted exclusively to the business of the state. It was in the Greek style, modeled on the Parthenon with soaring columns. An apparent afterthought was the large Roman dome rising from the center of the building, but even this incongruity could not destroy its air of dignified simplicity.[30]

This session could be appropriately dubbed the "Incorporation Session," for acts of incorporation were passed for ten bridge companies, eleven educational institutions, including Asbury (now De Pauw) University and Western University, nine industrial concerns, six turnpike companies, seven insurance companies, four savings institutions, ten towns, and three hotels. Even the New Albany Guards were incorporated. The state had passed out of the beginning stage of its growth when the legislators were completely occupied with the primary details of government and was now attempting to provide a sound business basis for all of its activities. There were fifty-three acts on roads passed, one of these containing over a hundred sections, each relating to a different road.[31]

The subject of internal improvements came up again. It had the persistency of Banquo's ghost. The pending bill was intricate, containing many parts, each one of which was voted upon separately. The whole situation was unsatisfactory, for the character of the improvements was unsettled, and the work was progressing so slowly that apparently many years would be required to complete it. The expenses were heavy—nearly four million dollars—and interest for which no provision had been made had to be met. Dark financial clouds were gathering.[32]

Conner now showed some anxiety about the situation. He asked for a statement from the Board of Internal Improvements as to how much interest the state would have to pay when the

The Old State House, Completed in 1835
From Burns and Polley, *Indianapolis, the Old Town and the New*

work was completed. That was a delicate situation, so the request was side-stepped. The canal politicians had assured the people that there would be no increase in taxation and that tolls would pay the interest—but the bald facts were that the state was borrowing money to pay the interest. Everybody seemed to be under the spell of the fantasy. Did not Noah Noble, whom everyone respected as governor, sign the January 1836 act? Had he not been a consistent and efficient promoter of canals? Was not Governor David Wallace at this time assuring the people that the outlook was very bright? The legislators were in a dilemma. The state needed these improvements and every section was clamoring for its share, but whether the state could afford the expense was a vital question. The *House Journal* discloses a medley of motions, bills, and resolutions on the subject—to repeal the act providing for the general system, to supplement it, to extend the internal improvements in the amount of $1,500,000, not to extend them, to amend the law—around they went in circles. Conner's position as interpreted from the records was to put through projects already passed but to oppose adding new ones. It took more than ten years to extricate the state from this mess, and much longer from the ill consequences of the Wabash and Erie Canal. The people as well as the politicians were to blame. If the backing given to canals had been devoted instead to railroads the story would have been different. The people were skeptical of the railroad and later, of the telegraph. The sordid fact was that bonds had been issued in amount of $15,000,000 for which the state received $8,593,000 cash: the balance was lost, or stolen by various state officers or agents.[33]

7.

When the legislature adjourned on February 6, 1837, William Conner's office holding was at an end. The previous week's advertisements in the Indianapolis newspapers announced that the stock and household equipment at his farm in Hamilton County would be placed on sale on March 1.[34] He was now preparing to retire from active business. His farm was turned over to one of his sons, and he removed not to Indianapolis, as might have been expected from his active association with the town, but to his farm of 150 acres adjoining Noblesville. The north line of his land was the present Cherry Street—the east line, the present Railroad Street. There were no buildings on it except his dwelling, a pretentious brick house set far back in the grounds, and a warehouse. On the site now stands a building which may be the remodeled Conner house, or perhaps a later structure. A number of small weather-stained cottages cluster about the present building. Formerly, towering forest trees sheltered the house. At a lofty height they spread their branches in a cool and inviting canopy, offering the generous hospitality so characteristic of their owner. As he had lived close to nature all his life, nothing less than such a setting could have drawn him from his prairie farm. The remaining acreage was arable land. It has since been converted into town lots devoted to homes, business, and a large factory. When William Conner moved there, the house and grounds resounded to children's voices and laughter, for Lavina, the oldest of seven, was then only fourteen years old. Three children were born in this house.

Not many months after his removal to Noblesville, Conner sold his entire collection of furs to the American Fur Company.[35] This virtually closed his career as a fur trader. In some of his ventures John D. Stephenson and Bicknell Cole were his partners.[36] He had an active interest in various kinds of trade to the end of his life.

A new impetus was given to Indiana railroading when the Madison Railroad Company in the autumn of 1847 ran its first train under steam power into Indianapolis. The Peru and Indianapolis Railroad was organized in that year, and surveyed the following year. Loud were the claims made for it. It was to be a feeder to the Wabash and Erie Canal. It would be seventy-three miles long and completed at less than one-third of the average cost of other roads. On January 8, 1849, William Conner, John Burk, Samuel Dale, and W. J. Holman notified the public that as a committee they would receive conditional donations and subscriptions for the location and erection of a depot in Indianapolis. The depot was located by the committee on property south of Washington Street between East and New Jersey streets.[37] The first section of the road, which was begun at Indianapolis, reached Noblesville in 1851— two years after it had been promised. The railroad station in the latter city was built on Conner's land, a short distance from his dwelling.

A visitor to the town the year the railroad was completed made the journey from Indianapolis, twenty-two miles, in one and one-half hours. Indianapolis was now accessible to Noblesville by a morning train, and persons could return by evening, an excellent arrangement. The six or eight stores visited, one of which was kept by Richard Conner, William's son, were well filled with goods and doing business. Richard's firm, called Conner and Massey, had an extensive dry goods store for the retail and wholesale trade on the present site of the American National Bank.[38]

By 1857 the railroad was ready for receivership, but it had reached Noblesville and for a time at least, satisfied one of Conner's hopes. This was his second and last venture in aiding and building of railroads. From now on Conner engaged in land deals—buying and selling town lots and farms, and operating a saw- and gristmill about four miles north of Noblesville.

William Conner had a building on the west side of the public square in which he conducted a general store for many years. It was something to occupy his time together with the management of nearly three thousand acres of land which he owned in Marion, Hamilton, Cass, and Wabash counties. He was now about eighty-two years old. Ten children had been born to him in his marriage with Elizabeth Chapman. Richard James, John Fayette, William Henry, Alexander Hamilton, George F., Elisha Harrington, Benjamin Franklin, Catherine Massey, Margaret Crans, Lavina—seven sons and three daughters—all living except Lavina. Most of them were near him. Alexander was in Nebraska. Not only his children, but his grandchildren were about him. He hoped they would remain here. He wrote his son Richard in 1848 that a large city was "a bad place for a young man to go to that is as little experienced in the world as you are. I would much rather you could get a situation in the country than to go to such a place [Louisville]," where there were "too many temptations to vice."[39]

On August 28, 1855, this sturdy pioneer took the last long trail. He did not execute a will, probably realizing that the determination of the legal rights of the two sets of children respectively, could be had with more exactitude by the law than by his judgment. This gives an impression of his character. He had purchased the interest of Mekinges and their children in a section of land granted by an act of Congress, as heretofore related. Were they also heirs to after acquired real estate along with his children by his marriage with Elizabeth Chapman? This was a question of equity as well as of law. He left it to the statute of descents. After his death his white children had a partition of his holdings among themselves. In 1861 the half-breed children—Mekinges was dead—brought suit against the children in possession and the title to all the land was quieted in the latter against the Indian plaintiffs.[40]

As gleaned from descriptions by his contemporaries, Conner was a large man, straight as an arrow. His homely sense of honesty and justice was reflected in his countenance and deeds. He was almost wholly self-educated. Of kindly disposition, he was generous not only to his friends but to strangers in need. He had an Indian characteristic in that he was implacable to his few enemies. He was held in popular esteem wherever he was known. He was modest, so much so that he seldom spoke of the adventures of his life—not a line was committed to paper—that was left to others. It was said of him that "with his natural powers of observation, which were remarkable" he was "one of the best woodsmen in the West, and one of the very best interpreters ever employed by the United States."[41] He had indomitable energy tempered with a kindliness of feeling exhibited first to his Indian friends and afterwards to his white neighbors. Notwithstanding his life with the Indians during forty-seven years, he had a natural love for his kind which asserted itself when he was detached from that life in 1820. He possessed "a more intimate knowledge" of the Indian "character and wants, than almost any other person of the same standing and respectability in the State," so wrote David Wallace, lieutenant governor, to John Tipton, United States senator.[42] General Harrison in 1826 wrote that he always considered Conner "as a man whose integrity & fidelity might be perfectly relied upon."[43] Placing side by side these recognitions of his traits of character, the conclusion of an early writer that he "was wrought of the finest human steel and endured to the end," seems a just one.[44]

Sixty years after his death Richard C. Adams, son of Nancy Conner Adams, half-breed daughter of William Conner, spokesman and historian of the Delaware tribe, wrote: "there were many persons who were adopted into the Delaware Tribe who, either they or their descendants, came into prominence in the history of the United States, among them Wm. Connor of Indiana and William Anderson of Ohio, not all, however, of Indian blood, but all of whom stood loyal to the Tribe, and who were devoted to their traditions, training and belief."[45] Such opinions and tributes from representatives of two races fundamentally and historically antagonistic to each other, set him apart from other men of his time.

For the purposes of understanding a man his character and his work are inseparable—the former fashions the latter, which in turn reflects the former. By this formula the Conners may be judged. Enveloped in barbarism or savagery from birth to their mid years they held the confidence and loyalty of the Indians. When they, John first and William later, gradually dissociated themselves from the Indians and more and more allied themselves with those of their own race, that fact did not alter the attitude of the Indians toward them. Their transformation came gradually as though they were stepping slowly out of the darkness and mists of their Indian life into the dawning day of civilization. Their past life in the wilderness with its tenants of savage men and wild beasts receded. Sons of the wilderness though they were, they helped to fashion a new state out of the primeval forest and virgin prairie.

NOTES

I

[1]Winsor, Justin, *The Mississippi Basin, 1697-1763*, 228-58 (Boston and New York, 1895); King, Rufus, *Ohio. First Fruits of the Ordinance of 1787*, 20-28, 44-45, 53-63 (*American Commonwealths*, Riverside Press, Cambridge, 1888).

[2]Thwaites, Reuben Gold, and Kellogg, Louise Phelps (eds.), *Documentary History of Dunmore's War, 1774*, 153n, 290n (Wisconsin Historical Society, Madison, 1905); De Schweinitz, Edmund, *The Life and Times of David Zeisberger . . .*, 374 (Philadelphia, 1870).

[3]Winsor, *Mississippi Basin*, 347; Dillon, John B., *A History of Indiana . . .*, 51 (Indianapolis, 1859).

[4]Volwiler, Albert T., *George Croghan and the Westward Movement, 1741-1782*, 17, 20-21, 30-32 (Cleveland, 1926).

[5]King, *Ohio*, 72-79; Volwiler, *op. cit.*, 115-89; Hinsdale, B. A., *The Old Northwest . . .*, 57-69 (New York, 1888); Parkman, Francis, *The Conspiracy of Pontiac . . .*, I, 232 ff. (Boston, 1924).

[6]Alvord, Clarence Walworth, *The Mississippi Valley in British Politics*, II, 52-61 (Cleveland, 1917); Volwiler, *op. cit.*, 189-204.

[7]*Ibid.*, 148-49, 172-75, 204-8; Alvord, *op. cit.*, I, 103-33, 210 ff., 226-27, 237-40; II, 59-61.

[8]*Ibid.*, II, 190 ff. See Introduction to Thwaites and Kellogg (eds.), *Documentary History of Dunmore's War*; Roosevelt, Theodore, *The Winning of the West*, I, pt. 2, 34 (New York and London, 1889).

[9]A tablet at Hockingport, Ohio, on the site of Fort Gower records this "spirit of American Independence," November 5, 1774. See King, *Ohio*, 111.

[10]Hinsdale, *The Old Northwest*, 147-61; Alvord, Clarence Walworth, *The Illinois Country*, 310-57 (*Centennial History of Illinois*, I, Springfield, 1920); King, *Ohio*, 141 ff.; Winsor, Justin, *The Westward Movement . . .*, 111-43, 170-78, 190 ff. (Boston and New York, 1897). The original "gaol" containing the cell where Hamilton, "the Hair-Buyer," was confined is now a part of the restoration of Williamsburg, Virginia. *A Handbook for the Exhibition Buildings of Colonial Williamsburg Incorporated . . .*, 37 (Williamsburg, Va., 1936). An accurate and comprehensive account of Hamilton's misdeeds and imprisonment are given in William H. English's *Conquest of the Country Northwest of the River Ohio 1778-1783 . . .*, I, 215 ff. and II, 605 ff. (Indianapolis and Kansas City, 1897). See also Marshall, John, *The Life of George Washington . . .*, I, 332-33 (Walton Book Co., New York, 1930); Bancroft, George, *History of the United States of America . . .*, V, 312-13 (New York, 1892).

[11]King, *Ohio*, 230-66; Hinsdale, *The Old Northwest*, 184-86. Roosevelt, *Winning of the West*, III, pt. 1, ch. 5.

[12]Esarey, Logan, *A History of Indiana from its Exploration to 1850*, I, 204-29 (3d ed., Fort Wayne, 1924).

(183)

II

¹*The Maryland Calendar of Wills,* compiled by Jane Baldwin and Roberta Bolling Henry, V, 92 (Baltimore, 1917) ; Fletcher, James C., "Early Days," in *Indianapolis News,* May 11, 1881 ; Cole, Ernest B., "The Conner Family," in *Indianapolis Sunday Star,* September 19, 1920; *History of Macomb County, Michigan . . .,* 229 ff. (M. A. Leeson & Co., Chicago, 1882) ; Ross, Robert B., and Catlin, George B., *Landmarks of Detroit . . .,* 674 (rev. ed., Detroit, 1898) ; De Schweinitz, *David Zeisberger,* 425; Jones, David, *A Journal of Two Visits Made to Some Nations of Indians on the West Side of the River Ohio, in the Year 1772 and 1773 . . .,* 88 (New York, 1865) ; entry for May 8, 1775, in Diary of the Moravian Mission to the Indians, Schoenbrunn on the Muskingum (hereafter referred to as Schoenbrunn Diary), manuscript in archives of Moravian Church, Bethlehem, Pennsylvania: "He [Richard Conner] was born in Maryland, his brothers and friends still live there in Frederickstown and according to his statement know of the brethren"; *Michigan Pioneer and Historical Collections,* IV, 308; V, 453; Loskiel, George Henry, *History of the Mission of the United Brethren among the Indians . . .,* pt. 3, 104 (London, 1794) ; Mitchener, C. H. (ed.), *Ohio Annals . . .,* 184-85 (Dayton, 1876).

²Alvord, *Mississippi Valley in British Politics,* I, 121-27, 161-67, 169-73, 178-88, 199 ff.; Volwiler, *George Croghan,* 139, 166-72.

³Margaret Boyer's name appears variously in the records, but she was known as Margaret Boyer to her descendants, as shown (1) in a letter from her grandson, George F. Conner, to Julia Conner Thompson, January 31, 1899, (2) in another, from Mary Conner Haimbaugh to Ernest B. Cole, October 19, 1920, which says: "Richard Conner's wife's name was Margaret Boyer. When it was written Bouvir, it was French. I had the name from our grandmother Conner, widow of William," and (3) in a written statement of another granddaughter, Alice Conner Cottingham, dated December 21, 1934. James C. Fletcher, whose article, "Early Days," in *Indianapolis News,* May 11, 1881, gives the name as Boyer, received his information from Elizabeth Chapman (Mrs. William) Conner.

In the register of St. Anne's Church, Detroit, she is twice mentioned in relation to her sons: February 12, 1792, her son James was baptized, "fils de Richard Connor et de Marguerite Connor, ses pere et mere, irlandois de nation"; February 23, 1808, her son Henry, who married Therese Tremblé, is described as "fils majeur de Defunct Richard Connor et de Marguerite Boiver." The spelling "Boivir," is used by Ernest B. Cole in his article on "The Conner Family," *Indianapolis Sunday Star,* September 19, 1920.

According to Father Christian Denissen's genealogical compilation (Burton Historical Collection, Detroit), Richard Conner married Margaret Bower (probably Bauer, of Pennsylvania Dutch parentage), Vol. C, 2930-31.

The following works list her surname as Myers, which is obviously incorrect: *History of Macomb County, Michigan* (Leeson), 229; *Michigan Pioneer and Historical Collections,* V, 453; XXVIII, 133-35; Kellogg, Louise Phelps (ed.), *Frontier Advance on the Upper Ohio, 1778-1779,* 246n (Wisconsin Historical *Collections,* XXIII, Madison, 1916); Quaife, Milo M. (ed.), *The John Askin Papers,* I, 228n (Detroit, 1928); Eldredge, Robert F., *Past and Present of Macomb County, Michigan,* 564 ff. (Chicago, 1905).

⁴Jones, *Journal of Two Visits,* 88, quoted *ante,* 12-13, and citations to Michigan and Wisconsin publications in note 3.

⁵This account is based upon the story told in the *Report of the Commission to Locate the Site of the Frontier Forts of Pennsylvania,* edited by Thomas Lynch Montgomery, I, 158-59 (2d ed., Harrisburg, 1916). His information was procured from Colonel John Craig, an old resident of Lehigh Gap. Craig received it from his father, who had it direct from Frederick Boyer, who was born December 31, 1742, and died October 31, 1832, at the age of nearly ninety years. Since Frederick Boyer was thirteen years old at the time of his capture, the date is fixed as 1756. C. Hale Sipe, in his *Fort Ligonier and Its Times* . . ., 139 (Harrisburg, 1932), mentions 1756 as the year when this happened. The *History of Lehigh County, Pennsylvania* . . ., edited by Charles Rhoads Roberts and others, II, 139 (Allentown, 1914), adds the name of the slain father and mentions a lad who later returned, and a daughter who was never heard of again. The sources for these statements are not given. The ancestry of John Jacob Boyer is outlined in a genealogical compilation issued by the Association of American Boyers at Reading, Pennsylvania (4th ed., 1915), entitled *The American Boyers.* This book states that there were three children, Frederick, Dorothea, and Catherine. This is the first time that the names of the little girls occur. They are not authenticated in any way. In 1762 many captives were released by western Indians at the Lancaster treaty, among them a Hans Boyer, who was, perhaps, the Frederick Boyer of Lehigh Gap. Sipe, *op. cit.* In *The American Boyers,* 211, appears the story of the Boyer girl who married the Indian chief, with a "Western paper" cited as authority. Diligent effort to identify this paper has been unsuccessful. The fate of her sister is not referred to in any of these books.

⁶The marriage customs of. the Indians are described as follows: "Marriages are performed in three different ways. 1st. If the male and female agree, they may cohabit with each other without any further ceremony. 2d. When a young man loves a girl, and she will not consent to have him without he first obtains the consent of her parents, which must be done with a present adequate to the character of the girl. If his present is received by the girl's friends, the marriage is fixed; if the present is returned, it is understood that they are not willing for the match. 3d. This is considered by much the most honorable and binding on the parties concerned. When an Indian has a son that he wishes to be married to a good and virtuous woman, he assembles his friends and relations, and consults with them what woman his son shall marry. When a choice is made, the relations of the young man collect what presents they think are sufficient for the occasion, and take them to the parents of the girl or intended bride;

they make known their business, leave the articles, and return home without an answer. The relations of the girl then assemble together, and con-
sult each other on the subject. If they agree to the match, they collect
suitable presents, dress the girl in her best clothing, and take her to the
persons that made application for the match, where she and the presents
are left. The marriage is then considered complete, as all the ceremony
for the occasion has been regularly gone through. But if the friends of
the girl or herself do not approve of the proposals, the presents that
were given by the young man's relations are returned, which is considered
a refusal." See "The Manners and Customs of the North-Western Indians," in *Fergus' Historical Series*, no. 26, p. 89; see also Seaver, James E.,
A Narrative of the Life of Mrs. Mary Jemison . . ., 180 (Random House,
New York, 1929); Heckewelder, John, *History, Manners, and Customs of
the Indian Nations . . .*, 161 (Historical Society of Pennsylvania, *Memoirs*,
XII, Philadelphia, 1876).

[7]Schoenbrunn Diary, May 4, 1775. In 1764, Margaret Boyer was a
captive with the Shawnee. One of Colonel Bouquet's demands when the
Shawnee and Delawares sued for peace was that all prisoners must be
delivered at Fort Pitt by October 29. By November 9, two hundred and
six had been brought in, and the Shawnee promised to return a hundred
more in the spring. *Historical Account of Bouquet's Expedition Against
the Ohio Indians, in 1764*, 52-76 (Cincinnati, 1868). The Shawnee never
delivered all their prisoners. Force, Peter (ed.), *American Archives . . .*,
I, 1015 (Washington, 1837).

[8]Jones, *A Journal of Two Visits*, 87-88. Jones, minister of the Baptist
Church at Freehold, New Jersey, visited the Moravian towns in 1772 and
1773, and preached there. He saw service in the Revolution, and was chap-
lain under General Wayne in 1777, and again in 1794. In December, 1789,
or January, 1790, he preached the first sermon ever preached in the settlement at Fort Miami, near the mouth of the Little Miami. *Ibid.*, v-xi; De
Schweinitz, *David Zeisberger*, 386n; Ferris, Ezra, *The Early Settlement of
the Miami Country*, 267-68 (*Indiana Historical Society Publications*, I, no. 9,
Indianapolis, 1897); Hill, N. N. (comp.), *History of Coshocton County,
Ohio . . .*, 243-44 (Newark, Ohio, 1881).

[9]Netawatwees, chief of the Unami or Turtle division of the Delawares,
often called King Newcomer, became principal chief of the Delawares in
1772, succeeding Beaver. His capital was at Gekelemukpechünk, near the
present site of Newcomerstown, and later at Goschachgünk, at the junction
of the Tuscarawas and Walhonding. He lived in a "roomy dwelling [which],
with its shingle-roof and board-floors, its staircase and stone-chimney,
formed one of those Delaware lodges that rivaled the homesteads of the
settlers." In this house the first Protestant sermon in the state of Ohio was
preached by Zeisberger on March 14, 1771. Netawatwees' son, John Killbuck, opposed Christianity, but his grandson, John Killbuck, Jr., or Gelelemend, embraced it. Upon his baptism in 1788 by Zeisberger, Gelelemend
was named William Henry, at his own request. Just before his death in
1776, Netawatwees besought White Eyes, his chief counselor, "to uphold
neutrality and the Christian religion." De Schweinitz, *David Zeisberger,*

348-49, 366-67, 372, 386n, 390, 394, 426, 436, 442, 604; Thwaites, Reuben Gold, and Kellogg, Louise Phelps (eds.), *The Revolution on the Upper Ohio, 1775-1777,* 38n, 46n (Madison, Wis., 1908).

[10]Schoenbrunn Diary, May 4, 1775. For the removal of the Indians, the founding of Schoenbrunn, and Zeisberger's subsequent journeys among the Shawnee, see De Schweinitz, *op. cit.,* 370-93. See also the chapter on "The Moravians," in King, *Ohio,* 119 ff.

[11]The register of St. Anne's Church (Detroit) records the baptism of James Conner at the age of twenty years and five months on February 12, 1792. See also Statement Concerning James Conner, the First White Child Born in Ohio, an unpublished manuscript by the Reverend Joseph E. Weinland, approved by the Executive Committee of the Moravian Historical Society, August 13, 1934, Bethlehem, Pa.

[12]Conner's presence at Snakestown as late as June, 1774, is mentioned in "Extract Taken from Alexander M'Kee, Esqr's, Journal of Transactions with the Indians at Pittsburg, &c., from the 1st May, to the 10th June, 1774," in Rupp, Isaac Daniel, *Early History of Western Pennsylvania . . . ,* Appendix, 211 (Harrisburg and Pittsburgh, 1846). The Shawnee were friendly with the Pennsylvania, but not the Virginia, traders. About thirty of the former were supposed to be in some danger, but Conner reported that he found them unharmed and making canoes. Snake was with the British Indians in the raid on the Moravian towns in 1781.

[13]De Schweinitz, *David Zeisberger,* 399-409; Thwaites and Kellogg (eds.), *Documentary History of Dunmore's War,* xxii-xxiii.

[14]De Schweinitz, *op. cit.,* 425. For a description of Pittsburgh in 1775 see *The Journal of Nicholas Cresswell, 1774-1777,* 65-66 (New York, 1924).

[15]Schoenbrunn Diary, February 24, 1775.

[16]Descriptions of the establishment of Schoenbrunn and its appearance at this period are given in De Schweinitz, *David Zeisberger,* 371-73, 375-76, 380n, 423; *Journal of Nicholas Cresswell,* 106-7. A map and photographs of the town as restored under the auspices of the Ohio State Archaeological and Historical Society appear in Weinland, Rev. Joseph E., *The Romantic Story of Schoenbrunn . . . ,* 7-23 (Ohio State Archaeological and Historical Society, 2d ed., 1929). The restored cabin of Richard and Margaret Conner was dedicated in Schoenbrunn Memorial State Park on May 12, 1935. *Museum Echoes,* VIII, 21 (June, 1935). See also the description of Gnadenhütten in 1775, in Captain James Wood's Journal, Thwaites and Kellogg (eds.), *Revolution on the Upper Ohio,* 64.

[17]White Eyes, as early as 1772, made a trip to New Orleans, New York, and Philadelphia which opened his eyes to the benefits of civilization. Thereafter he was dominated by the desire to achieve them for the Indians. He lived on the Tuscarawas River, six miles below Gekelemukpechünk near White Eyes Plains. He advocated neutrality in Dunmore's War and urged peace after the battle of Point Pleasant. He supported the enterprise of the Moravian missionaries and wanted the Delawares to accept Christianity and turn away from war. White Eyes favored the cause of the Americans in the Revolution and joined the American forces. He died of smallpox, November 10, 1778. De Schweinitz refers to him as "one of the greatest

and best of the later Indians" and says, "No unbaptized native, of any tribe or name, did so much for the Mission and the Gospel." His widow was baptized into Christian faith in March, 1799. In 1801, she and her second husband, Jacob Pemahoaland, accompanied the Moravian missionaries Kluge and Luckenbach to Indiana. De Schweinitz, *David Zeisberger*, 390-91, 408-9, 413-19, 428-30, 463, 468-70, 656; Dillon, *History of Indiana*, 100-1; Stocker, Harry Emilius (tr.), "The Autobiography of Abraham Luckenbach," in Moravian Historical Society, *Transactions*, X, pts. 3 and 4, 374 (Bethlehem, Pa., 1917).

[18]"At the children's service Bro. David [Zeisberger] baptized the little son born to the Conners, the child receiving the name of John." Schoenbrunn Diary, August 27, 1775.

[19]*Journals of the Continental Congress. 1774-1789*, II, 178-82 (Library of Congress ed., Washington, 1905); De Schweinitz, *David Zeisberger*, 430-31.

[20]*Ibid.*, 431; Schoenbrunn Diary, March 18, 1776, which says, "He is a little boy, four years of age, and can speak only the Shawnee language." Loskiel, *History of the Mission of the United Brethren*, pt. 3, 104-5.

[21]Schoenbrunn Diary, May 4, 1775.

[22]De Schweinitz, *op. cit.*, 380-81, 394, 424n-25n, 433-35; Loskiel, *op. cit.*, pt. 3, 113. Colonel George Morgan was born at Philadelphia in 1743. He became first an employee, then a partner, in the Philadelphia firm of Baynton and Wharton, which dealt in goods for the Indians. After Pontiac's war he represented the firm in the Illinois country. During the Revolution he served as Indian agent for the United States in the middle department and as deputy commissary-general of purchases for the western department. His headquarters were at Fort Pitt. Colonel Morgan was adopted by the Delawares, who called him Tamenend. *Dictionary of American Biography*, XIII, 169-70; De Schweinitz, *op. cit.*, 439; Heckeweder, John, *A Narrative of the Mission of the United Brethren among the Delaware and Mohegan Indians, from . . . 1740, to . . . 1808 . . .*, 150 (Philadelphia, 1820). To a letter to Morgan from John Leith, dated Moravian Town, August 19, 1778, there is appended a note recommending Leith as a "real friend to the United States." It is signed by Zeisberger, William Edwards, Heckewelder, and Richard Conner. Morgan Letter Book, III, 123, in Carnegie Library, Pittsburgh.

[23]See sketches of Elliot and McKee in Quaife (ed.), *John Askin Papers*, I, 257n and 300n. See also King, *Ohio*, 146 ff.; De Schweinitz, *op. cit.*, 447 ff., 462. Girty's activities are covered at length in Butterfield, Consul Willshire, *History of the Girtys . . .* (Cincinnati, 1890). See especially pages 178, 183, 184, 187-88, 199, 201, 389. In July, 1779, when Conner was at the Delaware capital, he met Girty, who told him to tell his brethren, the Americans, that he did not desire them to show him any favor, nor would he show them any. Hazard, Samuel (ed.), *Pennsylvania Archives*, 1 series, VII, 542 (Pennsylvania, 1853). Girty maintained this hostile attitude toward the Americans. In a letter of August 6, 1792, Anthony Wayne states that Girty had left Detroit on June 15 saying that he would attack the Americans near Fort Jefferson and either kill or be killed. Rufus Putnam Collection,

Marietta College. Rev. O. M. Spencer says in his *Indian Captivity: A True Narrative* . . ., 88 (New York, 1834) : "Simon Girty, whether it was from prejudice . . . or not, his dark shaggy hair; his low forehead; his brows contracted, and meeting above his short flat nose; his grey sunken eyes, averting the ingenuous gaze; his lips thin and compressed, and the dark and sinister expression of his countenance, to me, seemed the very picture of a villain."

[24]De Schweinitz, *David Zeisberger,* 449 ff.; Schoenbrunn Diary, April 19, 1777; Loskiel, *History of the Mission of the United Brethren,* pt. 3, 116; Weinland, *Romantic Story of Schoenbrunn,* 6-7; "Journal of John G. Jungman," in Charles Cist, *The Cincinnati Miscellany* . . ., II, 186 (Cincinnati, November, 1845).

[25]The place and date of William Conner's birth are not certain, but it is probable that he was born in 1773. According to the statement of Richard J. Conner, his son, William Conner was about eight years old in 1781. Draper MSS. VIII, yy21. The oldest son, James, was born in 1771, John in 1775, Henry in 1780, and Susanna in 1783. These were all of Richard Conner's other children. Living descendants believe William was born at Fort Pitt, although there is no record of any child with Richard and Margaret Conner at Fort Pitt in 1774 or at Schoenbrunn in 1775 before John's birth. William's tombstone at Noblesville, Indiana, gives his age as seventy-two years at the time of his death in 1855; this would place his birth in the year 1783, which is obviously incorrect. According to family tradition he was older than John, which is in agreement with the statement of Richard J. Conner, mentioned above.

[26]Diary of Moravian Mission to Indian Congregation at Lichtenau, two and one-half miles from Coshocton, Ohio, from April, 1776, to March 30, 1780. Unpublished manuscript in archives of Moravian Church, Bethlehem.

[27]"Oct. 8, 1780. The little son born to Bro. and Sr. Conner last night was baptized into the death of Jesus receiving the name Henry." Diary of the New Schoenbrunn Indian Mission, manuscript in the archives of the Moravian Church, Bethlehem. Henry Conner became government interpreter for the northern tribes and related Indian traditions to both Parkman and Schoolcraft. Parkman, *Conspiracy of Pontiac,* I, 373, II, 358. His name is attached to old landmarks in Detroit, such as Conners Creek.

III

[1]Loskiel, *History of the Mission of the United Brethren,* pt. 3, 135-37; King, *Ohio,* 148-51.

[2]Kellogg, Louise Phelps (ed.), *Frontier Retreat on the Upper Ohio, 1779-1781,* 320-21 (Wisconsin Historical *Collections,* XXIV, Madison, 1917). Brodhead's activities are discussed in *ibid.,* Introduction, *passim.*

[3]Butterfield, Consul Willshire (ed.), *Washington-Irvine Correspondence . . . 1781 to 1783,* 51-53 (Madison, Wis., 1882); Sipe, *Fort Ligonier,* 509 ff.; Butterfield, *History of the Girtys,* 126-29; Hazard (ed.), *Pennsylvania Archives,* 1 series, IX, 161-62.

[4]Butterfield, *Washington-Irvine Correspondence,* 58-63; De Schweinitz, *David Zeisberger,* 487 ff.; *Pennsylvania Magazine of History,* IV, 247-48 (1880); Doddridge, Joseph, *Notes on the Settlement and Indian Wars of the Western Parts of Virginia and Pennsylvania . . .,* 195-98 (3d ed., Pittsburgh, 1912); Sipe, *op. cit.,* 522-23. Some of Heckewelder's letters are printed in Hazard (ed.), *Pennsylvania Archives,* 1 series, VII, 516-18, 524-26, 541-42, VIII, 152, 158-59. Alexander McCormick is not to be confused with Alexander McKee. McCormick was a trader among the Wyandot, and gave Heckewelder secret warning of Elliot's intentions. De Schweinitz, *op. cit.,* 473, 492; Butterfield, Consul Willshire, *An Historical Account of the Expedition against Sandusky under Col. William Crawford in 1782 . . .,* 166, 189-91 (Cincinnati, 1873).

[5]John Leith (sometimes spelled Leath or Leeth) was born in South Carolina, March 15, 1755. In his eighteenth year he hired out to a Pittsburgh fur trader, but within a year was made prisoner by a Delaware chief with a white wife, who adopted him. He regained his liberty at Camp Charlotte and resumed his fur trading. In 1776 he was captured by the Shawnee and sold to the Wyandot, who released him because he was an adopted Delaware. The following year he was trading in Detroit. In the spring of 1778 his adopted father, the old Delaware chief, persuaded him to return to his tribe. He went to Coshocton, the capital of the Delawares, and in March, 1779, married Sally Lowry, or Lowrey, a white girl who had been taken captive when less than two years old. They went to live at the Moravian town of Gnadenhütten. He was living at the Moravian town in 1781 and was carried away captive with the Moravians. He resumed his trading operations at Upper Sandusky under the surveillance of the British. His biography, called *Leeth's Narrative,* is a rare book, containing the only extant account of some of the incidents of this period. His life is a close parallel to that of Richard Conner in many respects. Both were released at Camp Charlotte, both lived in the Moravian towns, and both were taken captive by the British Wyandot in 1781. Thwaites, Reuben Gold (ed.), *A Short Biography of John Leeth . . ., passim* (Cleveland, 1904); Butterfield, *Expedition against Sandusky,* 178n-79n; Loskiel, *History of the Mission of the United Brethren,* pt. 3, 140-41; Bliss, Eugene F. (tr. and ed.), *Diary of David Zeisberger . . .,* I, xxviii (Cincinnati, 1885).

[6]De Schweinitz, *David Zeisberger*, 493-511; Heckewelder, *Narrative of the Mission among the Indians*, 232-76; King, *Ohio*, 153-55; Loskiel, *History of the Mission of the United Brethren*, pt. 3, 151-61; Bliss (ed.), *Diary of David Zeisberger*, I, 3-16.

[7]*History of Macomb County, Michigan* (Leeson), 229, 231; letter of George F. Conner to Julia Conner Thompson, January 31, 1899.

[8]Bliss (ed.), *Diary of David Zeisberger*, I, 16-23; Heckewelder, *op. cit.*, 276-83; De Schweinitz, *op. cit.*, 513-17; Loskiel, *op. cit.*, pt. 3, 161-64; Burton Historical Collection, *Manuscripts*, I, 277-78; statement of R. J. Conner, June 17, 1891, in Draper MSS. VIII, yy21; Rice, William H., *David Zeisberger and His Brown Brethren*, 40 (Bethlehem, Pa., 1897). Zeisberger gives the date of arrival at Sandusky as October 1; Loskiel, and Heckewelder, who followed Loskiel, give the date as October 11. For a discussion of the location of the Moravian camping ground and Captives' Town, see Butterfield, *Expedition against Sandusky*, 162n, 163n, 180-81, n. 3. See also Wilcox, Frank, *Ohio Indian Trails*, 138 (Cleveland, 1933). Half King's town was at Indian Mill, a few miles north of the present Upper Sandusky. Butterfield, *op. cit.*, 162n, 163n.

The route followed was from Salem by land and water to Goschachgünk, now Coshocton; up the Walhonding, or White Woman's Creek, to the mouth of the Gokhosing or Owl Creek, now the Vernon River; by land to the vicinity of Upper Sandusky. This route can be traced by following U. S. Road 36 from Gnadenhütten to Coshocton and Mt. Vernon; by State Roads 13 and 95 through Mt. Gilead to Marion; then by U. S. Road 23 to Upper Sandusky. This route will trace or parallel the original Indian trails, the Muskingum, Walhonding, Owl River, and Scioto trails. It was through this country and likely over these trails that the Conner family and their fellow captives were led. A very informative book on *Ohio Indian Trails* has been written by Frank Wilcox. References to the above trails will be found on pages 91 ff., 131 ff., 147 ff., 158 ff. In 1934, by automobile, the writer in a few hours traversed this route which took the captives twenty days, 153 years before.

[9]The journey to Detroit, the trial and its outcome are described in De Schweinitz, *David Zeisberger*, 517-29; Loskiel, *History of the Mission of the United Brethren*, pt. 3, 164-69; Heckewelder, *Narrative of the Mission of the United Brethren*, 283-99; Bliss (ed.), *Diary of David Zeisberger*, I, 29-46. There are many discrepancies between Heckewelder's *Narrative* and Zeisberger's *Diary*. The latter is considerably more moderate in its account of the discomforts on the journey and the manner of reception. Pipe's ceremonial speech is quoted in Heckewelder, *History of the Indian Nations*, 134-36.

[10]De Peyster had arrived in Detroit in 1779 to succeed Hamilton as commandant, and remained until 1784. A man of some distinction, he was favorably regarded by the Moravian missionaries. He was a good officer, although arbitrary in his methods. Some of his land deals subjected him to criticism. Campbell, James V., *Outlines of the Political History of Michigan*, 178-84, 186 (Detroit, 1876); De Schweinitz, *David Zeisberger*, 528-29;

Quaife (ed.), *John Askin Papers*, I, 72n; *Michigan Pioneer and Historical Collections*, XX, 296-99.

[11]Bliss (ed.), *Diary of David Zeisberger*, I, xx; Loskiel, *History of the Mission of the United Brethren*, pt. 3, 116.

[12]On November 11, 1781, De Peyster wrote McKee: "Captain Pipe brought in four Teachers, leaving the other two to take care of their Wives and Children, and build huts for the winter. The four who came in appear to be harmless people. They make no secret to have written several letters for the Cooshocking Delawares to Fort Pitt, which they say they were obliged to do in their own Defence, but that those who dictated the letters always carried them themselves." J. Watts de Peyster (ed.), *Miscellanies, by an Officer. (Colonel Arent Schuyler de Peyster, B. A.), 1774-1813 . . .*, pt. 2, XXX (New York, 1888).

[13]Bliss (ed.), *op. cit.*, I, 21, 48, 75-76.

[14]De Schweinitz, *David Zeisberger*, 530-33; Loskiel, *op. cit.*, pt. 3, 169-71; Heckewelder, *Narrative of the Mission of the United Brethren*, 298 ff.

[15]De Schweinitz, *op. cit.*, 533-34; Bliss (ed.), *op. cit.*, I, 68-74, 76-78. Bliss quotes De Peyster's letter to Girty: "You will please present the strings I send you to the Half King and tell him I have listened to his demand. I therefore hope he will give you such assistance as you may think necessary to enable you to bring the teachers and their families to this place. I will by no means allow you to suffer them to be plundered or any way ill-treated." Girty doubtless hoped for better results from the second hearing.

[16]De Schweinitz, *op. cit.*, 535-57. De Schweinitz says: "According to a careful computation made by the missionaries, with the aid of the national assistants, the whole number of victims was ninety. The militia brought back ninety-six scalps; hence six of the murdered ones must have been heathen Indians, probably visitors at Gnadenhütten." The number is often given as ninety-six. See *A True History of the Massacre of Ninety-six Christian Indians at Gnadenhuetten, Ohio, March 8th, 1782* (New Philadelphia, 1844), reprinted in Burton Historical Collection, *Manuscripts*, I, 275-86; Loskiel, *op. cit.*, pt. 3, 175-85; Bliss (ed.), *op. cit.*, I, 78-86.

[17]De Schweinitz, *op. cit.*, 558-62; Bliss (ed.), *Diary of David Zeisberger*, I, 74-78, 87 ff.; De Peyster (ed.), *Miscellanies, by an Officer*, pt. 2, CXXXn.

[18]Butterfield, *Expedition against Sandusky*, n. 2, 78-80, and 81 ff.; De Schweinitz, *op. cit.*, 564 ff.; Heckewelder, *op. cit.*, 337 ff.; Lang, Frank H., *The Burning of William Crawford . . . June 11, 1782 . . .* (Upper Sandusky, Ohio, 1931).

[19]Bliss (ed.), *op. cit.*, I, 96, 103 ff.; De Schweinitz, *op. cit.*, 578-79; Miscellaneous Genealogy Notes in the Burton Historical Collection, Detroit Public Library, I, 155; Loskiel, *History of the Mission of the United Brethren*, pt. 3, 193; Ford, Henry A., "The Old Moravian Mission at Mt. Clemens," in *Michigan Pioneer and Historical Collections*, X, 107-15.

[20]Bliss (ed.), *op. cit.*, I, 100, 110, 159.

[21]Loskiel, *op. cit.*, pt. 3, 193, 194, 199; Heckewelder, *Narrative of the Mission of the United Brethren*, 348-49, 352-56; Utley, Henry M., and

Cutcheon, Byron M., *Michigan As a Province, Territory and State* . . ., I, 343 (Publishing Society of Michigan, 1906).

[22]Bliss (ed.), *Diary of David Zeisberger*, I, 174. Susanna was the first white child born in Macomb County, Michigan, of English-speaking parents. *Michigan Pioneer and Historical Collections*, V, 453; XVIII, 487; Utley and Cutcheon, *op. cit.*

[23]Heckewelder, *op. cit.*, 356-63; Bliss (ed.), *op. cit.*, I, 206-8; De Schweinitz, *David Zeisberger*, 583-89; Loskiel, *op. cit.*, pt. 3, 201; *American State Papers. Public Lands*, I, 501; Campbell, *Political History of Michigan*, 187-88.

[24]De Schweinitz, *op. cit.*, 589; Bliss (ed.), *op. cit.*, I, 265-66, 434; Quaife (ed.), *John Askin Papers*, II, 206-7; *American State Papers, op. cit.* Richard Conner was the first English-speaking settler in the region where Mt. Clemens is situated. *History of Macomb County, Michigan* (Leeson), 522.

[25]The date of Richard Conner's death is erroneously given as April 22, 1808, on the family monument in the Mt. Clemens cemetery. Papers in the county clerk's office, Detroit, show that administration of his estate was begun May 28, 1807, by his son James. For material on the family claims, see *American State Papers. Public Lands*, I, 316, 317, 356, 376, 456, 464, 493, 499; *Michigan Pioneer and Historical Collections*, XVIII, 491, 493.

[26]Clark, Charles L., "The Old Connors Mansion," in *House Beautiful*, May, 1902. According to the Denissen Genealogy, Margaret Conner was buried at Detroit on June 9, 1813, aged seventy-five. This statement of her age conflicts with the hypothesis advanced in Chapter II, of her capture by the Indians in 1756 when only five or six years old, and is probably incorrect.

IV

[1]Captain James Wood, in his Journal (Thwaites and Kellogg [eds.], *Revolution on the Upper Ohio,* 64) describes a church service which he attended at Gnadenhütten, Ohio, on August 6, 1775: "the Minister who resides at this Town is a German of the Moravian Sect has Lived with them several Years has Acquired their Language and taught most of them the English and German he prayed in the Delaware Language Preached in the English and sung Psalms in the German in which the Indians joined. . . ."

[2]De Schweinitz, *David Zeisberger,* 487; Weinland, *Romantic Story of Schoenbrunn,* 19-21. As the object of the Moravian teachers was to enlighten the Indians, the instruction was on their level.

[3]William Conner's intelligence as a woodsman is commented on by a contemporary, S. W. Parker. Parker met Conner at the Potawatomi Treaty of 1832 and accompanied him from the treaty grounds on the Tippecanoe River to Noblesville. He says that he never spent three days more agreeably than on this jaunt, most of it through "pathless woods," and continues: "Conner was at home in those woods. He heeded no roads or traces whenever he could make a nigh cut or better ground . . . . we traveled the most of the day without any sign of an axe or a tree. The old woodsman, at no time discovered the least perplexity as to our position or true course—spoke of the hills and streams we would encounter, long before we reached them—and frequently observed . . . : 'It's several years since I was along here, but even the trees seem familiar to me.' " *Connersville Times,* August 29, 1855.

[4]*American State Papers. Public Lands,* I, 456, 493, 499.

[5]Major Hamtramck's letter of July 17, 1796, to General Wilkinson, announcing the evacuation of the fort by the British on July 11 is printed in Farmer, Silas, *The History of Detroit and Michigan . . .,* I, 268 (Detroit, 1889). See *ibid.,* 267-69, for a discussion of the transfer.

[6]Campbell, *Political History of Michigan,* 198 ff.; Cooley, Thomas McIntyre, *Michigan, A History of Governments,* 141 ff. (*American Commonwealths,* Boston, 1885).

[7]"Military Journal of Major Ebenezer Denny . . .," in Historical Society of Pennsylvania, *Memoirs,* VII, 475 (Philadelphia, 1860).

[8]The treaty appears in Kappler, Charles J. (ed.), *Indian Affairs. Laws and Treaties,* II, 39-45 (Washington, 1904). See also Barce, Elmore, *The Land of the Miamis . . .,* 238-44 (Fowler, Ind., 1922); Howe, Daniel Wait, *Making a Capital in the Wilderness,* 307 (*Indiana Historical Society Publications,* IV, no. 4, Indianapolis, 1908).

[9]"Sketch of the Life of William Conner, late of Noblesville," *Indianapolis Daily Journal,* August 22, 1855; *History of Fayette County Indiana . . .,* 36 (Warner, Beers & Co., Chicago, 1885); Fletcher, James C., "The Life and Services of William Conner," in *Indianapolis News,* June 23, 1881; Rave, Herman, "An Indiana Pioneer," a newspaper clipping in Finch

Scrapbook, Indiana State Library; Fletcher, James C., "Who Was He?" in *Indianapolis News,* April 13, 1881.

[10]John Conner, after leaving Michigan, conducted his land transactions through an attorney in fact. Deed Record A, Macomb County, 184, 280. William Conner returned to Michigan for a short time in 1801, and put his Detroit brothers in possession of his land. *American State Papers. Public Lands,* I, 356, 456.

[11]John Gibson was released from captivity among the Indians by Colonel Bouquet in his expedition against the Shawnee in 1764; is said to have married a sister of the Mingo chief, Logan; translated Logan's memorable speech; delivered the Congressional belt to the Indians in 1775, and met the Conner family at Schoenbrunn that year; had a good record in the Revolution; became secretary of Indiana Territory in 1800, and served as acting governor during the absences of Governor Harrison in the War of 1812. His services to Indiana in its formative period were valuable. He died in 1822. See sketch in *Dictionary of American Biography,* VII, 253-54.

[12]According to the census figures set out in Woollen, William W., *et al.* (eds.), *Executive Journal of Indiana Territory, 1800-1816,* 83 (*Indiana Historical Society Publications,* III, no. 3, Indianapolis, 1900), there were 5,641 persons in the territory in 1800, of whom 2,513 were within the limits of the present state of Indiana. Not until two years later was the Gore included in Indiana Territory. It had a population of more than a thousand in 1800. Dunn, Jacob P., *Indiana and Indianans . . .,* I, 226 (Chicago and New York, 1919).

[13]Dillon, John B., *The National Decline of the Miami Indians,* 121-43 (*Indiana Historical Society Publications,* I, no. 4, Indianapolis, 1897); Howe, *Making a Capital in the Wilderness,* 307-8; Barce, *Land of the Miamis,* 44, 46, 47-52; Dunn, Jacob P., *True Indian Stories with Glossary of Indiana Indian Names,* 280-82, 297-98, 308-9 (Indianapolis, 1909); Beckwith, Hiram W., *The Illinois and Indiana Indians,* 107-17 (*Fergus' Historical Series,* no. 27, Chicago, 1884); Harrison, William Henry, *A Discourse on the Aborigines of the Ohio Valley . . .,* 22-23 (*Fergus' Historical Series,* no. 26, Chicago, 1883); Hodge, Frederick W. (ed.), *Handbook of American Indians North of Mexico,* pt. 1, 385 (U. S. Bureau of American Ethnology, *Bulletin 30,* Washington, D. C., 1912).

[14]King, *Ohio,* 149-51; De Schweinitz, *David Zeisberger,* 484; Heckewelder, *History of the Indian Nations,* 80-81. A dark picture of the Delaware nation at this period and this place is presented in Stocker, Harry Emilius, "A History of the Moravian Mission Among the Indians on the White River in Indiana," in Moravian Historical Society, *Transactions,* X, pts. 3 and 4, 241-43 (Bethlehem, Pa., 1917). Degraded by drink, their appetite for it was insatiable. They were lazy, deceitful, lying, and without ambition. Their outstanding virtue was their attachment to their children and relatives.

[15]There were Delawares on White River in 1794. Burnet, Jacob, *Notes on the Early Settlement of the North-Western Territory,* 181n (Cincinnati, 1847); De Schweinitz, *op. cit.,* 659; Drake, Benjamin, *Life of Tecumseh, and of His Brother the Prophet . . .,* 83 (Cincinnati, 1850).

[16]The sites of Indian villages in Indiana are much in doubt. An attempt is here made to collect all the evidence, historical and archaeological, now available concerning the location of Delaware and other Indian villages on the headwaters of the West Fork of White River during the years 1801 to 1806, when John and William Conner settled and traded there. The evidence is not always definitive, and later information may change these tentative conclusions. The material given here summarizes present findings and presents a picture corresponding approximately, at least, to the surroundings amid which the Conners labored when they first came to White River. See map, facing page 42.

After the Treaty of Greenville (August 3, 1795), it was necessary for the Indians in Ohio to settle elsewhere. If the Delawares had not settled in Indiana before that date (and there is considerable evidence that they had) they did so shortly after. Howe, *Making a Capital in the Wilderness,* 307. That they and other tribes were established on the upper waters of the West Fork of White River before 1801 is definitely stated in the papers of the Moravian missionaries Kluge and Luckenbach, who began a mission among them in that year. That the Shawnee were invited to this locality by the Delawares in 1798, that they came with their chief Tecumseh, and remained until early in 1805 is stated in Drake's *Life of Tecumseh,* 83-86.

Since the Moravian mission papers are used as a main source for the location of the Indian villages, and since they set forth the site of the Mission Town and locate the other villages with reference to this town, its location will be given first.

The *Moravian Mission Town* (site 6) was located in Madison County three miles east of the present Anderson, then Andersontown, on the right bank of the West Fork of White River. It was eight miles downstream from Hockingpomsga's Town (site 4), and twenty miles downstream from Wapicomekoke (site 1). "Autobiography of Abraham Luckenbach," 376, 379; Stocker, "History of the Moravian Mission Among the Indians on the White River," 280; De Schweinitz, *David Zeisberger,* 659. Dunn, *True Indian Stories,* 272, states that the mission was about four miles east of Anderson, identifying the site with that of the later Delaware town called Little Munsee Town. This area was surveyed in 1821 by B. Bentley, deputy surveyor. His plat, Vol. 3, p. 94, Records of Surveys, Auditor's Office, State House, Indianapolis, shows Little Munsee Town on the north side of White River in the S. E. ¼ of the S. E. ¼ of Sec. 17, T. 19 N., R. 8 E. Frank M. Setzler, who visited the site in August, 1930, confirms this location, placing it on "the old S. Hughel farm." By river the site is less than two miles from Anderson, but it was usual for the Moravians to go to Andersontown by the Indian road which lay three miles north of the mission town. Luckenbach and Kluge to Van Vleck, September 24, 1802, translation in Brady Papers, Indiana Historical Society. In 1913 the Kikthawenund Chapter of the D. A. R. erected a marker in commemoration of the mission on the old Anderson-Muncie road, one and one-half miles east of Anderson.

According to the entry of June 3, 1801, in the Diary of the Little Indian Congregation on the White River (translation in Brady Papers, Indiana

Historical Society), there were, down the river from the mission town, seven Indian towns of different nations, most of them Delaware towns, and up the river, four Indian towns, also of various nations. A letter from Kluge and Luckenbach dated September 24, 1802, states that "Delaware towns of which there are *nine in all* lie from four to five miles apart and are scattered along the river. After these towns come other settlements of Indian nations as for instance the Nanticoke, Shawanos and others. After that there is nothing but meadow land as far as the eye can reach until the banks of the Wabash." De Schweinitz refers to six Delaware towns on White River "of which the largest were Woapikamikunk, Monsey-Anderson, and Sarah Town." *David Zeisberger,* 659. These three towns, Wapicomekoke (Buckongahelas' Town), Munsee Town (Tetepachsit's Town) and Sarah Town, and three others, Hockingpomsga's Town, Nancy Town, and Andersontown (Monsey-Anderson) can be located with a fair degree of accuracy. The three Delaware towns necessary to reach the number nine given by Kluge and Luckenbach, and the villages of other nations needed to reach the total of eleven village sites mentioned in the Diary of the Little Indian Congregation are not so easily identified.

There are fourteen sites of Indian villages between and including Wapicomekoke (farthermost eastern site) and Lower Delaware Town (farthermost western site) which show evidence of Indian occupation in the historical period or are established by historical references. At least two of these sites were not occupied when the mission was founded, namely, Buckstown and Connerstown. Cf. notes that follow. It is also extremely probable that the Delaware town four miles below Connerstown (between Connerstown and Lower Delaware Town) was not settled until after the War of 1812, for there is no reference to it until 1818. When these three are eliminated there remain the eleven sites referred to by the missionaries in the earliest pages of their Diary.

The evidence in regard to each of these sites beginning with Wapicomekoke is set forth below. The known Delaware villages are designated by (D).

(1). *Wapicomekoke, or Buckongahelas' Town* (D) was located on the left bank of the river about three miles southeast of the present town of Muncie, Delaware County. It was the first Indian village reached by the missionaries on their journey from Goshen, Tuscarawas County, Ohio, via the Muskingum, Ohio, Big Miami, and Whitewater rivers, and overland from the forks of Whitewater at the present site of Brookville to White River. Here, in 1801, lived the Delaware chief Buckongahelas (Buckengelaus, Buckengelis, Buchengelas, Packangahelis, Pakantschihilas, Pachgantschihillas, Packandgihhilles, Pokenchelah, Pokenchilah, Pochgantschilias, Bohengeehalus, Bokongehalas, Buckangalah) with about forty families. Here, too, lived John Conner with his Indian wife. "Autobiography of Abraham Luckenbach," 375, 376, 379. According to Dunn, *True Indian Stories,* 255, Buckongahelas is properly pronounced "Pŏch-gŏnt'-shē-hē'-los," and means "Breaker to Pieces." The name Wapicomekoke (Woapicamikunk, Wahpikomekunk) is said to mean "White River Town" (*ibid.,* 285), "White Grave" ("Autobiography of Abraham Luckenbach," 375), or "at the place where there is much white earth" (Hodge [ed.], *Handbook of American Indians,* pt. 2, 967). Stocker, page 241, says the town was "situated about three miles east of the present city of Muncie and lying on the same side of the river." The town was approached by the missionaries from the southeast, and there is no record of their crossing the river to reach it.

There is a site of an Indian town in the N. W. ¼ of the N. W. ¼ of the S. E. ¼ of Sec. 25, T. 20 N., R. 10 E., about four miles southeast of Munsee Town on the west bank of White River. Frank M. Setzler, Archaeological Report on Delaware County. It is on the Burlington Road on the Jacob Felton farm, formerly the old Cecil farm. Mr. Cecil, in the *Indiana Magazine of History,* I, 178-79, describes the location as three miles southeast of Muncie, Indiana. He states that the village stood on a hill, one hundred feet above White River with a deep gully on the southwest, and sloping south eighty rods to Juber Creek. Beyond this creek about forty rods stood an Indian trading post. According to Glenn A. Black, archaeologist for the Indiana Historical Society, the many trade objects found here indicate that the site was inhabited well into the historical period. Dunn, in *True Indian Stories,* 285-86, says that the original location of Wapicomekoke was "a short distance . . . up the river" from Munsee Town. He identifies this earlier location as "Outainink," sometimes spelled "Utenink," meaning "Old Town." There seems to be no doubt that when the missionaries arrived, the town was located at this site. It is probable that after the death of Buckongahelas in May, 1805, or the murder of Tetepachsit in the following year, the inhabitants of Wapicomekoke removed to Munsee Town.

According to the Diary of the Journey from Goshen to White River, March 24-May 25, 1801 (translation in Brady Papers, Indiana Historical Society), the missionaries reached Wapicomekoke on May 21. Here they met a trader named Fisher (entry of May 24). This was the Frederick Fisher who was licensed to trade with the Delaware nation at their town of "Buckengelis." Lasselle, Charles B., "The Old Indian Traders of Indiana," in *Indiana Magazine of History,* II, 7 (March, 1906).

A marker has been erected on this site by the Paul Revere Chapter of the D. A. R., Muncie, Indiana. It states that Tecumseh and the Prophet lived here in 1805. Stocker, "History of the Moravian Mission on the White River," 298, says that "for a number of years he [Tecumseh] had his headquarters in one of the Delaware towns." Stocker's source is probably Drake's *Life of Tecumseh,* 83-86. Neither Stocker nor Drake attempts to identify the particular town in which Tecumseh lived. Esarey, *History of Indiana,* I, 206-7, states that the Shawnee headquarters on White River was Anderson.

(2). *Munsee Town or Tetepachsit's Town (D)* lay on the right bank of the river about four miles downstream from Wapicomekoke, within the present limits of Muncie, Delaware County.

The missionaries, setting out from Wapicomekoke on May 24, some in a canoe borrowed with the help of the trader Fisher, and some on foot, arrived "towards noon" at Munsee Town. Diary of the Journey from Goshen to White River. Luckenbach in his "Autobiography," 379, states that Tetepachsit was the first and oldest chief of his nation and lived at

Munsee Town with about eight families, four miles downstream from Wapicomekoke. When the Indian emissaries came to White River in January, 1801, to announce the coming of the missionaries, they were received cordially by Buckongahelas "and another chief of an adjoining town, called Tedpachxit." *Periodical Accounts Relating to the Missions Established by the Protestant Church of the Unitas Fratrum,* III, 68-73. Tetepachsit is spelled variously Tedpachsit, Tedpachxit, Tetpachski, Tatapachkse, Tate-e-bock-o-she, Tatepahosect, Telabuxika, Toethteboxie, and Teta Buxika. Dunn, in Notes on the Moravian Diary (Brady Papers, Indiana Historical Society), says the proper form is Ta-ta-pach-sit or Te-te-pach-sit. He is often referred to as The Grand Glaize King. See also Dunn, *True Indian Stories,* 305-6. His town is sometimes referred to as Talapoxie or Telipockshy.

Munsee Town is exactly located on the 1821 map, Records of Surveys, Auditor's Office, State House, Indianapolis, as being in the N. E. ¼ of the N. E. ¼ of Sec. 9 and the N. W. ¼ of the N. W. ¼ of Sec. 10, T. 20 N., R. 10 E. within the present limits of the city of Muncie. The site is immediately north of the river and west of or bisected by the L. E. & W. railroad tracks.

A marker was erected by the Paul Revere Chapter of the D. A. R. on June 14, 1917, for this site on Minnetrista Boulevard at the corner of the grounds of Mrs. Edmund Burke Ball, Muncie. It states that this is the traditional site of Wah-pe-kah-me-kunk, or Wapicomekoke. See (1).

(3). *Unnamed site near Yorktown.* Since Setzler's survey of Delaware County in 1930, material evidence of Indian habitation has been found in the vicinity of Yorktown, Delaware County, particularly across the river from this little community. Corroborative evidence of a town here is found in an advertisement in the *Indiana Journal,* September 3, 1836: "The undersigned has laid out 'Yorktown' at the junction of White river and Big Buck creek . . . between Andersontown and Muncietown. The town is located on the ground where the old Indian village stood, immediately below the mouth of Buck creek." The advertisement is signed by O. H. Smith. Yorktown is about six miles west of Munsee Town and about three miles east of Hockingpomsga's Town. Dillon says: "Tate-e-bock-o-she was burned at the Indian village which stood at the site of Yorktown." *History of Indiana,* 425n. Luckenbach, in his "Autobiography," 386, says, however, that Tetepachsit was burned near the Mission Town. It is possible that Dillon confuses Yorktown with the Mission Town. If there was an Indian village near Yorktown, it probably belonged to some other nation than the Delawares. Since there were Shawnee in this vicinity it may have been their town.

(4). *Hockingpomsga's Town (D).* The town of the Delaware Chief Hockingpomsga (sometimes given as Hockingpomsa, Hocking, Hock-ink-pam-ska, Hackinpomka, Hockingponsa, Hockingpomskan, Hockingponsha, Owenachki) was located in the present Delaware County about eight miles east of the Mission Town. "Autobiography of Abraham Luckenbach," 379; Diary of the Little Indian Congregation, November 8, 1802. This would make the site about nine miles west of Munsee Town. No statement is given as to which side of the river it is on, but in the Diary of the Journey from Goshen to White River (entry of May 24, 1801), the missionaries mention crossing the river after they left Munsee Town. This would bring them to the south or left bank. They rested for half an hour and at three o'clock of the same day came to the town where Tetepachsit and Hockingpomsga lived. Here Hockingpomsga played host and his wife prepared food for them, which supports the assumption that this was Hockingpomsga's Town. It is natural that the missionaries, new to this country, might assume, on seeing the two chiefs together, that they lived in the same town. It is difficult to see how the missionaries could have traveled nine miles in the short time between their arrival at Munsee Town "towards noon" and three o'clock, with a half hour out for a rest. It is possible that the time of arrival at Hockingpomsga's Town was given incorrectly, or that there is an error in the translation.

The nearest site of an Indian village in this location disclosed by archaeological evidence is the one known as the Kilgore Village Site (so named because it is located on the Kilgore farm) which is on the south side of White River in the S. W. ¼ of the N. W. ¼ of Sec. 29, T. 20 N., R. 9 E. in Delaware County. This site is not more than eight and one-half miles east of the Mission Town. Evidence indicating some length of habitation here was found by Frank Setzler. T. B. Helm, in his *History of Delaware County, Indiana* . . ., 28 (Chicago, 1881), reports a fortification in the way of a wall and ditch near the north end of the ridge upon which the site is located. Setzler, however, did not believe the site was fortified. Dr. Rollo H. Bunch, of Muncie, has material removed from burials at this site.

(5). *Killbuck's Village or Buck's Town.* There is material evidence of an Indian village site in Madison County between Chief Hockingpomsga's Town and the Mission. This could not have been settled during the period under discussion, 1801-1806, for Hockingpomsga's village was then nearest the Mission on the east. This site is known as Killbuck's Village or Buck's Town and is shown in the government survey of 1821 in the S. E. ¼ of the N. E. ¼ of the N. E. ¼ of Sec. 9, T. 19 N., R. 8 E., Vol. 3, p. 94, Records of Surveys, Auditor's Office, State House, Indianapolis. Setzler states that the site produced broken flints and fire-cracked rocks at the time of his visit. The site is on a high bluff east of the river, one mile northwest of the town of Chesterfield "on the old C. Brannenberg farm."

E. Y. Guernsey in his map, *Indiana, Influence of the Indian* . . . (Department of Conservation, *Publication No. 122,* 1933), marks this site as the village of Charles Killbuck, a Delaware. In 1800 the old Indian chief Gelelemend, afterwards called William Henry Killbuck, was living with his three sons, John, Charles, and Gottlieb, at Zeisberger's town of Goshen in Ohio. Twice Charles Henry Killbuck came on a special mission to the White River towns but each time he returned to Goshen. The second mission was in the fall of 1805. The families of both White Eyes and Killbuck had been especially invited to settle on White River but they did not come. "Autobiography of Abraham Luckenbach," 370, 373, 387; Stocker, "History of the Moravian Missions on the White River," 331-32. Killbuck's town on White River was not then in existence. It belongs to a later period.

(6). *Moravian Mission Town* (*Little Munsee Town*). See *ante*, 196.

(7). *Anderson's Town, Andersontown, or Wapeminskink* (*D*), sometimes called by Anderson's Indian name, Koktowhanund (spelled variously Kiktuchwenind, Kiktheswemud, Kikthawenund, Keehlawhenund) was located on the left bank of White River on the site of the present town of Anderson, Madison County. This town is shown in the Records of Surveys, Vol. 3, p. 93, in the N. E. ¼ of the S. W. ¼ of the S. E. ¼ of Sec. 12, T. 19 N., R. 7 E., on the west bank of White River about one-half mile south of Buck (Killbuck) Creek. The Field Notes of the Survey, Auditor's Office, State House, Indianapolis, Vol. 15, North and East, p. 309, mention "a road" intersecting the east line of Section 13 (south of the town site) 62 chains (approximately four-fifths of a mile) north of the southeast section corner. This road undoubtedly led from Anderson's Town to others up the river.

The Delaware name of the town was Wapeminskink or Chestnut Tree Place. This was the home of Chief William Anderson, a half-breed Indian descended from an Indian trader by the name of Anderson. He was the father-in-law of William Conner. The town at this period contained fifteen or sixteen families. Later, it is said to have had one thousand inhabitants. Thomas Dean, who visited Chief Anderson in 1817, described his home as "good as any in the village," and Anderson as "a plain, majestic looking man, sixty or sixty-five years old." Dean, John Candee and Randle C. (eds.), *Journal of Thomas Dean*, 317 (*Indiana Historical Society Publications*, VI, no. 2, Indianapolis, 1918). "Autobiography of Abraham Luckenbach," 379; Dunn, *True Indian Stories*, 253; De Schweinitz, *David Zeisberger*, 659; Guernsey's map, *Indiana, Influence of the Indian* (1933); Advertisement, Sale of Lots in Andersontown, in *Indianapolis Gazette*, August 16, 1825; Hodge (ed.), *Handbook of American Indians*, pt. 2, 912.

(8). *Nancy Town, Nantico, Nantikoke, or Nanticoke* (*D*), in Madison County, four miles overland northwest of Anderson's Town is the last of the Indian towns shown on the government survey made by Bentley in 1821. It is in the S. E. ¼ of the S. E. ¼ of Sec. 5, T. 19 N., R. 7 E., on the west bank of the river. Records of Surveys, Auditor's Office, State House, Indianapolis, Vol. 3, p. 93.

Part of the Nanticoke Indians moved west "about 1784 and joined the Delawares of Ohio and Indiana, with whom they soon became incorporated." Hodge (ed.), *Handbook of American Indians*, pt. 2, 24; Lasselle, "Old Indian Traders of Indiana," in *Indiana Magazine of History*, II, 6, 11. Nancy Town was the home of James Nantikoke. Dunn, *True Indian Stories*, 287. The town is mentioned also in Dean and Dean (eds.), *Journal of Thomas Dean*, 317-18, and placed about nine miles west of Anderson. This seems to be an error in mileage. The site is six miles south and east of Perkinsville. When Isaac McCoy was making a tour of the towns on White River in 1818, his party reached this village on December 5, "procured a little corn for our horses, and dined at the house of an elderly couple, the wife being a woman of note, named Nancy, who could speak English tolerably well, and who was the principal manager of matters around her." McCoy, Isaac, *History of Baptist Indian Missions* . . ., 51 (Washington, 1840).

NOTE. Between Nancy Town and the village site discussed next there may, at one time, have been another village, called Greentown. So far, the distance between the known towns has been generally four or five miles, as Luckenbach stated. The advertisement for a Sale of Lots in Andersontown in *Indianapolis Gazette,* August 16, 1825, states that Andersontown "was surrounded by Buckstown, Nantikoke, Greentown and other Indian villages of less importance." In *Indiana Miscellany* . . ., p. 32, by William C. Smith (Cincinnati, 1867), the author speaks "of hearing of an Indian, whose English name was Green say he had killed enough white people for himself and pony to swim in their blood." See also Fox, Henry Clay (ed.), *Memoirs of Wayne County and the City of Richmond, Indiana* . . ., I, 75 (Madison, Wis., 1912).

No definite information about this Indian or Greentown has been found, but that such a town was in this vicinity is at least possible. The tribe to which the Indian belonged is unknown. It may not have been the Delaware.

(9). *Indian Strawtown (D)*. A site in Hamilton County nine miles west of Nancy Town was discovered in 1821 by Thomas Brown, deputy surveyor. Of this site he says (Field Notes, Vol. 14, North and East, 311, Auditor's Office, State House): "Intersected line between Sec. 1 & 2— 60.58 chains north of Sec. corner

Thence N 32 E	4.50 chains	
N 51 E	9.00	"
N 56 E	6.00	"

the remains of an Old Indian Village, Situated on a Beautifull Eminance which overlooks a fine Prairie on the opposite side of the River." This places the site in the N. W. ¼ of the N. E. ¼ of the N. W. ¼ of Sec. 1, T. 19 N., R. 5 E., a little over one and one-half miles east and north of the present Strawtown, on the right bank of the river. Glenn A. Black suggests the possibility that this was the original site of the Indian Strawtown, for the evidences of occupation found where Strawtown now stands are of a prehistoric nature. Nathaniel Bolton in his *Early History of Indianapolis and Central Indiana,* 173 *(Indiana Historical Society Publications,* I, no. 5, Indianapolis, 1897), states that in 1823: "There was another post-office at Strawtown, a prairie of considerable magnitude, where many remains of the Indian village that had been there located were still standing." In the Post Office Index, Indiana State Library, no post office is listed at Strawtown until April 8, 1834. The previous post office near this site was called Stevensburgh. It was established on October 13, 1829. The name was changed to Strawtown in 1834. Haines, John F., *History of Hamilton County* . . ., 189 ff. (Indianapolis, 1915), states that Isaac Stevens was an early settler in this vicinity. He lived two miles above Strawtown, the approximate location of the above site. Two derivations of the name, Strawtown, have been suggested: that it came from a house in the town thatched with straw (Chamberlain's *Indiana Gazetteer,* 1850, p. 394); that the town was once the residence of a Chief Straw or Strawbridge (Helm, T. B., *History of Hamilton County,*

Indiana . . ., 132 [Kingman Brothers, Chicago, 1880]). This may have been a Delaware village.

(10). *Sarah Town* (*D*). Evidences of habitation have been discovered by Glenn Black in Hamilton County on the left bank of White River about one mile south and west of the present Strawtown. The area is on the Morris farm in the N. E. ¼ of the N. E. ¼ of the S. E. ¼ of Sec. 9, T. 19 N., R. 5 E. It is of some size, and lies five miles south and west of the site we have considered as the original Indian village of Strawtown. It seems logical to assume that this is the site of Sarah Town, referred to by Luckenbach in his "Autobiography," 379, as the last of the small Indian villages below Anderson's Town. It was so named he says, "because Isaac and Sarah, two baptized Indians, had settled there with their sons, who had become heathen. The parents were dead, and the sons would not leave their heathenism." De Schweinitz (*David Zeisberger,* 659) refers to it as one of the three largest Delaware towns on White River, the other two being Wapicomekoke and Anderson's Town.

(11). *Upper Delaware Town* (*D*). The name Upper Delaware Town was used frequently during the War of 1812 and thereafter to designate an Indian village in Hamilton County in the vicinity of William Conner's Trading Post, about seven miles downstream from the site we have called Sarah Town. Dillon, *History of Indiana,* 524; *Journal of Thomas Dean,* 316.

Upper Delaware Town is not mentioned by the missionaries; either it was not settled by 1806, or it lay outside their field of work. On November 30, 1801, a license was granted to John and William Conner to trade with the Delawares at their town of Petchepencues (Lasselle, "Old Indian Traders of Indiana," in *Indiana Magazine of History,* II, 6, 12-13) and in 1802 William Conner established his post on Conner's Prairie. It is possible that the Upper Delaware Town was called Petchepencues at this time, although Lasselle believed that Petchepencues was located on Wild Cat Creek which flows into the Wabash above the present Lafayette. In this study no other reference has been found to Petchepencues. The name suggests Hengue Pushees, a Delaware chief and a contemporary of White Eyes and Gelelemend.

There are three sites in this vicinity on which Glenn Black has found evidence of Indian occupation. One, called to his attention by Mr. Clay Kinsey, is in Noblesville Township, Hamilton County, in the N. W. ¼ of the N. W. ¼ of the N. E. ¼ of Sec. 12, T. 18 N., R. 4 E. The second site is less than a mile south of the first in the S. E. ¼ of the N. E. ¼ of the S. E. ¼ of Sec. 12, T. 18 N., R. 4 E., at the curve in the river known as Horseshoe Bend. The third site is less than a mile south of the second, and marks a village of some size. It lay in the S. E. ¼ of the S. W. ¼ of the S. W. ¼ of Sec. 12 and the N. E. ¼ of the N. W. ¼ of the N. W. ¼ of Sec. 13, T. 18 N., R. 4 E., on the west side of the river. The government surveyor, in his Field Notes, Vol. 14, North and East, 97, records seeing remains of a village here in 1821. One of these sites or all three of them may have constituted the town known as Upper Delaware Town.

Another Indian site of considerable size located on the Rucker farm about one mile south of Noblesville and a quarter of a mile south of Stoney

Creek in the N. W. ¼ of the N. W. ¼ of the N. W. ¼ of Sec. 18, T. 18 N., R. 5 E., is not of historic date but is an archaeological site.

(12). *Connerstown* in Hamilton County, about two or three miles south of the Upper Delaware Town. William Conner established his trading post here in 1802.

The Records of Surveys, Package 14, North and East, Archives Division, Indiana State Library, show the site about one-eighth mile east of the line dividing Secs. 23 and 24 on the left or southeast bank of the river in the N. W. ¼ of the S. W. ¼ of Sec. 24, T. 18 N., R. 4 E.

(13). *Unnamed site (historic).* Another site of an Indian village about four miles south of Connerstown in Delaware Township, is on the farm of Frank and Perry St. Clair in the S. E. ¼ of the S. E. ¼ of the N. E. ¼ of Sec. 4, T. 17 N., R. 4 E. A burial found here in 1930 indicated historical occupation. The Survey Field Notes, Vol. 14, North and East, 96, mention an "Indian Trace" intersected by the south line of Section 34, 60.50 chains west of the section corner and 3.96 chains west of the river. As its course was south, it doubtless connected this site with the Upper Delaware Town. It ran through what is now Northern Woods Beach.

This may have been a Delaware town of a later date. Thomas Dean says in his *Journal*: "We . . . went to the house of William Conner. . . . We went down across the prairie about a mile, crossed the river and went about four miles to a settlement of the Delaware Indians, carried our packs, and then met them at the lower village."

(14). *Lower Delaware Town (D).* The references to this site are summed up in Jacob Piatt Dunn's *Greater Indianapolis*, I, 38 (Chicago, 1910). He says: "There was no Indian village at this point [Indianapolis]. The nearest one, some twelve miles north, was what Tipton calls 'the Lower Delaware Town', but it was not much of a town. On the east side of the river, a Delaware known as 'The Owl' had a clearing of about 17 acres, which he cultivated in a way, and he also raised some pigs and chickens. On the west side was a French half-breed doctor, named Brouett (?Brouillette)—often called Pruitt—who had a white wife that had been captured and brought up by the Indians. He practiced medicine after the Indian fashion, and had considerable patronage. Both of these were just north of the Hamilton County line, and they constituted the 'town'. Just south of the line, on an elevation on the east side, were traces of Indian occupancy, and the old settlers called that point 'the old Indian town'. The place was commonly called 'Brouettstown', and was somewhat noted for the wild plum thicket there." Sources cited by Dunn are Ignatius Brown's "History of Indianapolis from 1818 to 1868," in *Logan's Indianapolis Directory*, I (Indianapolis, 1868), and John H. B. Nowland's *Early Reminiscences of Indianapolis . . .*, 157 (Indianapolis, 1870). See also "The Journal of John Tipton," in *Indiana Magazine of History*, I, 11; "Indian Towns of Marion County," in *ibid.*, I, 15-17; letter of Joseph Bartholomew to Posey, in Dillon, *History of Indiana*, 524; Esarey, Logan (ed.), *Governors Messages and Letters. Messages and Letters of William Henry Harrison*, II, 44 (*Indiana Historical Collections*, IX, Indianapolis, 1922).

There are many references to this trader, and many variations in the spelling of his name, including Brennett, Bruitt, Brewitt, and Bennett. Shirts, Augustus Finch, *A History of the Formation, Settlement and Development of Hamilton County, Indiana,* 25, 49, 68, 117 (1901); Helm, *History of Hamilton County,* 34, 113. These variations seem to be attempts of the frontiersman to find a satisfactory substitute for the French name Michael Brouillette. The original bearer of this name came to Vincennes before 1783 and died there in 1801. He had a son Michael who became an Indian trader and served as interpreter for Harrison during the War of 1812. Lasselle Papers, 1783, 1790, Indiana State Library; Esarey (ed.), *Messages and Letters,* II, Index; Dillon, *History of Indiana,* 439; Barce, *Land of the Miamis,* 308-9; Lasselle, "Old Indian Traders of Indiana," in *Indiana Magazine of History,* II, 7, 8.

It is probable, however, that Brouillette did not settle here until after the War of 1812 and that the town before 1806 was only that of the Delaware Indian known as "The Owl." A Miami by the name of Owl or Long Beard is mentioned several times in Esarey (ed.), *Messages and Letters,* II. His village is noted on Guernsey's map, *Indiana, Influence of the Indian* (1933), near the mouth of the West Fork of White River in what is now Daviess County. Long Beard's name is linked with John Conner's in the French spy incident related by Moses Dawson, *Historical Narrative of the Civil and Military Services of Major-General William H. Harrison,* 50 (Cincinnati, 1824).

Material evidence of a prehistoric Indian village has been found in this neighborhood. The evidence does not preclude the possibility that the site was also occupied within historical times. Glenn A. Black locates it in Washington Township, Marion County, on the old John Oliver and Bosson farms. It lies on the north and south sides of the river in the N. E. ¼ of the N. W. ¼ of the N. E. ¼ of Sec. 20 and the S. W. ¼ of the S. E. ¼ of the N. W. ¼ of Sec. 20, T. 17 N., R. 4 E. The trail mentioned above probably continued south to this site.

[17]Stocker, "History of the Moravian Mission on the White River," 246 ff.; "Autobiography of Abraham Luckenbach," 373; De Schweinitz, *David Zeisberger,* 659.

[18]Stocker, *op. cit.,* 279-80; "Autobiography of Abraham Luckenbach," 373-81; Dunn, *Indiana and Indianans,* III, 1476.

[19]"Autobiography of Abraham Luckenbach," 379-81.

[20]Stocker, "History of the Moravian Mission on the White River," 298n-99n; Drake, *Life of Tecumseh,* 83-84, 86-88; Dillon, *History of Indiana,* 424-25. Dawson says in his *William Henry Harrison,* 82, that if Buckongahelas, whom he characterizes as a great Indian, had lived, he would not have suffered the Prophet to impose on the people as he did. See also Hamilton, John Taylor, *A History of the Church known as the Moravian . . .,* 319-20 (Bethlehem, Pa., 1900).

Tenskwatawa did not overemphasize the evil effects of the introduction of liquor among the Indians. As early as 1721, Charlevoix, writing from the trading post on the St. Joseph River, described the effect on the Indians of liquor brought in from the English colonies. Quoted in Dillon, *National Decline of the Miami Indians,* 130-31. Nearly one hundred years later, Governor Harrison said before the legislature of Indiana Territory: "You are witnesses to the abuses, you have seen our towns crowded with furious and drunken savages, our streets flowing with their blood, their arms and clothing bartered for the liquor that destroys them, and their miserable women and children enduring all the extremities of cold and hunger." Esarey (ed.), *Messages and Letters*, I, 154. Jefferson frequently warned the Indians against the use of liquor. *Ibid.*, I, 329.

[21]Mitchener (ed.), *Ohio Annals*, 185-86.

[22]Stocker, "History of the Moravian Mission on the White River," 281.

[23]*Ibid.*, 339-44; Dunn, Jacob P., "Centennial Anniversary of the Burning of Christians at Stake for Witchcraft on the banks of White River," in *Indianapolis News*, March 17, 1906. See also Dunn, *True Indian Stories*, 60-68.

[24]Lasselle, "Old Indian Traders of Indiana," in *Indiana Magazine of History*, II, 5-13; "Autobiography of Abraham Luckenbach," 375. On February 19, 1802, Harrison, believing that British traders were inciting the Indians against the United States, suggested to the secretary of war that an effort be made to divert the trade in furs and Indian goods from British to American ports. Esarey (ed.), *Messages and Letters*, I, 38-39.

[25]Fletcher, "Early Days," in *Indianapolis News*, May 11, 1881; "Sketch of the Life of William Conner," *Indianapolis Daily Journal*, August 22, 1855; letter of R. J. Conner, Draper MSS. VIII, yy21.

[26]De Schweinitz, *David Zeisberger*, 660n; entry for October 18, 1802, in Diary of the Little Indian Congregation on the White River.

[27]Dawson, *William Henry Harrison*, 50, 54.

[28]*Atlas of Franklin Co. Indiana* . . ., 12-13 (J. H. Beers & Co., Chicago, 1882), quoting an article written by Reverend Allen Wiley for the *Western Christian Advocate* of August 15, 1845, and an article by William McClure, written in 1879. McClure says that he went to school with Conner's half-breed son, James.

[29]"A Joke in Pioneer Days," in *Indianapolis News*, February 14, 1902.

[30]*Atlas of Franklin County* (1882), 93; Reifel, August J., *History of Franklin County, Indiana* . . ., 149-50 (Indianapolis, 1915).

[31]*Atlas of Franklin County* (1882), 12, 95; Heineman, J. L., *Two Chapters from the History of Fayette County* . . ., 50 (B. F. Bowen & Company, Indianapolis, 1917). Telier died in 1815, and a few years later Peltier left for the West.

[32]Interview with Judge F. M. Finch, "The Ways of the Red Man," in *Indianapolis Journal*, October 30, 1887; Griswold, Bert J. (ed.), *Fort Wayne, Gateway of the West, 1802-1813* . . ., 595 (*Indiana Historical Collections*, XV, Indianapolis, 1927); "Wild Animals of Indiana," in *Indiana Magazine of History*, II, 13-16; letter to Van Vleck from Luckenbach, September 30, 1802, Brady Papers, Indiana Historical Society; Cockrum, William M., *Pioneer History of Indiana* . . ., 444-53 (Oakland City, Ind., 1907); Shirts, *History of Hamilton County*, 7-8, 30-31. The only recorded loss by this method of transportation occurred in July, 1824, when James Backhouse, who was transporting merchandise for John Conner, lost a part of his load in crossing Taylor's Creek. Barrows, Frederic Irving (ed.), *History of*

Fayette County, Indiana . . ., 153 (B. F. Bowen & Co., Indianapolis, 1917).

[33]The following description of the trail up the Whitewater Valley used by the Conners is adapted in part from J. L. Heineman's account in *ibid.*, 121-23, 132-34, and in part from Haines, *History of Hamilton County*, 94-95. See map facing page 42 of this volume. This trail was probably used more than any other by the Delawares.

THE INDIAN TRAIL THROUGH THE WHITEWATER VALLEY

Start from Cedar Grove by present wagon road to Brookville; cross the East Fork of Whitewater over bridge below Brookville; take the road to the right leading up towards the Catholic church; pass the present Mill Street and the old graveyard; keep on this road along East Fork to Fairfield; leave East Fork at Eli Creek (no road here); thence along Crandel Creek (northwest arm of Eli Creek); across original Adam Pigman farm where the existing township road (from Quakertown) for a short distance coincides with the line to Connersville; angle across old Samuel Harlan farm, direct for the Sparks-Stoops neighborhood and for the ford of the West Fork at Connersville (near Roots' foundry at the foot of Water Street); north along Water Street turning left at street between Third and Fourth streets; angle over to Eastern Avenue, striking it opposite the street between Fifth and Sixth streets; proceed north and northwest through Fair Grounds and City Cemetery to Edgewood; take road from the northwest corner of Edgewood, passing along the east foot of Elephant Hill, through the Austin Ready farms; thence to the foot of the hill near Harrisburg; thence along Lick Creek to its source northward (instead of going up the hill westward), past the old Hackleman home to the old Florea home to land of Sanford Guard and David Gordon, who established themselves in reference to the creek bed rather than to the township road which was built later; across the highlands of Posey Township in the direction of New Castle; northwest to Anderson (exact location of trail uncertain); thence by road connecting Indian towns on White River to the mouth of Stoney Creek (Hamilton County), thence along White River to William Conner's Post.

Luckenbach describes the journey from Goshen to the mission town on White River, during which he followed part of this trail. Stocker (tr.), "Autobiography of Abraham Luckenbach," 374-76. The road connecting the Indian towns is mentioned also in a letter to Van Vleck from Luckenbach and Kluge, September 24, 1802.

[34]*Atlas of Franklin County* (1882), 12-13, 52, 61; Cole, Ernest B., "The Winship Family of Indiana," in *Indianapolis Star*, September 12, 1920.

[35]Conner's move is discussed in Heineman, *Two Chapters from the History of Fayette County*, 49-50.

[36]*Atlas of Franklin County* (1882), 88.

[1]See opinion of Chief Justice Marshall in *Johnson* v. *McIntosh*, 8 *Wheaton*, 543-604; Royce, Charles C. (comp.), "Indian Land Cessions in the United States," with an Introduction by Cyrus Thomas, in U. S. Bureau of American Ethnology, *Annual Report,* 1896-97, pt. 2, 528-641 *passim*. (Washington, 1899); Esarey (ed.), *Messages and Letters,* I, 372.

[2]See page 61.

[3]William Conner visited this country in 1800, before he built his cabin there. "He told his eldest son it was the loveliest land he had ever laid eyes on. He said that the upper valley of the west fork of White river was a series of little prairies near the river, natural openings in the forest, where the Indians lived in peaceful villages and from time immemorial planted their fields of 'squaw corn.'" Fletcher, "Early Days," in *Indianapolis News,* May 11, 1881.

[4]Dawson, *William Henry Harrison,* 116. See Harrison's addresses to the Indians in *The Writings of Thomas Jefferson,* XVI, 390, 395-96 (Memorial edition, Washington, D. C., 1904); letter to Benjamin Hawkins, February 18, 1803: "In truth, the ultimate point of rest & happiness for them is to let our settlements and theirs meet and blend together, to intermix, and become one people." Ford, Paul Leicester (ed.), *The Works of Thomas Jefferson,* IX, 447 (Federal edition, G. P. Putnam's Sons, 1905).

[5]Dorothy Burne Goebel discusses Harrison's Indian policy in her *William Henry Harrison . . .*, 89-127 (*Indiana Historical Collections,* XIV, Indianapolis, 1926). See also Adams, Henry, *History of the United States . . .*, VI, 73-75 (New York, 1890); Esarey (ed.), *Messages and Letters,* I, 70-73.

[6]*Ibid.,* I, 56-57; Dawson, *William Henry Harrison,* 21-28.

[7]Little Turtle had a splendid war record. His generalship at the defeat of St. Clair gave him, in the opinion of Dunn, the rank of greatest of the Miami. *True Indian Stories,* 15. His influence with the Indians was later impaired by his acceptance of a pension from the United States. Esarey (ed.), *Messages and Letters,* I, 164, 240n-41n.

[8]De Schweinitz, *David Zeisberger,* 660; *Writings of Thomas Jefferson* (Memorial ed.), XVI, 396-400; Goebel, *William Henry Harrison,* 102.

[9]Dawson, *William Henry Harrison,* 47-50; account of council incorporated in a letter from Harrison to the secretary of war, March 3, 1805, in Burton Historical Collection, *Manuscripts,* I, 65-66; *Kappler* (ed.), *Indian Affairs. Laws and Treaties,* II, 64-66. Goebel, *William Henry Harrison,* 104, estimates this cession at about 1,520,000 acres; Dillon, *History of Indiana,* 418, puts the figure at 1,600,000 acres.

[10]Dawson, *op. cit.,* 50; letter from Dearborn to Harrison, February 21, 1803, quoted in *Bulletin of the Chicago Historical Society,* II, 89 (March, 1937).

[11]The treaties are printed in Kappler (ed.), *op. cit.,* II, 66 ff. See also Dillon, *History of Indiana,* 418-19; map of Indian cessions in Esarey,

History of Indiana, I, 272; Esarey (ed.), *Messages and Letters,* I, 161-66.

In addition to these treaties, Harrison was successful in negotiating a treaty with the Kaskaskia, August 13, 1803, for their land in Illinois, involving about 8,600,000 acres; with the Sauk and Foxes, November 3, 1804, for land on both sides of the Mississippi in northwestern Illinois, the southern part of Wisconsin, and northern Missouri including about 14,000,000 acres, of which 5,000,000 were relinquished to the Indians in 1816; with the Piankashaw, December 30, 1805, involving about 2,600,000 acres west of the Wabash River.

[12]Esarey (ed.), *Messages and Letters,* I, 281. As early as 1789 the Delawares had considered moving westward. See entry of December 26, 1789, in Quaife, Milo M. (ed.), *Fort Wayne in 1790,* 317 (*Indiana Historical Society Publications,* VII, no. 7, Greenfield, Ind., 1921); see also Esarey (ed.), *op. cit.,* I, 165.

[13]According to a report of the Commissioner of Indian Affairs, covering the years 1820-1876, the average Indian population was 315,000. On the hypothesis that the family averaged five members, there would have been 63,000 Indian families in the United States. With an area of 3,025,000 square miles in the United States (exclusive of Alaska), each family could have had 30,720 acres. The requirements of the human race and the advance of civilization could not admit of such an apportionment of the soil. There were very few if any areas in the United States to which the Indians did not claim title. If this claim could not be admitted as a just bar to any settlements by other peoples, where should the restriction begin, and how should it be accomplished? Royce (comp.), "Indian Land Cessions," in U. S. Bureau of American Ethnology, *Annual Report,* 1896-97, pt. 2, 537. This analysis was made to meet criticisms by moralists of the government's Indian policies.

Jefferson was right when he told Harrison in 1803 that the Indians "will in time incorporate with us as citizens of the United States or remove beyond the Mississippi." Esarey (ed.), *Messages and Letters,* I, 71. What happened was that the Indians refused civilization and in less than twenty years they were crossing that river. Their leaders had a vision of an Indian confederacy given them by the British politicians for selfish purposes. England had lost a valuable possession in the War of the Revolution, but she hoped to recover part of it and to that end incited the Indians to warfare against the Americans. Blindly the Indians followed the destiny prophesied for them. No human instrument could prevent it. Alvord, *Mississippi Valley in British Politics,* I, 103; II, 76. Tecumseh, in his memorable speech of August 10, 1810, said, "Now we began to discover the treachery of the British   they never troubled us for our lands but they have done worse by inducing us to go to war." Esarey (ed.), *Messages and Letters,* I, 464. It is evident that Tecumseh, at least, understood the motive of the British even when about to be allied with them against the Americans.

[14]*Ibid.,* I, 346-78, 387-91; Dawson, *William Henry Harrison,* 129-37. By the Treaty of Greenville, 1795, permanent annuities of $1000 in goods had been granted to seven tribes, the Wyandot, Delawares, Shawnee, Miami,

Ottawa, Chippewa, and Potawatomi; permanent annuities of $500 were granted to five tribes, the Kickapoo, Wea, Eel River, Piankashaw, and Kaskaskia. Subsequently the Miami received an additional annual allowance of $600, the Kaskaskia, $500, the Piankashaw, $300, and the Eel River and Wea, $250. The Delawares, Potawatomi, and Piankashaw had received additional grants for limited periods. Kappler (ed.), *Indian Affairs. Laws and Treaties,* II, 41, 65, 67, 70, 72, 81, 89. For a statement of these annuities and others made in treaties not relating particularly to Indiana Indians, see *American State Papers. Indian Affairs,* I, 816-23; II, 73-74 (Washington, 1832, 1834).

[15]Esarey (ed.), *Messages and Letters,* I, 390-91, 476-80; Griswold (ed.), *Fort Wayne. Gateway of the West,* 312n; Dawson, *William Henry Harrison,* 137.

[16]*Ibid.,* 110-18; Esarey (ed.), *Messages and Letters,* I, 328-35.

[17]*Writings of Thomas Jefferson* (Memorial ed.), XIII, 142; Harrison characterized the Prophet as "a scoundrel"; John Baptiste Bruno, an Indian trader at Vincennes, says his personal appearance was repulsive. "Tecumseh and the Prophet," *Indianapolis Press,* September 29, 1900.

[18]Esarey (ed.), *Messages and Letters,* I, 182-84; Drake, *Life of Tecumseh,* 88-91.

[19]Esarey, *History of Indiana,* I, 208; Esarey (ed.), *Messages and Letters,* I, 417-19, 421, 436-37.

[20]The entry for May 7, 1805, in the Diary of the Little Indian Congregation on the White River reads as follows: "Mr. [John] Connor's workmen came to us to-day in order to split the rails which the Chiefs had promised our brethren. These people . . . had already made 14,000 rails in the Indian towns lying between us and Woapicamikunk. With these the cornfields of the Indians, according to the will and contract of the Government, shall be enclosed with good fences under the supervision of Mr. Connor, who undertook the work . . . . the work shall be inspected by a commission appointed for the purpose, and then Mr. Conner is to receive payment for his labors."

[21]Esarey (ed.), *Messages and Letters,* I, 239-43, 247-51.

[22]Dawson, *William Henry Harrison,* 106-7; Drake, *Life of Tecumseh,* 106. In July, 1808, John Conner made his trip to the Prophet's Town to look for horses which had been stolen from the settlers. He found almost twenty which he thought belonged to the whites, but he was unsuccessful in his effort to recover them. On his way back down the Wabash he encountered four of the Prophet's band with twelve horses which he also thought belonged to the whites. Statement of John Conner, July 18, 1808, in *Liberty Hall and Cincinnati Mercury,* July 23, 1808.

[23]Esarey (ed.), *Messages and Letters,* I, 290-92, 302, 337-39, 340-49, 418; Drake, *op. cit.,* 105-12.

[24]Esarey (ed.), *Messages and Letters,* I, 421.

[25]*Ibid.,* I, 456, 459-67; McAfee, Robert B., *History of the Late War in the Western Country,* 17-18, 407 (Bowling Green, Ohio, 1919); Barce, *Land of the Miamis,* 59-60.

[26]Among the offenders was a band of Potawatomi outlaws who lived

near the present town of Morocco, Newton County, Indiana. During a raid in the Illinois country, this band committed one of the worst murders of the period, falling upon and killing a camp of sleeping men who had pursued the Indians for stealing horses. The same band stole twelve horses near Vincennes on April 1, 1811. Harrison sent Wells and John Conner into the Indian country to reconnoiter and demand restitution for the horses. Their search took them to Prophet's Town where they conversed with Tecumseh and the Prophet, both of whom denied that they had any part in instigating these outrages, but admitted that the group of Potawatomi was under their influence. Four horses were returned and the restoration of the others promised. This promise was never fulfilled and the thefts continued.

Another incident in the spring of 1811 called forth all of Conner's adroitness. White Turkey, a Delaware, robbed the house of one of the Vawters, a settler near Madison. The Delawares refused to deliver the culprit, charging that white persons who had murdered Indians were not brought to justice. While they would not surrender White Turkey, they promised to punish him themselves and did actually put him to death—a severe penalty for the offense. John Conner, recovering most of the stolen articles, deposited them in a warehouse in Fort Wayne, but the warehouse was broken open and the goods again stolen. At this point the Indians refused to pay for them, saying they had delivered the articles once and punished the thief, thereby discharging their obligations under treaty agreements. These incidents are fairly illustrative of the irritation between the whites and Indians. Harrison admitted that the latter were often maltreated, and that it was rare that they could obtain any satisfaction for "the most unprovoked wrongs." Barce, *Land of the Miamis,* 336-38; Esarey (ed.), *Messages and Letters,* I, 506-7, 512, 515-16.

[27]The question of just how far Wells could be depended upon had bothered Harrison for a long time; his attitude toward Wells was not consistent, as he himself admitted. *Ibid.,* I, 81, 148, 393-95, 432, 478, 508-9. As for John Conner, it is not surprising, in view of his association with Wells, and his long and close connection with the Delawares, that he did not at first enjoy Harrison's complete confidence. By 1807, however, Harrison shared Gibson's good opinion of Conner, and wrote of him to the secretary of war: "I have entire confidence in his fidelity, and am confident that he can do us much service." *Ibid.,* I, 248, 509.

[28]*Ibid.,* I, 544, 550, 599-601, 604-5, 609, 611; Dawson, *William Henry Harrison,* 192-200.

[29]For accounts of the approach to Prophet's Town and the battle, see McAfee, *History of the Late War* (1919 ed.), 27 ff.; Adams, *History of the United States,* VI, 98ff.; Dawson, *op. cit.,* 202 ff.; Esarey (ed.), *Messages and Letters,* I, 608 ff. For Conner's part in the battle, see also *ante,* 144-45.

[30]Esarey (ed.), *Messages and Letters,* II, 30-31, 34-35; Dawson, *op. cit.,* 262.

[31]Esarey (ed.), *Messages and Letters,* II, 36-37. Cf. *ibid.,* II, 402.

[32]*Ibid.,* II, 39-40, 43-44, 57.

[33]Esarey (ed.), *Messages and Letters,* II, 45-47.

[34]*Ibid.,* II, 48.

[35]*Ibid.,* II, 52-53; Dillon, *History of Indiana,* 482-86; Dawson, *William Henry Harrison,* 265-68.

[36]*Indiana Magazine of History,* III, 46-47; VIII, 116-17.

[37]Esarey (ed.), *Messages and Letters,* II, 59, 228-31, 401, 402; Dillon, *History of Indiana,* 516.

VI

[1]Adams, *History of the United States,* VI, 133 ff.; McMaster, John Bach, *A History of the People of the United States . . .,* III, 432 ff. (New York, 1892).

[2]Pratt, Julius W., "Fur Trade Strategy and the American Left Flank in the War of 1812," in *American Historical Review,* XL, 246 ff. (January, 1935); Innis, Harold A., "Interrelations between the Fur Trade of Canada and the United States," in *Mississippi Valley Historical Review,* XX, 321-32 (December, 1933).

[3]Esarey (ed.), *Messages and Letters,* II, 76-77, 109; Dillon, *History of Indiana,* 486.

[4]Adams, *History of the United States,* VII, 72; Dillon, *op. cit.,* 487-88.

[5]In 1811 the strength of the militia was reported as 4,160; in 1814 it had increased to 5,010. *A History of the National Guard of Indiana . . .,* 34, 38 (Indianapolis, 1901); Esarey, *History of Indiana,* I, 224-26; Dillon, *op. cit.,* 520-21. Hargrove's instructions are printed in Esarey (ed.), *Messages and Letters,* II, 71-73, and in Cockrum, *Pioneer History of Indiana,* 348-51.

[6]Esarey (ed.), *Messages and Letters,* II, 91n; Goebel, *William Henry Harrison,* 133-42, 164; Adams, *History of the United States,* VII, 73-75.

[7]McAfee, *History of the Late War,* 143-48; Griswold (ed.), *Fort Wayne, Gateway of the West,* 57-74; Esarey (ed.), *Messages and Letters,* II, 143-45.

[8]*Ibid.,* II, 148.

[9]The following anecdote about the Conners was given to the press by Samuel W. Parker of Connersville at the time of William Conner's death. It had come to him some twenty-five years before from a casual acquaintance, a Kentuckian named Rankin, and its authenticity is not vouched for, though Parker saw no reason to question it. Rankin, a visitor in Connersville during the thirties, inquired about John and William Conner, whom he had met during the War of 1812. The story, briefly, is that when the Conners were acting as guides for Harrison's army near the lakes, they came to a deep and difficult fording place. Harrison told Rankin that he thought the Conners were true, but to watch them carefully, and if they led the troops into too deep water, to shoot them down. In the middle of the stream the guides' horses stepped into deep water, and Rankin had cocked his pistol to shoot when the guides shouted that the ford had changed, but that they would soon be all right. So they were, and Rankin commented that he afterwards found them to be "as true and noble Americans" as he had ever known. Parker, "William Conner," in *Connersville Times,* August 29, 1855. Another version of the story is given by Herman Rave in his article, "An Indiana Pioneer," in Finch Scrapbook, Indiana State Library. He says that William Conner told the story himself. The chief variations from the Parker story are that William Conner was the sole guide, and that Harrison was not present at the time.

(213)

[10]Dillon, *History of Indiana,* 492-94; Esarey, *History of Indiana,* I, 218-19.

[11]The attack on Fort Harrison occurred on the night of September 4. Esarey (ed.), *Messages and Letters,* II, 124-28; Dillon, *op. cit.,* 488-91.

[12]Esarey (ed.), *Messages and Letters,* II, 174-75; McAfee, *History of the Late War,* 195-96.

[13]*Ibid.,* 196; Esarey (ed.), *Messages and Letters,* II, 186.

[14]Hopkins' first expedition is covered in *ibid.,* II, 162-63, 192-93, 201-2; Dillon, *History of Indiana,* 496-500. On the second expedition, see *ibid.,* 501-5; Esarey (ed.), *Messages and Letters,* II, 231-34.

[15]*Ibid.,* II, 164, 186.

[16]For accounts of this battle, see *ibid.,* II, 228-29, 248-49, 252-65, 269-74, 287-89; McAfee, *History of the Late War,* 195-200. For the stories of Conner's horse, and the discovery of the Indians, see "Sketch of the Life of William Conner, late of Noblesville," *Indianapolis Daily Journal,* August 22, 1855, and "William Conner, A Notable Character in the Early History of Indiana," *Rochester Republican,* November 20, 1895; Lockridge, Ross F., "History on the Mississinewa," in *Indiana Magazine of History,* XXX, 41-45 (March, 1934).

[17]Esarey (ed.), *Messages and Letters,* II, 136-37, 297; McAfee, *op. cit.,* 263; Adams, *History of the United States,* VII, 84.

[18]*Ibid.,* VII, 79-81; Esarey (ed.), *op. cit.,* II, 369; McAfee, *op. cit.,* 183-84, 202-5; Goebel, *William Henry Harrison,* 146-52. For a description of the Black Swamp, see Power, Richard Lyle, "Wet Lands and the Hoosier Stereotype," in *Mississippi Valley Historical Review,* XXII, 38-39 (June, 1935).

[19]Esarey (ed.), *Messages and Letters,* II, 299 ff.; Goebel, *op. cit.,* 144-52, 155-62; Adams, *op. cit.,* VII, 76-101; McAfee, *History of the Late War,* 219-61. Secretary of War Eustis was incompetent. Early in December he resigned, and Monroe acted as secretary until February, when John Armstrong took over the office.

[20]McAfee, *op. cit.,* 243.

[21]Esarey (ed.), *Messages and Letters,* II, 419, 509, 533-35; McAfee, *op. cit.,* 329.

[22]*Ibid.,* 281 ff.; Adams, *History of the United States,* VII, 104-8; Goebel, *William Henry Harrison,* 168-71; Smith, Oliver H., *Early Indiana Trials: and Sketches,* 174 (Cincinnati, 1858).

[23]For accounts of Harrison's position and the Fort Stephenson episode, see Adams, *op. cit.,* VII, 108-14; McAfee, *History of the Late War,* 344-56; Goebel, *op. cit.,* 174-78; Esarey (ed.), *Messages and Letters,* II, 502, 503, 510-13, 514-16. Conner's part in the affair is mentioned by McAfee, *op. cit.,* 348; and by Croghan in a statement of August 27, 1813, printed in Burr, Samuel J., *The Life and Times of William Henry Harrison,* 276-79 (8th ed., New York and Philadelphia, 1840). In defense of Harrison, see *ibid.,* 275-76, and Hall, James, *A Memoir of the Public Services of William Henry Harrison, of Ohio,* 262-64 (Philadelphia, 1836).

[24]Goebel, *William Henry Harrison,* 178-79; Esarey (ed.), *Messages and Letters,* II, 539, 540, 541; McAfee, *History of the Late War,* 372. At this

time the town of Detroit contained about 160 houses and 700 inhabitants. Fort Detroit stood on a bit of high ground in the rear of the town, about 250 yards from the river. The inhabitants were largely of French descent and the Catholic faith.

[25]Dawson, *William Henry Harrison,* 430; McAfee, *History of the Late War,* 420-21, 426-28; Esarey (ed.), *Messages and Letters,* II, 554-56, 558-65. According to a statement of Richard J. Conner, Draper MSS. VIII, yy21, William Conner commanded 300 friendly Indians at this battle. Dawson fixes the number of Indians engaged at 30. About 260 Indians joined Harrison at Seneca, but their presence at the Thames is not mentioned. Dawson, *op. cit.,* 418; McAfee, *op. cit.,* 392.

[26]*Ibid.,* 428; Adams, *History of the United States,* VII, 137-38; McMaster, *History of the United States,* IV, 40; Smith, W. L. G., *Fifty Years of Public Life. The Life and Times of Lewis Cass,* 77 (New York, 1856).

[27]Statement of Richard J. Conner, Draper MSS. VIII, yy21, and of F. M. Finch, *ibid.,* VIII, yy18; Smith, *Early Indiana Trials,* 175; Dawson, *William Henry Harrison,* 438-39; Adams, *History of the United States,* VII, 140; McAfee, *History of the Late War,* 426; *Indiana Magazine of History,* XXIX, 30-31 (March, 1933); *Richardson's War of 1812; with Notes and a Life of the Author by Alexander Clark Casselman,* 212-14 (Historical Publishing Co., Toronto, 1902).

[28]The armistice is printed in Esarey (ed.), *Messages and Letters,* II, 577-79; for the treaty, see Kappler (ed.), *Indian Affairs. Laws and Treaties,* II, 105-7. When news of the treaty reached the peace commissioners of Great Britain and the United States at Ghent, interest in the Indian question was lessened. Adams, *History of the United States,* IX, 32.

[29]It is impossible to determine accurately the acreage involved in these treaties. Ten of them related to land in Indiana. In the eight principal treaties, Grouseland, Fort Wayne (1809), St. Mary's, Tippecanoe, and Mississinewa, there were probably 17,000,000 acres. In 1821 the Committee on Education reported to the General Assembly that its estimate of the number of acres in Indiana was 22,312,960, including Lake Michigan. It was estimated that 96,000 were covered by the waters of that lake. The net acreage including the beds of rivers and smaller lakes was 22,216,960. Esarey, Logan (ed.), *Governors Messages and Letters. Messages and Papers of Jonathan Jennings, Ratliff Boon, William Hendricks . . . 1816-1825,* 234-35 (*Indiana Historical Collections,* XII, Indianapolis, 1924), cited hereafter as Esarey (ed.), *Messages and Letters,* III.

[30]A great westward movement followed the War of 1812. Babcock, Kendric Charles, *The Rise of American Nationality, 1811-1819,* 243-44 (New York and London, 1906); Adams, *History of the United States,* IX, 170-74.

[31]The treaty negotiations are discussed in *ibid.,* IX, 1-53.

[32]*Ibid.,* IX, 46.

[1]Esarey (ed.), *Messages and Letters,* II, 186, 228-29.

[2]For a description of blockhouse construction, see Smith, *Indiana Miscellany,* 76-77. Some of the stockades and blockhouses built in the three counties are listed below.

Wayne County: "Rue's and Meek's stations on the east branch of White Water. One mile below the site of Abington . . . a block house, enclosed with pickets. On the west branch of White Water . . . Lewis's Station above the Walnut Level. Still further west . . . Jenneys' Station. At the upper end of the Walnut Level . . . Martindale's Station, a large block house with pickets. On the Walnut Level, below this one . . . a stockade fort known as Boyd's Station. . . . On an average . . . every fourth house was so strengthened as to be equal to block houses." (Fox, Henry Clay [ed.], *Memoirs of Wayne County* . . ., I, 74 [Madison, Wisconsin, 1912]) ; about 1812 Reverend John Strange preached at a blockhouse "on the present site of Cambridge" (Heineman, J. L., *The Indian Trail Down the White Water Valley* . . ., note 10, p. 43 [3d ed., Indianapolis, 1925]) ; "Joseph Holman served in the War of 1812 while his family lived in his blockhouse where Centerville later stood." Esarey, Logan, "Organizing a State," in *Indiana Historical Society Publications,* VI, 100; a blockhouse built in 1812 about two miles from the present site of Richmond by George Smith and others (*Indiana Magazine of History,* II, 162; Smith, *Indiana Miscellany,* 78; Ewbank, Louis B., "Blockhouse Stockades," in *Indiana History Bulletin,* III, extra no. 2, p. 96 [March, 1926]).

Franklin County (including present-day Fayette and Union counties) : "An important one . . . where the village of Brownsville now is," on the East Fork of Whitewater, northwest corner of present Union County (*History of Fayette County* [1885], 43) ; one in Sec. 30, T. 14 N., R. 14 E., just opposite the mouth of Richland Creek, erected in 1805 (Homsher, George W., "Remains on White Water River, Indiana," in Smithsonian Institution, *Annual Report,* 1882, p. 748) ; one near Dunlapsville, in Sec. 28, T. 11 N., R. 2 W., erected by William Nickles in 1805 (*ibid.*) ; "one in the northern part of Harrison Township," present Fayette County (*History of Fayette County* [1885]), on Lick Creek (*An Illustrated Historical Atlas of Fayette Co. Indiana,* 16 [Chicago, 1875]) ; Conner blockhouse on present site of Connersville (Heineman, *Indian Trail Down the White Water Valley,* note 10, pp. 43-44) ; Helm blockhouse, a few miles south of Connersville "just below Nulltown" (*History of Fayette County* [1885], 43; *A Biographical History of Eminent and Self-Made Men of . . . Indiana,* I, 6th district, 37 [Cincinnati, 1880] ; Mason, Dr. Philip, *A Legacy to my Children, including Family History, Autobiography* . . ., 369 [Cincinnati, 1868]) ; in Laurel Township, Franklin County, one on Garrison's Creek, near the county line; Martin's blockhouse on the Beggs farm; Conn's blockhouse on Seine's Creek; Brison's blockhouse in section 22; one known as Hawkins', Baker's, or Salt Creek blockhouse, on Salt Creek, southeast

quarter of section 33 (*Atlas of Franklin County* [1882], 102, 107) ; one on
Pipe Creek (*History of Fayette County* [1885], 43; Reifel, *History of
Franklin County*, 276) ; Mount blockhouse near Metamora (*Atlas of Frank-
lin County* [1882], 103) ; William Wilson's blockhouse on the west fork of
Whitewater, six miles above Brookville (Dunn, *Greater Indianapolis*, I, 44) ;
one in Sec. 33, T. 10 N., R. 2 W., Fairfield Township, erected by Obadiah
Eustes in 1804 (Homsher, *op. cit.*, 728) ; Benjamin McCarty's blockhouse,
two and one-half miles north of Brookville, on East Fork of Whitewater
(Reifel, *History of Franklin County*, 276) ; one in Sec. 21, T. 9 N., R. 2 W.
(Homsher, *op. cit.*, 728) ; "another, built by Conrad Saylor, three miles and
a half below Brookville, on White Water, one-half mile east of where the
Little Cedar church stands" called Little Cedar Blockhouse (Reifel, *History
of Franklin County*, 275-76).

Dearborn County (including present-day Ohio and Switzerland coun-
ties) : One "about one-half mile above Johnson's Fork" (*ibid.*, 275; see
also *History of Dearborn and Ohio Counties, Indiana*, 524 [F. E. Weakley
& Co., Chicago, 1885]). In the Guilford-Cambridge neighborhood, present
Miller Township, Dearborn County, a stockade with two blockhouses,
erected about 1811 on Tanner's Creek, and under command, for a time, of
Captain Blasdel (Ewbank, "Blockhouse Stockades," in *Indiana History
Bulletin*, III, extra no. 2, p. 95 ; *History of Dearborn and Ohio Counties*
[1885], 201, 462-64) ; a small stockade at Georgetown, not far from the
Cambridge neighborhood (Shaw, Archibald [ed.], *History of Dearborn
County, Indiana . . .*, 288 [Indianapolis, 1915]) ; a blockhouse about four
miles above the mouth of North Hogan Creek, "Capt. Jim Bruce, Amor and
Henry Bruce lived near" (*History of Dearborn and Ohio Counties* [1885],
552; Shaw [ed.], *op. cit.*, 174-75) ; a stockade in or near Sec. 36, T. 5
N., R. 3 W., on Laughery Creek, Cesar Creek Township, "back of an old
stone house called the Spears House, and near the foot of the hill close to
a large spring. . . . Within it were many small cabins, to which, when an
alarm was given, the women and children fled, the men going to the blockhouses, one opposite the mouth of South Fork and one lower down the
creek than the stockade. The stockade was built under the direction of Mr.
Purcell, in 1811 or 1812" (*History of Dearborn and Ohio Counties* [1885],
508; Shaw [ed.], *op. cit.*, 162) ; the McGuire blockhouse : "April 17, 1811,
James McGuire entered the southwest half of the quarter of Section 9,
Town 4, Range 3. . . . Here he moved into and occupied the blockhouse."
"His location was in Cesar Creek Township on the north side of Laughery
Creek, opposite the mouth of Bear Creek" (*History of Dearborn and Ohio
Counties* [1885], 508-9, 587-88) ; Robert Rickett's cabin, in or near Sec. 16,
T. 3 N., R. 1 W., on land later owned by Lester Lostutter, which, "during
the period of the Indian frights . . . was often used as a place of defense
and resort" (*ibid.*, 449) ; Samuel Curry's blockhouse in present Randolph
Township, Ohio County, on land where Peter Lostutter afterward lived
(*ibid.*, 450) ; McConnell's house, about two miles below Rising Sun. James
McConnell said that about 1812 "the neighbors forted at his father's house"
(*ibid.*, 448) ; a blockhouse "one half mile south of Aberdeen, built in 1814"
(*ibid.*, 587-88).

³See photostatic copies of Muster, Pay and Receipt Rolls of Indiana Territory, Volunteers or Militia, War of 1812, in Indiana State Library, II, 394, 395, 396; III, 464b, 465a, 466a, 468, 469, 470, 471, 472, 473; IV, 573, 574, 575.

⁴Esarey, *History of Indiana*, I, 238-39, 243-45; Wiley, Rev. Allen, "Introduction and Progress of Methodism in Southwestern Indiana," in *Western Christian Advocate*, August 15, 1845, file at Methodist Book Concern, Cincinnati.

⁵"To John Conner will ever be credited the honor of being the first white man to enter land in this township [Highland], but the record shows that he did not buy government land until August, 1810, although he had without question been a resident of this section a few years before that date." Reifel, *History of Franklin County*, 149. In 1810 John Conner entered two 160-acre tracts of land northwest of Cedar Grove, with appurtenances (S. W. ¼ of Sec. 11, T. 8 N., R. 2 W., and N. W. ¼ of Sec. 13, T. 8 N., R. 2 W.), *ibid.*, 88. He also entered a tract west of Cedar Grove containing something over 21 acres in the N. E. ¼ of the N. W. ¼ of Sec. 14, T. 8 N., R. 2 W. Land patents in possession of Miss Frieda Woerner, Indianapolis, for all of above. Final payment was made on these in 1813. Between 1811 and 1815 he entered parts of sections 23 and 25 near Connersville, in T. 14 N., R. 12 E. Barrows (ed.), *History of Fayette County*, 223.

⁶There are conflicting statements as to whether James or John left with the Delawares in 1820. James G. Finch in a letter of March 1, 1896, to Fabius M. Finch, speaks of the Conner boy who left Indiana as James. *History of Fayette County* (1885), 37, mentions only a son James, saying nothing of what became of him; Barrows (ed.), *History of Fayette County*, 143-44, says that James remained with his father and died in his youth; that John was reared by the Delawares and went with them to Missouri, where he became a wealthy landowner. He communicated with William Winship Conner in 1862.

⁷The marriage is recorded in the office of the County Clerk, Franklin County, Brookville, Indiana.

⁸One of these lots, No. 33, was contracted for by John McCormick, father of the three McCormick brothers who were the first settlers of Indianapolis. He came to the present site of Connersville in 1808, and is said to have built the first cabin in the settlement. Smith, Laura A., "McCormick Cabin's Story," in *Indianapolis Star*, June 28, 1925, pt. 5, p. 1; *History of Fayette County* (1885), 135-36. Conner's Trading Post was above the original site of the town.

⁹Mason, *Family History, Autobiography*, 369, quoted in *History of Fayette County* (1885), 136. "John Conner. By his Granddaughter, Mrs. Sarah C. Christian," in *Indiana Magazine of History*, III, 87 (June, 1907).

¹⁰Heineman, *Indian Trail Down the White Water Valley* (1925 ed.), 27-31, 44.

¹¹Mason, *Family History, Autobiography*, 113-17, 134.

¹²Esarey, *History of Indiana*, I, 239, 245.

[13]"Indianapolis is, therefore, a sort of colony of Connersville, and, as will be seen hereafter, had to depend for some time upon the mother settlement for support." Holloway, William R., *Indianapolis. A Historical and Statistical Sketch of the Railroad City* . . ., 3 (Indianapolis, 1870). See list of Franklin County officials during the territorial period in Ewbank, Louis B., and Riker, Dorothy L. (eds.), *Laws of Indiana Territory, 1809-1816*, 838-40 (*Indiana Historical Collections*, XX, Indianapolis, 1934).

[14]Fordham, Elias Pym, *Personal Narrative of Travels in Virginia, Maryland, Pennsylvania, Ohio, Indiana, Kentucky* . . ., edited by Frederic Austin Ogg, 109, 138, 153 (Cleveland, 1906). Fordham was one of the surveyors appointed to lay out the city of Indianapolis. Dunn, *Greater Indianapolis*, I, 28-29.

[15]Speaking of the difficulties faced by the legislators in attending meetings of the Assembly at Corydon, Logan Esarey says: "From the Whitewater, they traveled down the Ohio river, stopping at New Albany, or coming down to Evans Landing or Leavenworth, and thence by trail to the capital." *Internal Improvements in Early Indiana*, 50 (*Indiana Historical Society Publications*, V, no. 2, Indianapolis, 1912). It is stated, however, that Conner and two companions went to Jeffersonville by horseback in 1820, and it is assumed that this was his mode of travel four years earlier. *One Hundredth Anniversary, Warren Lodge No. 15 F. & A. M., Connersville, Indiana, 1822-1922*, 15.

[16]Moores, Charles W., "Old Corydon," in *Indiana Magazine of History*, XIII, 20-23 (March, 1917); Dunn, *Indiana and Indianans*, I, 295; Ridley, William, "The Old Capitol Building at Corydon—as Changed," in *Year Book of the Society of Indiana Pioneers, 1923-24*, 17-19; Cottman, George S., *The Corydon State House* . . ., 12-20 (Department of Conservation, State of Indiana, *Publication Number 94*, Indianapolis, 1930); photostatic copies of measured drawings of Old State Capitol, Corydon, in Smith Library, Indiana Historical Society.

[17]Indiana *Senate Journal*, 1816-1817, pp. 27, 32, 39, 41-42.

[18]*Ibid.*, 35, 36, 37, 42, 46; *Laws of Indiana*, 1816-1817, pp. 112-15.

[19]Indiana *House Journal*, 1816-1817, pp. 25, 29, 62, 71; 1817-1818, pp. 63, 66, 105, 108, 163; *Senate Journal*, 1817-1818, pp. 50, 53-54, 68, 69; *House Journal*, 1818-1819, pp. 53, 60, 68-69, 80-81; *Senate Journal*, 1818-1819, pp. 45, 48, 57, 59; *Laws of Indiana*, 1818-1819, pp. 103-7.

[20]For the act providing for appointment of sheriffs, see *ibid.*, 1816-1817, pp. 109-11. An act regulating the duties of sheriffs was passed at the second session (*ibid.*, 1817-1818 [general], 179-82), and an act for the relief of sheriffs at the third session (*ibid.*, 1818-1819, pp. 88-90). Conner's appointment as sheriff on December 30, 1818, is recorded in the Executive Proceedings of the State of Indiana, November 7, 1816—November 2, 1823, in Indiana State Library.

[21]Indiana *Senate Journal*, 1816-1817, pp. 62, 64, 67; *Laws of Indiana*, 1816-1817, pp. 169-70; 1817-1818 (general), pp. 317-19.

[22]On the condition of the roads, see Haimbaugh, Frank D. (ed.), *History of Delaware County, Indiana*, I, 209-11 (Indianapolis, 1924). For legislation on roads in 1816-1817, see Indiana *House Journal*, 16, 105, 106-7,

110, 119; *Senate Journal*, 35, 45, 49, 51, 78, 84, 85; *Laws of Indiana*, 72-84; in 1817-1818, *ibid.* (general), 273-85; in 1818-1819, *Senate Journal*, 6, 44, 52, 53-54; *House Journal*, 97, 133, 134; *Laws of Indiana*, 69-74.

[23]For John Conner's activities see the Indiana *Senate Journal*, 1816-1817 to 1818-1819, *passim*.

[24]Morse, Jedidiah, *A Report to the Secretary of War . . . on Indian Affairs, comprising a Narrative of a Tour performed in the Summer of 1820 . . .*, 108-12 (New Haven, Conn., 1822). Under the Fort Wayne Treaty of 1809 the Miami explicitly acknowledged the equal right of the Delawares to the country watered by White River. Kappler (ed.), *Indian Affairs. Laws and Treaties*, II, 101.

[25]For Stevens' motion, see Indiana *House Journal*, 1817-1818, pp. 88, 100, 115, 203. On the secret session, see *ibid.*, 1817-1818, pp. 93, 195; 1818-1819, pp. 7-8; *Senate Journal*, 1817-1818, pp. 59-60, 143; 1818-1819, pp. 6-7.

[26]The treaty of September 29, 1817, is printed in Kappler (ed.), *Indian Affairs. Laws and Treaties*, II, 145 ff. Comments appeared in the Vincennes *Western Sun* of March 14, 1818 (p. 3, col. 2), October 17, 1818 (p. 3, col. 4), and October 24, 1818 (p. 3, col. 3). The supplementary treaty appears in Kappler (ed.), *op. cit.*, II, 162 ff.

[27]See Chapter VIII for a discussion of these treaties.

[28]Esarey, Logan (ed.), *The Pioneers of Morgan County. Memoirs of Noah J. Major*, 454-55 (*Indiana Historical Society Publications*, V, no. 5, Indianapolis, 1915); Wilson, George R., *Early Indiana Trails and Surveys*, 399-401 (*Indiana Historical Society Publications*, VI, no. 3, Indianapolis, 1919).

[29]*Journal of the Executive Proceedings of the Senate of the United States . . .*, III, 135 (Washington, D. C., 1828); Kettleborough, Charles, *Constitution Making in Indiana . . .*, I, 97 (*Indiana Historical Collections*, Indianapolis, 1916).

[30]*Laws of Indiana Territory*, 1813-1814, pp. 442-45; *Laws of Indiana*, 1816-1817, pp. 180-82; Vincennes *Western Sun* (on the dueling incident), December 20, 1817, March 14, August 22, 29, October 3 and 10, 1818; (on the appointment as commissioner, and general politics), August 15, 29, September 5, 12, 19, 26, October 17, 24, 31, 1818. The constitutionality of the act of 1816-1817 was upheld by the Indiana Supreme Court (1 *Blackford*, 483-85). See also Order Book of the Supreme Court of Indiana, May Term, 1817, in Indiana State Library.

[31]Vincennes *Western Sun*, November 7, 14, 21, 28, December 19, 1818; January 2, 1819; Indiana *House Journal*, 1818-1819, 46-47; Dunn, *Indiana and Indianans*, I, 374-78.

[32]*Historical Atlas of Fayette County* (1875), 4-6; *History of Fayette County* (1885), pp. 57-58, 63.

[33]*Historical Atlas of Fayette County* (1875), 16; advertisement in *Indianapolis Gazette*, November 4, 1823; *History of Fayette County* (1885), 137.

[34]*Ibid.*, 138; record in Recorder's Office, Franklin County, Brookville, Indiana; Indiana *Senate Journal*, 1821-1822, p. 88.

[35]Heineman, *Two Chapters from the History of Fayette County*, 74.

[36]*Ibid.*, 60; *History of Fayette County* (1885), 143.

[37]*Laws of Indiana*, 1817-1818 (special), 33.

[38]Heineman, *Two Chapters from the History of Fayette County*, 61; Smith, *Early Indiana Trials*, 11.

[39]Cole, Ernest B., *The Winship Family in America* . . ., 12 (Indianapolis, 1905).

[40]*Laws of Indiana*, 1819-1820, pp. 97-112; 1821-1822, pp. 38-42, 45-46, 124-27, 152 ff.; *Senate Journal*, 1821-1822, pp. 65, 71, 72, 75, 79, 80, 81, 87-88, 131, 137, 144, 150, 175, 186, 189, 194, 199.

[41]*Ibid.*, 1821-1822, p. 163.

[42]*Ibid.*, 1821-1822, p. 107; Kettleborough, *Constitution Making in Indiana*, 108.

VIII

[1]For a description of St. Mary's during the treaty, see McMurray, William J. (ed.), *History of Auglaize County, Ohio,* I, 124-30 (Indianapolis, 1923). Esarey (ed.), *Messages and Letters,* II, 148, mentions the building of the road to Fort Defiance.

[2]Jennings to John C. Calhoun, October 28, 1818. Photostat in Indiana State Library.

[3]Barce, *Land of the Miamis,* 48.

[4]Esarey (ed.), *Messages and Letters,* III, 56-57.

[5]Cass's letter of January 20, 1823, and Jennings' letter of January 23, 1823, are printed in U. S. *Senate Documents,* 20 Congress, 2 session, report 25.

[6]The treaties are printed in Kappler (ed.), *Indian Affairs. Laws and Treaties,* II, 168-74. Article 3 of the treaty with the Miami made twenty-one grants to individuals, totaling 31,360 acres. These lands, with the exception of the nine sections (5,760 acres) granted by patent in fee simple to Richardville, were transferable only with the approval of the president of the United States. These grants were in addition to large reserves made to the Miami nation. The 640 acres reserved to Rebecca Hackley, half-breed daughter of William Wells, later became the site of Muncie. Haimbaugh (ed.), *History of Delaware County,* 433.

[7]According to an interview with Robert B. Duncan, printed in the *Indianapolis Journal,* September 25, 1887, under the title "Before the Red Men Left," William Conner was deputized to distribute annuities to the Delawares. "He had an odd way of paying them, which he used in order to keep their accounts so that they would understand. They were divided into three grades. The older ones were to receive so many dollars; the next younger so many half dollars, and the youngest so many quarter dollars. He would give to the old ones as many sticks of a certain length, as they were to receive dollars; to the next class shorter sticks, and to the next, still shorter. Then they would all take places, grouped in families, on the prairie between Conner's house and the river, covering an acre or two of it, where all could see and be seen, and Conner and his assistants would go about and give a dollar, or a part of a dollar, as the case might be, and take a stick. This was continued until the sticks were all taken up and the money paid." See also Sulgrove, Berry R., *History of Indianapolis and Marion County, Indiana,* 9 (Philadelphia, 1884).

[8]U. S. *Senate Documents,* 16 Congress, 1 session, report 84; *ibid.,* 20 Congress, 2 session, report 25, p. 3; *Annals of Congress,* 16 Congress, 1 session, 436, 494, 498, 598. John F. Ross and some thirty other citizens joined in Conner's memorial.

[9]U. S. *Statutes at Large,* VI, 271. *Annals of Congress,* 17 Congress, 1 session, 58, 212, 221, 310, 312, 1324, 1381, 1868, 1871; U. S. *Senate Documents,* 20 Congress, 2 session, report 25, p. 5.

[10]*Annals of Congress,* 17 Congress, 2 session, 97, 99, 105, 106-7, 192,

196; 18 Congress, 1 session, 1215, 1808; U. S. *Senate Journal*, 19 Congress, 1 session, 93, 97, 115, 121; 20 Congress, 1 session, 64, 78, 126-27, 229, 298, 302; U. S. *House Journal*, 20 Congress, 1 session, 585, 600, 729, 846.

[11]Conner's petition, Mekinges' memorial, and the letters of Cass and Jennings are printed in the report of the Committee on the Judiciary, *Senate Documents*, 20 Congress, 2 session, report 25. See also U. S. *Senate Journal*, 20 Congress, 2 session, 22, 26-27, 63, 67, 191. For some years prior to 1827 Noble and Jennings were at outs. This may have had something to do with the failure of Conner's various petitions. Smith, *Early Indiana Trials*, 88.

[12]William G. to George W. Ewing, December 11, 1852, in Ewing Papers, Indiana State Library.

[13]"We . . . went to the house of William Conner. . . . The women could not speak English." Dean and Dean (eds.), *Journal of Thomas Dean*, 315-16.

[14]"William Conner. A Notable Character in the Early History of Indiana," *Rochester Republican*, November 20, 1895.

[15]Fletcher, James C., "Old Events," in *Indianapolis News*, April 26, 1881.

[16]It is now generally conceded that the North American Indian belongs to the Mongoloid division of the human race which includes the Mongolian and Malaysian. His progenitors probably came to America by way of the Bering Straits after the retreat of several ice invasions. Shetrone, Henry Clyde, *The Mound-Builders . . .*, 481 (New York and London, 1930). Some of the early writers who attempted to explain the origin of the American Indian offered the fantastic theory that they were descended from the Israelites. See for example, Adair, James, *The History of the North American Indians . . .* (London, 1775). For a study of various aspects of the question, see Jenness, Diamond (ed.), *The American Aborigines, Their Origin and Antiquity* (University of Toronto Press, 1933).

[17]For accounts of this early settlement of Hamilton County, see Helm, *History of Hamilton County*, 33; Shirts, *History of Hamilton County*, 9-19; Finch, *Story of the First Settlement of Hamilton County*; letter of James G. Finch to Fabius M. Finch, July 1, 1893, copy in Indiana State Library; "Reminiscences of Judge Finch," reprinted from the *Indianapolis Journal*, May 30, 1885, in *Indiana Magazine of History*, VII, 155-65 (December, 1911); Duncan, Robert B., *"Old Settlers"* (*Indiana Historical Society Publications*, II, no. 10, Indianapolis, 1894).

[18]"Sketch of the Life of William Conner, late of Noblesville," in *Indianapolis Daily Journal*, August 22, 1855.

[19]The horse mill has been described as follows: "First they put up a little frame 6 or 8 feet high   on this was placed the hopper and stones   From this frame running North 25 or 30 feet was a plate framed into a post which stood in the ground. About the middle of this plate was a shaft into which arms were framed. These arms carried a rawhide tug around which gave power to the mill stones. This structure was not enclosed in any way." Letter of James G. Finch to Fabius M. Finch, March 1, 1896. Cf. with description in Duncan, *"Old Settlers,"* 379. In the "Reminiscences of Judge Finch," *Indiana Magazine of History*, VII, 159-60,

we find the following description: "The stones were made out of the bowlders which then strewed the uplands, laboriously hewed and split into the proper shapes, and with their faces ridged into furrows, so that a fine quality of meal was produced to the amount of thirty or forty bushels a day."

[20]Finch, Story of the First Settlement of Hamilton County, 7.

[21]For the act appointing commissioners, see *Laws of Indiana,* 1819-1820, pp. 18-20; see also Indiana *House Journal,* 1819-1820, pp. 134, 176, 193; *Senate Journal,* 1819-1820, pp. 18, 139-40, 142, 147-48. For the provisions in the Enabling Act see Kettleborough, *Constitution Making in Indiana,* I, 76-77; Jennings' proclamation for the meeting of the commissioners to select a capital site, and the official report of the commission are printed in Esarey (ed.), *Messages and Letters,* III, 109-12.

[22]Tipton's "Journal" is printed in the *Indiana Magazine of History,* I, 9-15, 74-79 (1905). For other accounts of the activities of the commissioners, see "Reminiscences of Judge Finch," in *Indiana Magazine of History,* VII, 160-62; Bolton, *Early History of Indianapolis and Central Indiana,* 153-54; Duncan, *"Old Settlers,"* 379-80; Dunn, *Indiana and Indianans,* I, 361-63; Holloway, *Indianapolis,* 9-10; Sulgrove, *History of Indianapolis and Marion County,* 23-24.

[23]Cottman, George S., "Internal Improvements in Indiana, No. I—The First Thoroughfares," in *Indiana Magazine of History,* III, 12-20 (March, 1907).

[24]See pages 176-77; Blank, Ralph, "Early Railroad Building in Indiana," in *Indiana Historical Society Publications,* VI, 134.

[25]"The Games of Moccasin and Bullet," in *Indiana Magazine of History,* I, 17 (1905). Deer hunting at night in a canoe with a torch was a fascinating sport in those days on White River. There is a story that William Conner once invited a guest, Colonel Eaton, to go on a fire hunt. As soon as the night set in they lighted the torch in the bow of the canoe and cut cable. Eaton was a good marksman. After proceeding some distance down stream Conner, who was steering, saw one of his own cattle in the river. He decided to have a good joke on Eaton. "Look," said he, pointing to the animal, "at that noble buck; when I say fire, you must be sure to shoot." The blaze of the torch blinded the animal and at the proper time the word was given. The animal bawled as it made for the shore, and the Colonel discovered his mistake. It was a fat bullock of the choicest flavor. The joke was so good that Conner sent for his neighbors and liberally divided the animal free of cost. "Indianapolis—the Past and the Present," in *Indiana Democrat,* May 15, 1839.

[26]Finch, James G., "Early Days at Noblesville," in *Indianapolis Journal,* December 18, 1898.

[27]The signing of the report by nine commissioners and B. I. Blythe, clerk, took place at McCormick's cabin. "Journal of John Tipton," in *Indiana Magazine of History,* I, 77-78. To have returned to William Conner's home for this official act would have involved a hard journey of about thirty-five miles. There is no record of the individual preferences of the commissioners. It has often been stated that only five commissioners

voted, three for the present site and two for the Bluffs. Brown, "History of Indianapolis," 2; Sulgrove, *History of Indianapolis and Marion County*, 24; Holloway, *Indianapolis*, 9; Bolton, *Early History of Indianapolis and Central Indiana*, 153. Tipton's statement clearly implies that nine were present, and the report gives no evidence of division among the members. Dunn's *Greater Indianapolis*, 5, 6, confirms this view. Rev. James C. Fletcher, in an article, "The Beginning of Indianapolis," in *Indianapolis News*, March 15, 1879, speaks of the "spirited contest whether the seat of government of Indiana should be located at the 'Bluffs' of White river, or near the mouth of Fall creek. After much debate and examination the choice fell upon the woody plain near the mouth of Fall Creek."

[28]Story of the First Settlement of Hamilton County, 9. Finch, "Early Days at Noblesville," in *Indianapolis Journal*, December 18, 1898.

[29]The feud became acute after an incident involving the Willison cat. A kettle of lard had been cooked and set to cool at the corner of the Willison cabin. A cat, undertaking to climb the wall to the clapboard roof, slipped and went into the lard up to the neck. It was said that the owner took the cat by the ears, raised it up with one hand and with the other scraped the lard back into the kettle. This proceeding was ridiculed by one of the Finches in a doggerel which ran as follows:

"Katy's cat fell in the fat,
And there she lay a-foaming
Jimmie's lice are big as mice
And round his head they're roaming."

It is said that John Finch very shortly found one of his yoke of large oxen with its throat cut and later a red muley cow with a bullet hole in its head. Finch, Story of the First Settlement of Hamilton County, 10.

[30]"Early Days at Noblesville," in *Indianapolis Journal*, December 18, 1898. "Most of the money in those days was silver. There were times when Wm. Conner had a good deal of it. He kept his money in a trunk at the head of his bed, and a rifle within easy reach. The trunk would hold a bushel and a half, and I have seen it full of silver dollars. There was little or no thought of thieves then. I do not remember to have heard a case of house-breaking in all the years I lived there." Fabius M. Finch's "Recollections," in *Indianapolis News*, March 19, 1896. See also James G. Finch to Fabius M. Finch, May 3, 1896.

"It is worthy of remark, that in their villages the Indians use neither bolts nor locks, and that when they leave for a time their cabins, either empty or with any articles in them, a log placed against its door affords ample protection to its contents, and abundant evidence of the right of possession." Spencer, *Indian Captivity*, 67.

[31]During the summer of 1820 "there were a great many Indians collecting there [at Conner's] preparatory to leaving the country. They came down the river in canoes and from the surrounding country on their ponies. Marshall and James Conner (half-breed Indian) [see note 6, chapter 7], son of John Conner, went with them when they left; which I think was the last of Aug. or first of Sept." Letter of James G. Finch to Fabius M. Finch, March 1, 1896. See also Shirts, *History of Hamilton County*, 24-25;

Finch, "Early Days at Noblesville," in *Indianapolis Journal,* December 18, 1898. Esarey, citing the Vincennes *Centinel* of November 4, 1820, says in his *History of Indiana,* I, 260: "In the fall of 1820 the remnant of this once powerful tribe . . . took up their western march, the disheartened train passing Kaskaskia about the middle of October." Isaac McCoy, a Baptist missionary, who made a tour of the Delaware villages in 1818-1819, tells of the effect on the Indians of the late treaty and the prospect of their removal westward. In December, 1818, he suggested a mission to William Anderson and found him more receptive than he had dared hope. He spoke to William Conner, asking his help, which Conner would have given except that the Indians were dispersed at their hunting camps. By the next May, McCoy found Anderson's attitude changed. He was embittered at what he felt to be unjust treatment of his people, and seemed eager to be free of all contact with the whites. McCoy was disgusted by the drunken frolicking in Anderson's village. *History of Baptist Indian Missions,* 50-53, 58-60.

[32]Adams' more important writings are: *A Brief History of the Delaware Indians,* U. S. *Senate Documents,* 59 Congress, 1 session, report 501; *A Delaware Indian Legend* (1899); *The Adoption of Mew - Seu - Qua, Tecumseh's Father, and the Philosophy of the Delaware Indians . . .* (Washington, D. C., 1917).

[1]"Old Events," an interview by Rev. James C. Fletcher with Elizabeth Chapman Conner, in *Indianapolis News*, April 26, 1881; article by Laura A. Smith on "William Conner's Station," in *Indianapolis Star*, January 17, 1926. "Reminiscences of Judge Finch," in *Indiana Magazine of History*, VII, 164-65, describes the type of clothing in vogue. The act providing a penalty of $500 for any clerk granting a marriage license to persons resident outside the county appears in *Laws of Indiana*, 1817-1818 (general), pp. 224-26.

[2]"Mr. Finch's Recollections," in *Indianapolis News*, March 19, 1896; Shirts, Augustus F., "'Horse Shoe Prairie' Settlers," in *Indianapolis News*, April 2, 1896; letters of James G. Finch to Fabius M. Finch, February 5, 1892, March 1, 1896, May 3, 1896; Shirts, *History of Hamilton County*, 16, 22, 123-24; Duncan, *"Old Settlers,"* 377-79.

[3]See varying accounts of the incident in Helm, *History of Hamilton County*, 131; letter of James G. Finch to Fabius M. Finch, August 31, 1893; Shirts, *op. cit.*, 127-29; "Early Days at Noblesville," article by James G. Finch in *Indianapolis Journal*, December 18, 1898.

[4]Howe, *Making a Capital in the Wilderness*, 328; James G. Finch to Fabius M. Finch, March 1, 1896; "Wilderness of Indiana Conquered by Pioneers," *Indianapolis News*, November 25, 1931.

[5]James G. Finch to Fabius M. Finch, February 1, 1899; James G. Finch, "Early Days at Noblesville," *Indianapolis Journal*, December 18, 1898; Shirts, "'Horse Shoe Prairie' Settlers," in *Indianapolis News*, April 2, 1896.

[6]Shirts, *History of Hamilton County*, 18, 21, 27-28; James G. Finch to Fabius M. Finch, February 5 and March 2, 1892; "Reminiscences of Judge Finch," in *Indiana Magazine of History*, VII, 160; Fletcher, James C., "Indianapolis," in *Indianapolis News*, March 22, 1879.

[7]*Laws of Indiana*, 1822-1823, pp. 15-18.

[8]Forkner, John L., and Dyson, Byron H., *Historical Sketches and Reminiscences of Madison County, Indiana*, 372 (Anderson, Ind., 1897).

[9]The house is described in an article by Laura A. Smith on "William Conner's Station," *Indianapolis Star*, January 17, 1926; see also article on the unveiling of a monument to Conner, *ibid.*, July 3, 1927. In the Indianapolis *Western Censor*, June 18, 1823, we find the statement that Conner "is building an elegant house of brick, and making other extensive improvements suitable for a large farm, from which he has a commanding view of all the land under fence, and can see very distinctly with the naked eye to the most distant part of his domains." Bolton's lecture is printed in the *Indiana Historical Society Publications*, I, 151 ff. See pages 172-73 for an account of Conner's hospitality.

[10]On the formation of Hamilton County, the selection of a county seat, and the first courts, see *Laws of Indiana*, 1822-1823, pp. 100-1; Shirts, *History of Hamilton County*, 45 ff., 60 ff.; Helm, *History of Hamilton*

County, 38-39; Haines, *History of Hamilton County,* 119-24; Monks, Leander J., Esarey, Logan, and Shockley, Ernest V. (eds.), *Courts and Lawyers of Indiana,* II, 713 (Indianapolis, 1916). Order Book A, county clerk's office, Noblesville, contains a record of the April session of the Circuit Court, 1824, held at the house of William Conner.

[11]Various explanations have been given for the naming of Noblesville. There is a sentimental story that the town was named for Lavina Noble, Polk's fiancée. Helm, *op. cit.,* 33; Shirts, *op. cit.,* 171. Noah and James Noble were both well known to the Conners and it is more likely that the town was named for one of them. "William Conner. A Notable Character in the Early History of Indiana," in *Rochester Republican,* November 20, 1895.

[12]This tradition, and another to the effect that Washington Irving once visited Conner on a trip to the West, are mentioned in an article by Laura A. Smith on "William Conner's Station," in *Indianapolis Star,* January 17, 1926.

[13]Canby, Henry Seidel, *Classic Americans* . . ., 130 (New York, 1931); Rusk, Ralph Leslie, *The Literature of the Middle Western Frontier,* I, 96; II, 34 (New York, 1925); "Structure of the Indian Language . . .," in *North American Review,* XXVI, 373-76 (April, 1828), cited by Rusk; page 12 of a "miscellaneous" wallet of the C. C. Trowbridge Papers, Burton Historical Collection, Detroit Public Library. For Conner's opinion of the Delawares, see "William Conner. A Notable Character in the Early History of Indiana," in *Rochester Republican,* November 20, 1895.

[14]For the correspondence between Du Ponceau, Wistar, and Heckewelder, see the latter's *History of the Indian Nations,* 349 ff. A short account of Trowbridge's visit to Conner is given by James V. Campbell in his "Biographical Sketch of Charles C. Trowbridge," in *Michigan Pioneer and Historical Collections,* VI, 486; letter of Trowbridge to Lyman C. Draper, March 14, 1874, Draper MSS. V, yy6; C. C. Trowbridge Papers, page 12, cited *ante,* note 13.

[15]Rice, *David Zeisberger and His Brown Brethren,* 56.

[16]Woodburn, James Albert (ed.), *The New Purchase or, Seven and a Half Years in the Far West,* by Robert Carlton, 247-48 (Princeton University Press, 1916).

[1]Smith, Laura A., "McCormick Cabin's Story," in *Indianapolis Star*, June 28, 1925, pt. 5, p. 1; Bolton, *Early History of Indianapolis and Central Indiana*, 155; "Journal of John Tipton," in *Indiana Magazine of History*, I, 9-15, 74-79; Brown, "History of Indianapolis," 2-3; Holloway, *Indianapolis*, 3-4, 7-11; Dunn, *Greater Indianapolis*, I, 36-39; Fletcher, "Early Days," in *Indianapolis News*, July 5, 1879; letter of E. K. Barnhill, of Plymouth, in the *Indianapolis News*, March 22, 1879.

[2]*Laws of Indiana*, 1821-1822, pp. 135-39; Dunn, *op. cit.*, 74-75; Brown, *op. cit.*, 13; *Revised Laws of Indiana*, 1823-1824, p. 370. Indiana *Senate Journal*, 1823-1824, pp. 94, 98, 101, 123; *House Journal*, 1823-1824, pp. 178, 187-88.

[3]Nowland, *Early Reminiscences of Indianapolis*, in a sketch of Phipps, 154-56; cf. Dunn, *Greater Indianapolis*, I, 445-46; see advertisements of Conner, Tyner, and Co. in Indianapolis *Western Censor, & Emigrants Guide*, July 2-September 29, 1823.

[4]Advertisement in Indianapolis *Indiana Journal*, May 10-June 21, 1825; Fletcher, "Early Days," in *Indianapolis News*, July 12, 1879. For a description of a pioneer store, see Young, Andrew W., *History of Wayne County, Indiana . . .*, 62-63 (Cincinnati, 1872).

[5]This story is told in Dunn, *True Indian Stories*, 197-212; Nowland, *op. cit.*, 165-67; Smith, *Early Indiana Trials*, 51-53; Sulgrove, *History of Indianapolis and Marion County*, 54-56. See also Helm, *History of Hamilton County*, 34. Governor Hendricks, in his annual message to the General Assembly in 1825, referred to this affair as a "melancholy occurrence," and recommended that the expense of safekeeping of the prisoners be paid out of the state treasury. Esarey (ed.), *Messages and Letters*, III, 512.

[6]*Western Censor*, April 19, July 20, 27, August 10, 1824; *Indianapolis Gazette*, July 20, 27, 1824; Pirtle, Alfred, *The Battle of Tippecanoe*, 117 (*Filson Club Publications*, no. 15, Louisville, 1900); Esarey (ed.), *Messages and Letters*, I, 627. For an anecdote concerning John Wyant, see Nowland, *Early Reminiscences of Indianapolis*, 127.

[7]*Indianapolis Gazette*, July 6, 1824; *Western Censor*, July 6, 13, 1824. Ninian Edwards was senator from Illinois, a critic of Jackson, Clay, and Crawford. For a description of earlier Fourth of July celebrations in Indianapolis, see *Indianapolis Gazette*, July 6, 1822, and July 8, 1823.

[8]Brown, "History of Indianapolis," 13; Holloway, *Indianapolis*, 15, 20; "Remarks . . . from Dr. S. G. Mitchell's Manuscript Historical Notes on Indiana," in *Indianapolis Gazette*, February 11, 1822; descriptions of the first courthouse in Dunn, *Greater Indianapolis*, I, 61-62, and Sulgrove, *History of Indianapolis and Marion County*, 44, 251; descriptions of the jail, in Dunn, *op. cit.*, 57, and Sulgrove, *op. cit.*, 41-42.

[9]*Locations in Indianapolis in 1825.*

These locations have been gathered from many sources, as noted below, and carefully checked with a card file of the names of first purchasers of lots compiled by Willis N. Coval, president of the Union Title Company of Indianapolis.

About the length of three city blocks beyond West Street was White River. In this space near the river were grouped the very first dwellings in the town. Here was the cabin which had been the tavern of Matthias Nowland and in which General Carr had held the sale for the first lots in Indianapolis. It was not occupied by either in 1825. Holloway, *Indianapolis*, 13.

Here was the double log cabin used by the families of the two brothers, John and James McCormick, who lived here only two years (1820-1822). Smith, "McCormick Cabin's Story," in *Indianapolis Star,* June 28, 1925, pt. 5, p. 1. Around it were grouped huts for the accommodation of overnight guests. Brown, "History of Indianapolis," 36.

There was also the cabin of the ferryman (1825), Asael Dunning, who had a store and tavern. "Reminiscences of Amos Hanway," in *Indiana Magazine of History,* II, 39 (March, 1906); *Indianapolis Gazette,* May 10 and 24, 1823.

Samuel McGeorge had a tavern here also in 1821 and may have been here in 1825. Nowland, *Early Reminiscences of Indianapolis,* 173; Fletcher, James C., "First Days," in *Indianapolis News,* April 12, 1879.

Amos Griffith, cabinetmaker, opened a shop at the west end of Washington Street in 1824. *Western Censor,* January 12, 1824.

Sam Reed's shop, where bacon and lard were sold, adjoined Dunning's tavern and ferry.

Locations on the Circle and between Market and Ohio streets.

The first market house was built in the maple grove on the Governor's Circle in May, 1822. *Indianapolis Gazette,* June 22, 1822; Brown, "History of Indianapolis," 8.

Block 44   between Delaware and Pennsylvania streets and Ohio and Market streets.

Lot 7   George Taffe, first purchaser (1821); assigned by Armstrong Brandon to John Johnson (1830). This was the site of John Johnson's brick house built in 1822-1823, the first brick house in Indianapolis. Sulgrove, *History of Indianapolis and Marion County,* 32; Brown, *op. cit.,* with illustration, 8.

Block 45   between Pennsylvania and Meridian streets and Ohio and Market streets.

Lot 2   Jacob G. Capp, first purchaser (1821); the Presbyterian Church, second purchaser (1827). The church building was erected here in 1824. Sulgrove, *History of Indianapolis and Marion County,* 32. See Brown, "History of Indianapolis," 12, for a picture of the church.

Lots 12   Isaac Coe, first purchaser and early resident. On one of these
13 and   lots was the home of Isaac Coe, but the date he moved here is
14   not certain.

Block 46   between Meridian and Illinois streets and Ohio and Market streets.

Lot 11 Judge James McIlvain, first purchaser (1821) and early resi-
dent. He lived here in a log house. *Centennial Memorial. First
Presbyterian Church, Indianapolis, Ind.* . . ., 187 (Greenfield,
Ind., 1925) ; Dunn, *Greater Indianapolis*, I, 47.

Block 47 between Illinois and Tennessee streets and Ohio and Market
streets.

Lot 12 Robert Gibson, Jr., first purchaser (1821) ; Matthias Scudder,
second purchaser (1827). Gibson died less than two years after
his purchase. In 1822 he had started an earthenware or potting
business here. His wife, Margaret Gibson, took it over at his
death, employing J. R. Crumbaugh. On July 19, 1825, she married Matthias Scudder. *Indianapolis Gazette*, June 8, 1822; June
21 and July 15, 1823; July 19, 1825.

*Locations on the north side of Washington Street beginning at West
Street with Block 51 and proceeding east to Block 60.*

Block 51 between the western boundary of the Plat, now West Street, and
Missouri Street.

Lot 12 Skinner and Crumbaugh, first purchasers (1821). Jacob R.
Crumbaugh was an early resident and built on this lot a neat
two-story frame house 31 by 20 feet with a good log house adjoining. *Indianapolis Gazette*, September 2, 1823; Sulgrove,
History of Indianapolis and Marion County, 44. The lot was
advertised for sale in 1823 but not sold until 1827. Fletcher,
"Early Days," in *Indianapolis News*, May 17, 1879. The house
was moved in 1825 to a site opposite the courthouse. Nowland,
Early Reminiscences of Indianapolis, 64-65.

Block 52 between Missouri and Mississippi streets.

Lot 6 Luke Walpole, first purchaser and early resident (1821). He
had his house and tavern here in the spring of 1823. Cf. Block
53, the State House Square. It was his second business location
in Indianapolis. *Indianapolis Gazette*, April 3, 1827.

Block 53 State House Square between Market and Washington streets;
Mississippi and Tennessee streets.

On the southeast corner of this block, corner of Washington
and Tennessee streets, was the second location of the *Gazette*
from 1822 to 1824. It is specifically stated in the *Gazette* of
October 5, 1822, that the office would be "removed to the corner of Washington and Tennessee streets, on the State House
square, opposite the residence of Dr. Mitchell." Dr. Mitchell's
residence at that time is mentioned in Nowland, *Early Reminiscences of Indianapolis*, 108. Nowland's statement, page 92, locating the *Gazette* office on the northeast corner of the Square,
and Holloway's statement, page 18, placing its location in Block
54, lot 6 or 7 (site of Metropolitan Theatre) are obviously incorrect.

On the south side of this square about opposite lots 2, 3, or 4
in Block 68 was located Caleb Scudder's cabinet shop, where the

first Sunday school was established in 1823. Nowland, *op. cit.*, 81; *Indianapolis Gazette*, February 25, 1822 ff.; February 22, 1823.

West of Scudder's shop, nearer Mississippi than Tennessee Street, was the grocery store of Jacob Landis, which was established here from 1822 to about 1824. Nowland, *op. cit.*, 144; *Indianapolis Gazette*, February 15, 1823. Cf. Sulgrove, *History of Indianapolis and Marion County*, 31.

Jonathan Clifton, tailor, started his business one door west of Jacob Landis but he was here only a few months in 1823. *Indianapolis Gazette*, March 8 and May 17, 1823.

On the northwest corner of the State House Square, Isaac Wilson, who came to Indianapolis in 1820, built his double log cabin, "the first house of any kind built on the original town plat." Luke Walpole, who arrived here in 1822, resided in this cabin, as Isaac Wilson had moved to a farm. Walpole had a store on the southwest corner of the Square, and remained here for a year when his store was advertised for sale. *Indianapolis Gazette*, July 6, 1822; *Western Censor*, August 11, 1823; Nowland, *op. cit.*, 25, 147; Sulgrove, *History of Indianapolis and Marion County*, 31. Cf. notes on Block 52, lot 6.

Block 54   between Market and Washington streets; Tennessee and Illinois streets.

Lot 7   James Linton, first purchaser and early resident (1821). Linton was a sawyer and millwright who built the first sawmill on Fall Creek, near the Crawfordsville road bridge, in September, 1821. He also built the first gristmill for Isaac Wilson on Fall Creek. On his Indianapolis lot he built the first two-story frame house, 76 West Washington Street, 1822. Brown, "History of Indianapolis," 7-8; Sulgrove, *op. cit.*, 32; Fletcher, "Early Days," in *Indianapolis News*, May 17, 1879.

Block 55   between Illinois and Meridian streets.

Lot 5   Not sold until 1827 (George Norwood). Here he conducted his wagon-making establishment about 1822. Fletcher, "Early Days," in *Indianapolis News*, August 2, 1879; Nowland, *op. cit.*, 152. Peter Harmonson and Company opened a blacksmith shop here in August, 1824. *Indianapolis Gazette*, August 17, 1824. Norwood's location in 1823 was the corner of Maryland and Illinois streets. *Ibid.*, July 22, 1823.

Lot 6   Thomas Carter, first purchaser (1821). This may have been the site of the "Rosebush" tavern operated by Carter for a short time. Nowland, *Early Reminiscences of Indianapolis*, 64. See Block 63, lot 4 for Carter's location in 1825.

Lot 9   Not sold until 1827. Nathaniel (Nathan) Davis, who bought it then, probably had his hat shop here in 1825. Cf. Nowland, *op. cit.*, 187.

Lot 10   Armstrong Brandon, first purchaser and probably nonresident (1821). Dr. Samuel G. Mitchell, the first physician who came

to Indianapolis in 1821, built on this site his second house, a
frame one. The lot was assigned by A. Brandon to Elizabeth
Mitchell (wife of Dr. Mitchell), who assigned it to Henry Porter, her father (1826). Nowland, *op. cit.*, 108-9; Dunn, *Greater
Indianapolis*, I, 71.

Block 56 between Meridian and Pennsylvania streets.

Lot 1 Not sold until May, 1825, to Israel Phillips, shoemaker, and
James Luster (Lester), tailor. Lester had his shop here in 1823.
See *Indianapolis Gazette*, December 9, 1823. In the *Gazette* of
February 15, 1825, John Ambrozene advertised the opening of a
watch and clock repair shop on the east corner of Washington
and Meridian streets, the second door below John Hawkins'
tavern.

Lot 2 Armstrong Brandon, first purchaser and probably nonresident
(1821). John Hawkins was the second owner (1826). He had
his home and tavern (the latter called the Eagle Tavern) on
this site. *Western Censor*, July 2, 1823; Sulgrove, *op. cit.*, 32.
By 1827, John Hawkins had purchased two more lots, 12 and 13,
in this block.

Lot 4 Harvey Gregg, first purchaser, with others, and early resident
(1821). Mr. Gregg was among the first lawyers to practice in
Indianapolis. In 1823 he formed a partnership with Douglass
Maguire to publish the second newspaper in Indianapolis, called
the *Western Censor, & Emigrants Guide*. It was on this site in
a house owned by Gregg that the newspaper was published. This
house was located just west of the alley in this block. Just west
of the newspaper building on this lot was the law office of Harvey Gregg and Gabriel Johnston. Nowland, *op. cit.*, 141-44.

Lot 5 Not sold until May, 1825, to Jacob Whitinger, probably a non-
resident. This was the site of the store of Conner, Tyner, and
Company, which was opened in July, 1823. *Western Censor*,
July 2, 1823. The partnership was dissolved in 1824, and busi-
ness continued by John Conner until his death in 1826. *Ibid.*,
April 19 and June 22, 1824.

NOTE: Between lots 5 and 6, that is between Paxton and
Bates general store and Conner's Store on lot 5, was the barber
shop of "Fancy Tom," a colored barber who followed the legislators up from Corydon. Nowland, *Early Reminiscences of Indianapolis*, 169.

Lot 6 William Earle, first purchaser, probably nonresident (1821).
Hervey Bates, second purchaser and early resident (January,
1825). On this site the Paxton and Bates general store was
established prior to 1825. Part of this lot was sold to James
Paxton in February, 1825. The other part was sold at the same
time to James D. Conerty or Conery. In 1827 when it was the
property of Jonathan Conery it was sold to William Conner and
Alfred Harrison. *Indianapolis Gazette*, February 28 and August
1, 1826.

Block 57 between Pennsylvania and Delaware streets.

Lot 7 James McClure, first purchaser, and probably nonresident (1821). William Conner, second purchaser in 1828. In January, 1825, this was the site of the shoe shop of Israel Phillips and Dennis I. White, which was located at the corner of Pennsylvania and Washington streets. *Western Censor,* December 29, 1823; *Indianapolis Gazette,* May 10 and September 13, 1825.

Lot 8 Daniel Stevens, first purchaser (1821).

Lot 9 Not sold until May, 1825 (Bishop and Stevens). Isaac Stevens had a general store at this location with Austin Bishop. *Indianapolis Gazette,* September 23, 1823, and April 5, 1825. In 1825 the partnership was dissolved and a new firm organized as I. Stevens and J. L. Sloan at the same location. *Ibid.*

Lot 10 Obed Foote, first purchaser and early resident (1821). Foote was one of the first lawyers and a justice of the peace. He lived in a cabin on this site. Nowland, *op. cit.,* 136; *Indianapolis Gazette,* March 8, 1823.

Lot 11 John Givan, first purchaser and early resident (1821); James Givan, second purchaser and early resident (1823). This was the site of a store kept by John Givan and later by James Givan and Son. *Indianapolis Gazette,* April 3, 1822, and February 22, 1823.

Lot 12 John Carr, first purchaser and resident (1821). General Carr was the first agent of Indianapolis and his double log cabin stood on this lot. Brown, "History of Indianapolis," 4; Sulgrove, *History of Indianapolis and Marion County,* 44.

Block 58 between Delaware and Alabama streets.
Occupied by the courthouse, jail, and pound.

Block 60 between New Jersey and East streets.

Lot 12 Wilkes Reagan, first purchaser and early resident (1821). He was a butcher and this the site of his slaughterhouse. Nowland, *Early Reminiscences of Indianapolis,* 133-34.

Locations on the south side of Washington Street from East Street proceeding west to the western boundary of the Plat at West Street.

Block 61 between East and New Jersey streets.

Lot 6 Thomas Chinn, first purchaser (1821) and early resident. He came to Indianapolis in 1821, settling near Pogue's cabin. Dunn, *Greater Indianapolis,* I, 45. He opened a tavern called Travellers' Hall on this lot which he owned, January 1, 1824. In the fall of 1825 he sold the tavern to David Buchanan and a year later, the lot on which it stood. *Western Censor,* January 5, 1824; *Indianapolis Gazette,* October 18, 1825.

Block 62 between New Jersey and Alabama streets.

Lot 6 Abraham Barnett, first purchaser (1821). This was the site of Andrew W. Reed's cabinet shop. *Indianapolis Gazette,* June 22, 1824.

NOTE: Samuel S. Rooker moved his house and sign painting

shop to the south side of Washington Street, east of the court-house, in 1825. *Indianapolis Gazette,* May 10, 1825.

Lots 7 and 8   Yandes and Wilkins, first purchasers (1821). This was the site of the first tanyard, which was started in 1822. Nowland, *op. cit.,* 76-78.

Block 63   between Alabama and Delaware streets.

Lot 1   Daniel Yandes, first purchaser, 1825. In 1822 Yandes erected a double log cabin near the southwest corner of Alabama and Washington streets. The following year, 1823, he built a frame house of three rooms in that locality. Sulgrove, *History of Indianapolis and Marion County,* 101.

Lot 3   James M. Ray, first purchaser (1821).

Lot 4   Armstrong Brandon, first purchaser (1821). This was probably the location of Major Carter's tavern, called the Indianapolis Hotel, a two-story frame building which was erected in 1823 and burned in January, 1825, during the legislative session. In the spring of this year he purchased the two-story frame house of Jacob R. Crumbaugh on Washington Street down by the river and moved it to the site of the burned tavern. Nowland, *Early Reminiscences of Indianapolis,* 64-65; Brown, "History of Indianapolis," 36; *Indianapolis Gazette,* October 7, 1823, November 9, 1824, January 18 and April 19, 1825.

Block 64   between Delaware and Pennsylvania streets.

Lot 9   Unsold until May, 1825 (John E. Baker, first purchaser). This was the site of the law office of Bethuel F. Morris, who was agent of Indianapolis, 1822-February, 1825. *Indianapolis Gazette,* March 29, 1823; October 26, 1824. Brown, "History of Indianapolis," 4.

Lot 10   William Earle, first purchaser (1821), probably nonresident. Calvin Fletcher announced formation of a law partnership with James Rariden in the *Indianapolis Gazette* of March 8, 1825. According to the notice, "Mr. Fletcher keeps his office on Washington street opposite to Messrs. Bishop and Steven's store, and one door east of the Gazette printing office.".

David Mallory's barbershop was probably close by. Nowland, *Early Reminiscences of Indianapolis,* 163.

Lot 11   William Earle, first purchaser (1821), probably nonresident. To this lot the office of the *Indianapolis Gazette* was moved in 1824 from the corner of Washington and Tennessee streets. *Indianapolis Gazette,* October 5, 1822, October 26, 1824, June 14, 1825.

Lot 1   Not sold until May, 1825 (Fleming T. Luse, first purchaser). Luse was a cabinetmaker, and had his shop here prior to April, 1826, at which time he built a new shop on this same lot where his old one had burned. *Indianapolis Gazette,* April 11, 1826.

Block 65   between Pennsylvania and Meridian streets.

Lot 1   Nicholas McCarty, first purchaser (May, 1825). McCarty was a merchant who came to Indianapolis in the fall of 1823, and established his store at this location. James Blake was his part-

ner at one time. See *Indianapolis Gazette,* November 15, 1825;
Nowland, *op. cit.,* 158-59; Fletcher, "Early Days," in *Indianapolis
News,* July 26, 1879; Sulgrove, *History of Indianapolis and
Marion County,* 99.

Lot 2 Maxwell Chambers, first purchaser (1821), probably a nonresident. This lot was occupied by Joseph K. Looney, tailor, from
November, 1823, to October, 1825, when Masey and Stewart
opened a tailoring shop at the same location. *Indianapolis Gazette,* November 25, 1823, and October 4, 1825.

Lot 3 Daniel Yandes, first purchaser (1821), and early resident. On
this location in January, 1824, Henderson and Blake opened a
tavern, Washington Hall. This partnership was dissolved in
1826, Henderson continuing the tavern alone. *Western Censor,*
January 12, 1824; *Indianapolis Gazette,* May 9, 1826. This was
a two-story frame building. Previous to this Henderson had a
tavern here in a log house. Brown, *op. cit.,* 13.

Lot 5 Elizabeth Nowland, first purchaser (1825), and early resident.
She was the widow of Matthias R. Nowland, who died in 1822.
They first lived near the river, but in 1823 Mrs. Nowland moved
to this location and opened a boarding house here. She bought
the lot in May, 1825, and erected a brick house here about 1828.
Holloway, *Indianapolis,* 13; Nowland, *Early Reminiscences of
Indianapolis,* 53, 447; Brown, "History of Indianapolis," 36.

Block 66 between Meridian and Illinois streets.

Lot 1 Not sold until 1827 (Jeremiah Collins). Jerry Collins had a
whisky shop and small lunchroom at this location from about
1821. Nowland, *op. cit.,* 109-11.

Block 67 between Illinois and Tennessee streets.

Lot 1 The first log schoolhouse was located in 1821 about the place
where Kentucky Avenue enters Illinois Street. Joseph C. Reed
was the first teacher. Sulgrove, *History of Indianapolis and
Marion County,* 31. For a description of the schoolhouse, see
Rabb, Kate Milner, and Herschell, William (eds.), *An Account
of Indianapolis and Marion County,* 45 (Dayton, Ohio, 1924).

Lot 3 Peter H. Patterson, first purchaser (1821); certificate assigned
to Hays and by Hays to Kenneth A. Scudder, who received
patent (1826). He had a drugstore here. Calvin Fletcher's
family lived here for a short time during 1824-1825. Sulgrove,
History of Indianapolis and Marion County, 29; Fletcher, "Early
Days," in *Indianapolis News,* July 5, 1879.

Lot 12 James Blake, first purchaser (1821) and early resident. When
Blake bought it, Colonel Paxton had half finished a frame house
of one story and two rooms connected by a covered space for a
kitchen on this lot. It was leased in 1822-23 by Calvin Fletcher,
a lawyer. The following year he shared it with the family of
Samuel Merrill, state treasurer. James Blake roomed and
boarded with the Fletchers, who lived here until 1824, when they
moved to Kenneth Scudder's house (Cf. Block 67, lot 3), but

they returned to this location before Miles Fletcher was born here in September, 1828. "Early Indianapolis," in *Indiana Magazine of History*, II, 33; *Biographical History of Eminent and Self-Made Men of Indiana*, II, 7th district, 273; Graydon, Katharine Merrill (ed.), *Catharine Merrill . . .* (Greenfield, Ind., 1934); Fletcher, articles on early Indianapolis, in *Indianapolis News*, March 10, April 4, July 5, 1879.

Lot 11 Thomas McOuat, first purchaser (1821). He did not remove here until 1830. Nowland, *op. cit.*, 229.

Lot 10 John Hall, first purchaser (1821).

Lot 9 Not sold until 1838 (James M. Smith).

Lot 8 Jesse McKay, first purchaser (1821).

Block 68 between Tennessee and Mississippi streets.

Lot 1 In February, 1825, the Assembly appropriated $1,000 to build on lot 1, Block 68, "a substantial brick house for the residence of the treasurer of state, to contain the offices of the treasurer and auditor, and a fire-proof vault." *Laws of Indiana*, 1825, p. 11; Brown, "History of Indianapolis," 13.

Lot 2 Armstrong Brandon, first purchaser (1821); lot 3 not sold until 1832 to Isaac Blackford; and lot 4, Armstrong Brandon, first purchaser (1821). On one of these lots Caleb Scudder had his house opposite his shop, and Abraham Beasly, tinker, had his shop. Nowland, *op. cit.*, 81; *Indianapolis Gazette*, July 20, 1824.

Lot 5 Not sold until 1832 (Isaac Blackford).

Lot 6 Samuel Patterson, first purchaser (1821). Probably occupied by the spinning wheel factory of Samuel Walton. *Indianapolis Gazette*, October 21, 1823.

Locations south of Washington Street.

Block 76 south of Maryland Street, between Meridian and Pennsylvania streets.

The Methodists had no church building until 1825 when they bought a lot and hewed log house for $300 on the south side of Maryland Street east of Meridian. They occupied this place for four years. Brown, "History of Indianapolis," 14. Dunn, *Greater Indianapolis*, I, 86, gives the location as west of Meridian Street.

[10]Seven years later, Alfred Harrison, who was then managing the Conner store, moved to La Porte, because he felt that "there was no prospect . . . that Indianapolis would be anything more than an inland mud town." Autobiographical sketch of Harrison under the title "An Old Man's Career," in *Indianapolis Journal*, February 1, 1885.

[11]The courthouse is described in Dunn, *Greater Indianapolis*, I, 62; for a picture, see Sulgrove, *op. cit.*, 251.

[12]*Indianapolis Gazette*, February 15, 1825.

[13]Indiana *House Journal*, 1825, pp. 9, 20.

[14]*Ibid.*, 23.

[15]*Indiana Journal*, October 11, 1825; the act appears in the *Laws*, 1825,

pp. 84-86. For a discussion of the road problem and description of first road between Indianapolis and William Conner's, see Dunn, *Greater Indianapolis*, I, 76-81.

[16]Indiana *House Journal*, 1825, pp. 79, 82; the act providing for the examining of White River was approved February 12, 1825. *Laws of Indiana*, 1825, p. 63. Ralston's manuscript report, dated December 13, 1825, is in the Indiana State Library; act for improving navigation of White River, *Laws of Indiana*, 1825-1826, pp. 47-49. See also Dunn, *Greater Indianapolis*, I, 16-25; Ewbank and Riker (eds.), *Laws of Indiana Territory, 1809-1816*, 45-52.

[17]County libraries, *Laws of Indiana*, 1825, pp. 46-47; State Library, *ibid.*, 47-49; medical societies, *ibid.*, 36-40, and Indiana *House Journal*, 1825, p. 239; joint resolution disapproving constitutional amendment proposed by the state of Georgia, "on the subject of the ingress of people of color into the several states of the Union," *Laws of Indiana*, 1825, p. 105, and *House Journal*, 1825, p. 224; joint resolution respecting the gradual emancipation of slaves and colonization of people of color within the United States, *Laws of Indiana*, 1825, pp. 105-6.

[18]Joint resolution on Lafayette's visit, *Laws of Indiana*, 1825, pp. 108-9; account of his visit, Vincennes *Western Sun*, April 16, 30, May 28, July 2, 1825; Thompson, Charles N., "General La Fayette in Indiana," in *Indiana Magazine of History*, XXIV, 57-77 (June, 1928); entries for May 8 to 13, 1825, in Nolan, James Bennett, *Lafayette in America Day by Day*, 286-87 (Historical Documents, Institut Français de Washington, *Cahier VII*, Baltimore, 1934).

[19]Tipton to the secretary of war, July 31, 1825; Thomas L. McKenney to Tipton, August 16, September 29, 1825; Tipton to McKenney, September 10, 1825; Cass to Tipton, October 12, 1825, in Tipton Papers, Indiana State Library.

[20]Quaife (ed.), *Fort Wayne in 1790*, 311n, 312, 320; Dunn, *True Indian Stories*, 272, 303-4.

[21]Tipton's Journal, January 3-February 24, 1826, in Indiana State Library; letters of Noble to Cass, February 3 and 4, 1826, William Hendricks to Cass, March 7, 1828; and McKenney to Peter B. Porter, July 31, 1829, photostats in possession of Eli Lilly, Indianapolis.

[22]Letter of George W. Ewing to John Tipton, January 1, 1830, Ewing Papers, Indiana State Library; Kappler (ed.), *Indian Affairs. Laws and Treaties*, II, 278-81; Weesner, Clarkson W. (ed.), *History of Wabash County, Indiana* . . ., I, 65 (Chicago and New York, 1914).

[23]*Indiana Journal*, April 25, 1826; *Indianapolis Gazette,* issue dated Tuesday, April 18, 1826, on page 1, and Wednesday, April 19, on editorial page.

[24]Smith, *Early Indiana Trials*, 174. Smith tells a story which Conner told at his own expense: "On one occasion, as he told me, he came to Andersontown, then the lodge of a large band of Indians, under Chief Anderson. He was dressed and painted as a Shawnee, and pretended to be a Representative of Tecumseh. As is usual with the Indians, he took his seat on a log barely in sight of the Indian encampment, quietly smoked his pipe, waiting the action of Anderson and his under chiefs. After an hour

he saw approaching the old chief himself, in full dress, smoking his pipe. I give his language. 'As the old chief walked up to me I rose from my seat, looked him in the eyes, we exchanged pipes, and walked down to the lodge smoking, without a word. I was pointed to a bear skin—took my seat, with my back to the chiefs. A few minutes after, I noticed an ·Indian by the name of Gillaway, who knew me well, eyeing me closely. I tried to evade his glance, when he bawled out in the Indian language, at the top of his voice, interpreted, "You great Shawnee Indian, you John Conner." The next moment the camp was in a perfect roar of laughter. Chief Anderson ran up to me, throwing off his dignity. "You great Representative of Tecumseh," and burst out in a loud laugh.' "

²⁵Conner's house at Connersville was a rendezvous for all the settlers. "They came there for social times and to learn the latest obtainable news. On one occasion, when there was an unusual number present and all the chairs and stools were in use, in came a big, bashful, awkward young fellow. Endeavoring to keep in the background he sidled around the wall to the corner near the great fireplace. The blue dye kettle stood there with a cloth over it. Mistaking it for a stool in his embarrassment he sat down, went under and came up with his tow linen suit dripping blue dye. The poor fellow made a shot for the door and the shouting men saw a literal 'blue streak' vanishing into the moonlit forest." It must have been a recurrent source of amusement to Conner, and it was impressed on the memory of his son, William Winship, who is said to have referred to the incident fifty years later in a political speech at Connersville. An old man then and there admitted he was the victim. Smith, Laura A., "Native Hoosiers Urged to Keep Pioneer Relics," *Indianapolis Star*, January 10, 1926.

[1]Miscellaneous Genealogy Notes in the Burton Historical Collection, Detroit Public Library.

[2]The records of Zion Lodge, No. 1, Detroit, show that John Conner was initiated as a member on December 6, 1802. The Zion Lodge was then No. 10. For failure to attend meetings, he was suspended for two years. In December, 1806, he was reinstated. On February 3, 1807, he was made a Master Mason. Zion Lodge was called a military lodge because it was instituted by English army officers (1764), but it never was really a military lodge. It was the first lodge on Michigan soil and had the only Masonic charter in the territory for some years. For the brothers' records in Indiana masonry, see *One Hundredth Anniversary, Warren Lodge No. 15, Connersville,* 14-16; *Atlas of Franklin County* (1882), 61; McDonald, Daniel, *A History of Freemasonry in Indiana From 1806 to 1898,* 80-82 (Indianapolis, 1898); English, Will E., *A History of Early Indianapolis Masonry . . .,* 13, 19 ff. (*Indiana Historical Society Publications,* III, no. 1, Indianapolis, 1895); Shirts, *History of Hamilton County,* 191-92; Helm, *History of Hamilton County,* 87.

[3]Will of John Conner, and inventory and appraisement of his personal estate, in possession of Miss Frieda Woerner, Indianapolis.

[4]Advertisements of Conner's store, *Indiana Journal,* April 25-August 1, 1826; *Indianapolis Gazette,* April 25-July 18, 1826; Conner and Harrison's new store, *Indiana Journal,* October 16, 1826-January 2, 1827; *Indianapolis Gazette,* October 17-November 30, 1826; advertisements of Conner and Harrison's store, *Indiana Journal,* April 9, 16, 1829; *Indianapolis Gazette,* April 9-23, 1829; *Indiana Democrat,* October 16, 1830-January 1, 1831, and May 5, 1832 ff.; notice of dissolution of partnership between A. W. Russell and the firm of Conner and Harrison, *Indiana Journal,* September 8, 1832-January 23, 1833; *Indiana Democrat,* September 22, 1832 ff.; notice of dissolution of firm of Harrison and Conner, and the occupancy of their quarters by the firm of A. W. Russell and Company, *Indiana Journal,* August 10-December 4, 1833; *Indiana Democrat,* August 10, 1833 ff. See "An Old Man's Career. Outline of the Busy and Successful Business Life of Mr. Alfred Harrison," in *Indianapolis Journal,* February 1, 1885; sketch of Harrison in Nowland, John H. B., *Sketches of Prominent Citizens of 1876 . . .,* 482 (Indianapolis, 1877). See Dunn, *Greater Indianapolis,* I, 377-78, and files in Union Title Company, Indianapolis, on various locations of the store.

[5]William Conner advertised the Hamilton County properties for rent in the *Indiana Journal,* February 29, 1840. James M. Ray, as agent, offered the Fayette County mills for sale in 1830. Advertisement quoted in *History of Fayette County* (1885), 138.

[6]Article 9 of the Constitution of 1816 is printed in Kettleborough, *Constitution Making in Indiana,* I, 112-15.

[7]Esarey, *History of Indiana,* I, 329.

⁸See letter from the group "To the Editors of the Democrat and the Journal," in *Indiana Democrat*, November 12, 1831.

⁹*Indiana Journal*, November 9, 1833; Dunn, *Indiana and Indianans*, II, 877-78, 886.

¹⁰Article by Laura A. Smith on "William Conner's Station," in *Indianapolis Star*, January 17, 1926; Finch, "Early Days at Noblesville," in *Indianapolis Journal*, December 18, 1898.

¹¹*Proceedings of the Indiana Historical Society, 1830-1886*, 9-10, 13, 17 (*Indiana Historical Society Publications*, I, no. 1, Indianapolis, 1897); Holloway, *Indianapolis*, 33, 41.

¹²The treaty appears in Kappler (ed.), *Indian Affairs. Laws and Treaties*, II, 273-77.

¹³*McRoberts* v. *Vogel*, 100 *Ind. App.*, 303-10. See also Esarey, *History of Indiana*, I, 292 ff.

¹⁴Esarey, *History of Indiana*, I, 367-70. Claims against the government found in the Ewing Manuscripts, Indiana State Library, show specific amounts paid to certain influential persons in connection with Indian treaties.

¹⁵Indiana *House Journal*, 1829-1830, p. 5.

¹⁶See sketches of Tipton in Woollen, *Biographical and Historical Sketches*, 185-95; Smith, *Early Indiana Trials*, 478-79; sketches of John Ewing in *ibid.*, 362, and in Cauthorn, Henry S., *A History of the City of Vincennes . . .*, 210 (Terre Haute, Ind., 1902); the newspaper controversy between Ewing and Tipton appears in the *Indiana Journal*, December 8, 11-12, 15-16, 1829. See also Dunn, *Indiana and Indianans*, I, 380-81, for comment on Ray's activities at the treaty.

¹⁷The election for clerk is described in "Reminiscences of Judge Finch," in *Indiana Magazine of History*, VII, 162-63; Dunn, *Greater Indianapolis*, I, 49-50; Holloway, *Indianapolis*, 19; Fletcher, "First Days," in *Indianapolis News*, April 26, 1879, and "Early Days," in *ibid.*, May 10, 1879. See "Sketch of the Life of William Conner, late of Noblesville," in *Indianapolis Daily Journal*, August 22, 1855, for Conner's opinion of political practices.

¹⁸Esarey, *History of Indiana*, I, 402 ff.; Dunn, *Indiana and Indianans*, I, 385 ff.

¹⁹*Ibid.*, I, 381-82; Indiana *House Journal*, 1829-1830, pp. 101, 224, 265-73, 275-85; *Laws of Indiana*, 1829-1830, pp. 111-14.

²⁰*House Journal*, 1829-1830, pp. 538-39; *Senate Journal*, 1829-1830, p. 428; *Laws of Indiana*, 1830-1831 (special), 153-54; Dunn, *Greater Indianapolis*, I, 103; Sulgrove, *History of Indianapolis and Marion County*, 103. Conner was a member of the joint standing committee on public buildings.

²¹The Indiana convention is described in the *Indiana Journal*, November 12, 1831. For a discussion of the first national political conventions, see Fess, Simeon D., *The History of Political Theory and Party Organization in the United States*, 144 ff. (Ginn and Company, 1910).

²²Laws incorporating railroads appear in *Laws of Indiana*, 1831-1832, pp. 173-236. The supplementary Wabash and Erie Canal act is printed in *ibid.*, 1-8.

²³*Indiana Journal*, June 16, 1832; Sulgrove, *History of Indianapolis and Marion County*, 109-10; Holloway, *Indianapolis*, 43-44; Dunn, *Greater*

Indianapolis, I, 135; Masters, Edgar Lee, *The Tale of Chicago,* 38, 55-59 (New York, 1933).

[24]Union Inn Register, 1833-1836, Smith Library, Indiana Historical Society; advertisement, *Indiana Journal,* November 9, 1833, and following issues; Loucks, Kenneth, "John Elder: Pioneer Builder," in *Indiana Magazine of History,* XXVI, 28-29 (March, 1930), and "A Hoosier Hostelry a Hundred Years Ago," in *Indiana History Bulletin,* VIII, 308-15 (April, 1931).

[25]Report of the meeting in *Indiana Journal,* March 29, 1834; see also Holloway, *Indianapolis,* 41-42, 48; Brown, "History of Indianapolis," 30-31; Dunn, *Indiana and Indianans,* I, 391 ff.

[26]Indiana *Senate Journal,* 1816-1817, p. 86.

[27]For discussions of the movement for internal improvements, see Esarey, *History of Indiana,* I, 412-14; Dunn, *op. cit.,* I, 382 ff.

[28]Advertisement in *Indiana Journal,* May 7, 1836, and subsequent issues.

[29]Indiana *House Journal,* 1836-1837, p. 4.

[30]Dunn, *Greater Indianapolis,* I, 105; Dunn, *Indiana and Indianans,* I, 455.

[31]See list of incorporations, *Laws of Indiana,* 1836-1837 (local), Index.

[32]Esarey, *History of Indiana,* I, 417.

[33]Indiana *House Journal,* 1836-1837, p. 136, and following pages *passim.* See also Esarey, *History of Indiana,* I, 414-36.

[34]Advertisement in *Indiana Democrat,* January 31, 1837.

[35]George Hunt, a buyer for the American Fur Company, reported the purchase of the furs on May 16, 1838. Calendar of American Fur Company Papers, item 4494, in Indiana State Library.

[36]For information on Conner's business partnerships, see note 35, *supra;* records in office of county clerk, Hamilton County; letter of Ernest B. Cole to Mary C. Haimbaugh, October 8, 1920.

[37]*Indiana State Journal,* July 12, 1847; January 8, 27, 1849.

[38]"A Trip to Noblesville," *Indiana State Journal,* April 23, 1851.

[39]William Conner to Richard Conner, February 11, 1848, in possession of Mary Conner Haimbaugh.

[40]The suit was brought July 3, 1861, in the United States Circuit Court in Indianapolis by John P. Usher, Cause No. 44. The jury returned a verdict for the defendant and judgment was accordingly entered January 6, 1863. Among the papers in the files in the clerk's office is an undated memorandum signed by Usher and addressed to Thomas A. Hendricks to the effect that upon execution of ten notes of $700 each by defendant heirs, judgment could be rendered for the defendants. The notes were to be sent by Hendricks to Usher at Washington. Presumably the rights of all the children were determined in this manner. It is noteworthy that Caleb B. Smith, the judge, was afterwards secretary of the interior in Lincoln's first cabinet. Usher had the same portfolio in his second cabinet. Hendricks became governor of Indiana and vice-president of the United States.

[41]"Sketch of the Life of William Conner, late of Noblesville," in *Indianapolis Daily Journal,* August 22, 1855.

[42]Wallace to Tipton, January 3, 1832, Tipton Papers.

[43]Harrison to Lewis Cass, December 17, 1826, photostat in possession of Eli Lilly, Indianapolis.

[44]James C. Fletcher, "Early Days in Indiana," in *Indianapolis News,* June 23, 1881. Fletcher tells this story: "Some thirty years ago, while men were engaged in digging a cellar on East Market street, for the late John Wilkins, the laborers found, at the depth of several feet beneath the ground, a beautiful tomahawk, with silver devices—one of which was the rising sun—and with William Conner's name in *intaglio,* evidently of French workmanship." This is now in the possession of Charles Conner.

[45]Adams, Richard C., *The Adoption of Mew-Seu-Qua . . .,* 48 (Washington, D. C., 1917).

BIBLIOGRAPHY

BIBLIOGRAPHY

[This bibliography is limited to materials cited.]

MANUSCRIPTS

Arthur W. Brady Papers, Indiana Historical Society, Indianapolis, containing translations of Diary of a Journey from Goshen to White River, March 24-May 25, 1801; Diary of the Little Indian Congregation on the White River; correspondence of Kluge and Luckenbach with Van Vleck; Notes on the Diary of the Little Indian Congregation, by Jacob P. Dunn.

Calendar of American Fur Company Papers, in Indiana State Library. The manuscripts for which the calendar was made are in possession of the New York Historical Society.

Cole, Ernest B., to Mary C. Haimbaugh, October 8, 1920.

Conner, George F., to Julia Conner Thompson, January 31, 1899.

Conner, Richard J., statement of June 17, 1891, in Draper Manuscripts, Wisconsin State Historical Society, Madison.

Conner, William, to Richard Conner, February 11, 1848, in possession of Mary Conner Haimbaugh.

Cottingham, Alice Conner, statement of December 21, 1934, in Indiana State Library.

Coval, Willis N., Card file of first purchasers of lots in Indianapolis, in office of the Union Title Company, Indianapolis.

Father Christian Denissen Genealogical Compilation, in Burton Historical Collection, Detroit Public Library.

Draper Manuscripts, in Wisconsin State Historical Society Library, Madison.

W. G. and G. W. Ewing Manuscripts, in Indiana State Library, Indianapolis.

Executive Proceedings of the State of Indiana, November 7, 1816-November 2, 1823, in Indiana State Library.

Field Notes of the Survey, Volumes 14 and 15, North and East, in Auditor's Office, State House, Indianapolis.

Finch, Fabius M., statement in Draper Manuscripts, Wisconsin State Historical Society, Madison.

Finch, James G., letters to Fabius M. Finch, February 5 and March 2, 1892; July 1 and August 31, 1893; March 1 and May 3, 1896; and February 1, 1899, in Indiana State Library.

———, Story of the First Settlement of Hamilton County Indiana, December 18, 1893. Typewritten manuscript in Indiana State Library.

Franklin County, Indiana. Connersville Library Association, record of incorporation in recorder's office, Brookville, Ind.

———, Marriage Records, in clerk's office, Brookville, Ind.

Freemasons. Records of Zion Lodge No. 1, Detroit.

Haimbaugh, Mary Conner, to Ernest B. Cole, October 19, 1920, in possession of Mary Conner Haimbaugh.

Hamilton County, Indiana. Order Book A, clerk's office, Noblesville, Ind.
————, Record of William Conner's business partnerships in clerk's office, Noblesville, Ind.
Index of Indiana Post Offices, in Indiana State Library.
Jennings, Jonathan, to John C. Calhoun, October 28, 1818. U. S. War Department, Supplementary Calendar, Letters Received. Photostat in Indiana State Library.
Hyacinthe and Charles B. Lasselle Papers, in Indiana State Library.
Eli Lilly Collection of photostats from U. S. Indian Office, Michigan-Indiana Superintendency, Letters Received, 1826-1829, Indianapolis, Ind.
Macomb County, Michigan. Deed Record A, in recorder's office, Mt. Clemens, Mich.
Miscellaneous Genealogy Notes, in Burton Historical Collection, Detroit Public Library.
Moravian Mission Diaries. Diary of Moravian Mission to Indian Congregation at Lichtenau, April, 1776, to March 30, 1780; Diary of the Moravian Mission to the Indians, Schoenbrunn on the Muskingum; Diary of the New Schoenbrunn Indian Mission, in Archives of the Moravian Church, Bethlehem, Pa.
George Morgan Letter Books, in Carnegie Library, Pittsburgh.
Muster, Pay and Receipt Rolls of Indiana Territory, Volunteers or Militia, War of 1812. Photostatic copies in Indiana State Library.
Order Book of the Supreme Court of Indiana, May Term, 1817, in Indiana State Library.
Rufus Putnam Collection, in Marietta College Library, Marietta, Ohio.
Ralston, Alexander, report of survey of West Fork of White River, in Indiana State Library.
Records of Surveys, Volume 3, in Auditor's Office, State House, Indianapolis.
Records of Surveys, Package 14, North and East, in Indiana State Library.
St. Anne's Church, Detroit. Register.
Setzler, Frank M., Archaeological Report on Delaware and Madison counties, Indiana, in Indiana Historical Bureau.
John Tipton Papers, in Indiana State Library.
C. C. Trowbridge Papers, in Burton Historical Collection, Detroit Public Library.
Union Inn Register, 1833-1836, in William Henry Smith Memorial Library, Indiana Historical Society, Indianapolis.
United States Circuit Court Records, in Federal Building, Indianapolis. Cause No. 44, July 3, 1861.
Weinland, Joseph E., statement concerning James Conner. An unpublished manuscript approved by the Executive Committee of the Moravian Historical Society, August 13, 1934, Bethlehem, Pa.
Frieda Woerner Collection of papers of John Conner, Indianapolis.

PUBLISHED COLLECTIONS, GOVERNMENT RECORDS, AND PERIODICALS

American Archives, see Force, Peter (ed.).
The American Historical Review (Washington, 1895-   ). *See* volume XL.

American State Papers. Indian Affairs. 2 volumes (Washington, D. C., 1832, 1834).

———. *Public Lands.* 8 volumes (Washington, D. C., 1834-1861).

Bulletin of the Chicago Historical Society (Chicago, 1934-   ). *See* volume II.

Burton Historical Collection, *Manuscripts and Records,* I, numbers 1-8 (Detroit, 1916-1918).

Dictionary of American Biography. 20 volumes (New York, 1926-1936). *See* volumes VII and XIII.

Fergus' Historical Series. 35 numbers (Chicago, 1876-1914). *See* numbers 26 and 27.

Filson Club *Publications* (Louisville, 1884-   ). *See* numbers 13 and 15.

Force, Peter (ed.), *American Archives: Fourth Series. Containing a Documentary History of the English Colonies in North America, from the King's Message to Parliament, of March 7, 1774, to the Declaration of Independence by the United States.* 6 volumes (Washington, D. C., 1837-1846).

Hazard, Samuel (ed.), *Pennsylvania Archives. Selected and Arranged from Original Documents,* 1 series, 12 volumes (Philadelphia, 1852-1856). *See* volumes VII-IX.

Historical Society of Pennsylvania, *Memoirs.* 14 volumes (Philadelphia, 1826-1895). *See* volumes VII and XII.

House Beautiful (Boston and Chicago, 1896-   ). *See* issue for May, 1902.

Indiana Documents. Appellate Court Reports. *See* 100 *Indiana Appellate.*

———, General Assembly. *House Journal,* 1816-1817 to 1819-1820, 1823-1824, 1825, 1829-1830, 1836-1837. *Senate Journal,* 1816-1817 to 1819-1820, 1821-1822, 1823-1824, 1829-1830.

———, *Laws of Indiana,* 1816-1817 to 1819-1820, 1821-1822, 1822-1823, 1825, 1825-1826, 1831-1832, 1836-1837. *Revised Laws of Indiana,* 1823-1824.

———, Supreme Court Reports. *See* 1 *Blackford.*

Indiana Historical Collections (Indianapolis, 1916-   ). *See* volumes VII, IX, XII, XIV, XV, XX.

Indiana Historical Society Publications (Indianapolis, 1886-   ). *See* volumes I-VII.

Indiana History Bulletin (Indianapolis, 1923-   ). *See* volumes III, extra number 2, and VIII.

Indiana Magazine of History (Indianapolis and Bloomington, 1905-   ). *See* volumes I-III, VII, VIII, IX, XIII, XXIV, XXVI, XXIX, XXX.

Michigan Pioneer and Historical Collections (Lansing, 1877-   ). *See* volumes IV-VI, X, XVIII, XX, XXVIII.

The Mississippi Valley Historical Review (Cedar Rapids, Iowa, 1914-   ). *See* volumes III, XIX-XXII.

Moravian Historical Society, *Transactions.* 11 volumes (Nazareth, Pa., 1857-1934). *See* volumes VI and X, parts 3 and 4.

Museum Echoes (Columbus, Ohio, 1928-   ). *See* volume VIII (June, 1935).

North American Review (New York and Boston, 1815-). *See* volume XXVI.

Pennsylvania Archives, see Hazard, Samuel (ed.).

Pennsylvania Magazine of History (Philadelphia, 1877-). *See* volumes IV, XI, XII.

Periodical Accounts Relating to the Missions Established by the Protestant Church of the Unitas Fratrum (quarterly. London, 1790-1894).

Society of Indiana Pioneers, *Year Book* (1921-). *See* 1923-1924.

United States Congress. *The Debates and Proceedings in the Congress of the United States* . . . . 1-18 Congress, March 3, 1789-May 27, 1824 (Washington, 1834-1856). Cited as *Annals of Congress. See* 16 Cong., 1 sess., 17 Cong., 1 and 2 sess., 18 Cong., 1 sess.

———. *Journal of the Executive Proceedings of the Senate of the United States* . . . 1789-1829. 3 volumes (Washington, 1828). *See* volume III.

———. *Journal of the House of Representatives of the United States* . . . (1789-). Cited as U. S. *House Journal. See* 20 Cong., 1 sess.

———. *Journal of the Senate of the United States* . . . (1789-). Cited as U. S. *Senate Journal. See* 19 Cong., 1 sess., 20 Cong., 1 and 2 sess.

———. *Journals of the Continental Congress. 1774-1789* (Library of Congress ed., Washington, 1905-). *See* volume II.

———. *Senate Documents. See* 16 Cong., 1 sess., report 84; 20 Cong., 2 sess., report 25.

United States Laws, Statutes, etc. *The Public Statutes at Large from the Organization of the Government in 1789, to March 3, 1845* . . ., edited by Richard Peters. 8 volumes (Boston, 1848-1856). *See* volume VI, *Private Statutes at Large.*

United States Supreme Court Reports (1790-). See 8 *Wheaton.*

Western Christian Advocate (Cincinnati, 1834-). *See* issue for August 15, 1845.

Wisconsin Historical *Collections* (Madison, 1855-). *See* volumes XXIII and XXIV.

GENERAL WORKS, MONOGRAPHS, AND ARTICLES

Adair, James, *The History of the American Indians; particularly Those Nations adjoining to the Missisippi, East and West Florida, Georgia, South and North Carolina, and Virginia* . . . (London, 1775). An edition edited by Samuel Cole Williams was published in 1930.

Adams, Henry, *History of the United States of America.* 9 volumes (New York, 1889-1891).

Adams, Richard C., *The Adoption of Mew-seu-Qua, Tecumseh's Father, and the Philosophy of the Delaware Indians* . . . (Washington, D. C., 1917).

Albach, James R. (comp.), *Annals of the West: Embracing a Concise Account of Principal Events which Have Occurred in the Western States and Territories, from the Discovery of the Mississippi Valley to the Year Eighteen Hundred and Fifty-Six* . . . (Pittsburgh, 1857).

Alvord, Clarence Walworth, *The Illinois Country, 1673-1818* (*Centennial History of Illinois*, I, Springfield, 1920).

——, *The Mississippi Valley in British Politics. A Study of the Trade, Land Speculation, and Experiments in Imperialism culminating in the American Revolution.* 2 volumes (Cleveland, 1917).

Askin, John, *see* Quaife, Milo M.

Atlas of Franklin Co. Indiana, to which are added various general maps, History, Statistics Illustrations, &c. &c. &c. (J. H. Beers & Co., Chicago, 1882).

Babcock, Kendric Charles, *The Rise of American Nationality, 1811-1819* (*American Nation Series*, XIII, New York and London, 1906).

Baldwin, Jane (comp.), *see The Maryland Calendar of Wills.*

Bancroft, George, *History of the United States of America, from the Discovery of the Continent.* 6 volumes (D. Appleton and Co., New York, 1891-92).

Barce, Elmore, *The Land of the Miamis. An Account of the Struggle to Secure Possession of the North-West from the End of the Revolution until 1812* (Fowler, Ind., 1922).

Barnhill, E. K., letter in *Indianapolis News*, March 22, 1879.

Barrows, Frederic Irving (ed.), *History of Fayette County, Indiana. Her People, Industries and Institutions* (B. F. Bowen & Co., Indianapolis, 1917).

Beckwith, Hiram W., *The Illinois and Indiana Indians* (*Fergus' Historical Series*, no. 27, Chicago, 1884).

A Biographical History of Eminent and Self-Made Men of the State of Indiana. . . . 2 volumes (Cincinnati, 1880).

Bissell, H. N., "The Early Settlement of Mt. Clemens and Vicinity," in *Michigan Pioneer and Historical Collections*, V, 450-69 (Lansing, 1884).

Blank, Ralph, "Early Railroad Building in Indiana," in Lindley, Harlow (ed.), *Proceedings of the Tenth Annual Meeting of the Ohio Valley Historical Association held at Indianapolis, Indiana October 4 and 5, 1916 . . .* (*Indiana Historical Society Publications*, VI, no. 1 [Indianapolis, 1917]).

Bliss, Eugene Frederick (tr. and ed.), *Diary of David Zeisberger, a Moravian Missionary among the Indians of Ohio.* 2 volumes (Cincinnati, 1885).

Bolton, Nathaniel, *Early History of Indianapolis and Central Indiana* (*Indiana Historical Society Publications*, I, no. 5, Indianapolis, 1897).

Bouquet, Henry. *Historical Account of Bouquet's Expedition against the Ohio Indians, in 1764*, with preface by Francis Parkman (*Ohio Valley Historical Series*, Cincinnati, 1868).

Boyer, Charles C., *The American Boyers* (4th ed., Kutztown, Pa., 1915).

Brown, Ignatius, "History of Indiana from 1818 to 1868," in *Logan's Indianapolis Directory . . .* (Indianapolis, 1868).

Burnet, Jacob, *Notes on the Early Settlement of the North-Western Territory* (Cincinnati, 1847).

Burr, Samuel J., *The Life and Times of William Henry Harrison* (8th ed., New York and Philadelphia, 1840).

Butterfield, Consul Willshire, *An Historical Account of the Expedition against Sandusky under Col. William Crawford in 1782* . . . (Cincinnati, 1873).

———, *History of the Girtys, Being a Concise Account of the Girty Brothers—Thomas, Simon, James and George, and of their half-brother John Turner—also of the part taken by them in Lord Dunmore's War, in the Western Border War of the Revolution, and in the Indian War of 1790-95* (Cincinnati, 1890).

——— (ed.), *Washington-Irvine Correspondence. The Official Letters which passed between Washington and Brig.-Gen. William Irvine and between Irvine and Others concerning Military Affairs in the West from 1781 to 1783* . . . (Madison, Wis., 1882).

Campbell, James V., "Biographical Sketch of Charles C. Trowbridge," in *Michigan Pioneer and Historical Collections,* VI, 478-91 (Lansing, 1884).

———, *Outlines of the Political History of Michigan* (Detroit, 1876).

Canby, Henry Seidel, *Classic Americans. A Study of Eminent American Writers from Irving to Whitman* . . . (New York, 1931).

Carlton, Robert, *see* Woodburn, James A.

[Cass, Lewis], "Structure of the Indian Language . . .," in *North American Review,* XXVI, 357-402 (April, 1828).

Casselman, Alexander Clark, *see* Richardson, John.

Catlin, George B., *see* Ross, Robert B.

Cauthorn, Henry S., *A History of the City of Vincennes, Indiana, from 1702 to 1901* (Terre Haute, Ind., 1902).

Centennial Memorial. First Presbyterian Church, Indianapolis, Ind. . . . (Greenfield, Ind., 1925).

Christian, Mrs. Sarah C., *see* Conner, John.

Clark, Charles L., "The Old Connors Mansion," in *House Beautiful* (May, 1902).

Cockrum, William M., *Pioneer History of Indiana including Stories, Incidents and Customs of the Early Settlers* (Oakland City, Ind., 1907).

Cole, Ernest B., "The Conner Family," in *Indianapolis Star,* September 19, 1920.

———, "The Finch Family," in *Indianapolis Star,* October 3, 1920.

———, *The Winship Family in America* . . . (Indianapolis, Ind., 1905).

———, "The Winship Family of Indiana," in *Indianapolis Star,* September 12, 1920.

"John Conner. By his granddaughter, Mrs. Sarah C. Christian," in *Indiana Magazine of History,* III, 87-88 (June, 1907).

Conner, William. "Sketch of the Life of William Conner, late of Noblesville," in *Indianapolis Daily Journal,* August 22, 1855.

———, "William Conner. A Notable Character in the Early History of Indiana," in *Rochester Republican,* November 20, 1895.

Cooley, Thomas McIntyre, *Michigan, A History of Governments (American Commonwealths,* Boston, 1885).

Cottman, George S., *The Corydon State House. A Hoosier Shrine* (Department of Conservation, State of Indiana, *Publication Number 94*, Indianapolis, 1930).

———, "Internal Improvements in Indiana. No. I—The First Thoroughfares," in *Indiana Magazine of History*, III, 12-20 (March, 1907).

Cresswell, Nicholas. *The Journal of Nicholas Cresswell, 1774-1777* (New York, 1924).

Croghan, George, "A Selection of George Croghan's Letters and Journals Relating to Tours into the Western Country—November 16, 1750-November, 1765," in Thwaites, Reuben Gold (ed.), *Early Western Travels*, I, 45-173 (Cleveland, 1904).

Cutcheon, Byron M., *see* Utley, Henry M.

Dawson, Moses, *A Historical Narrative of the Civil and Military Services of Major-General William H. Harrison, and a Vindication of his Character and Conduct as a Statesman, a Citizen, and a Soldier* . . . (Cincinnati, 1824).

Dean, John Candee and Randle C. (eds.), *Journal of Thomas Dean. A Voyage to Indiana in 1817* (*Indiana Historical Society Publications*, VI, no. 2, Indianapolis, 1918).

Dearborn, Henry, to William Henry Harrison, February 21, 1803, in *Bulletin of the Chicago Historical Society*, II, 88-90 (March, 1937).

"Dedication of the Conner Cabin," in *Museum Echoes*, VIII, 21 (June, 1935).

Denny, Ebenezer. "Military Journal of Major Ebenezer Denny . . . with an Introductory Memoir by William H. Denny," in Historical Society of Pennsylvania, *Memoirs*, VII, 205-492 (Philadelphia, 1860).

De Peyster, J. Watts (ed.), *Miscellanies, by an Officer. (Colonel Arent Schuyler de Peyster, B. A.), 1774-1813* . . ., pt. 2 (New York, 1888).

De Schweinitz, Edmund, *The Life and Times of David Zeisberger, the Western Pioneer and Apostle of the Indians* (Philadelphia, 1870).

Dietrich, William J., *see* Roberts, Charles Rhoads.

Dillon, John B., *A History of Indiana, from its Earliest Exploration by Europeans to the Close of the Territorial Government, in 1816* . . . (Indianapolis, 1859).

———, *The National Decline of the Miami Indians* (*Indiana Historical Society Publications*, I, no. 4, Indianapolis, 1897).

Doddridge, Joseph, *Notes on the Settlement and Indian Wars of the Western Parts of Virginia and Pennsylvania from 1763 to 1783, inclusive, together with a Review of the State of Society and Manners of the First Settlers of the Western Country* (3d ed., Pittsburgh, 1912).

Downes, Randolph C., "Dunmore's War: An Interpretation," in *Mississippi Valley Historical Review*, XXI, 311-30 (December, 1934).

Drake, Benjamin, *Life of Tecumseh, and of His Brother the Prophet; with a Historical Sketch of the Shawanoe Indians* (Cincinnati, 1850).

Duncan, Robert B., *"Old Settlers"* (*Indiana Historical Society Publications*, II, no. 10, Indianapolis, 1894).

———. Interview with Robert B. Duncan, "Before the Red Men Left," in *Indianapolis Journal*, September 25, 1887.

Dunn, Jacob P., "Centennial Anniversary of the Burning of Christians at Stake for Witchcraft on the banks of White River," in *Indianapolis News*, March 17, 1906.

——, *Documents Relating to the French Settlements on the Wabash* (*Indiana Historical Society Publications*, II, no. 11, Indianapolis, 1894).

——, *Greater Indianapolis. The History, the Industries, the Institutions, and the People of a City of Homes.* 2 volumes (Chicago, 1910).

——, *Indiana; a Redemption from Slavery* (*American Commonwealths*, rev. ed., Boston and New York, 1905).

——, *Indiana and Indianans. A History of Aboriginal and Territorial Indiana and the Century of Statehood.* 5 volumes (Chicago and New York, 1919).

——, "The Moravian Mission near Anderson," in *Indiana Magazine of History*, IX, 73-83 (June, 1913).

——, *True Indian Stories, with Glossary of Indiana Indian Names* (Indianapolis, 1909).

Eldredge, Robert F., *Past and Present of Macomb County, Michigan* (S. J. Clarke Publishing Co., Chicago, 1905).

English, Will E., *A History of Early Indianapolis Masonry and of Center Lodge* (*Indiana Historical Society Publications*, III, no. 1, Indianapolis, 1895).

English, William H., *Conquest of the Country Northwest of the River Ohio 1778-1783 and Life of Gen. George Rogers Clark. . . .* 2 volumes (Indianapolis and Kansas City, 1897).

Esarey, Logan (ed.), *Governors Messages and Letters. Messages and Letters of William Henry Harrison.* 2 volumes (*Indiana Historical Collections*, VII, IX, Indianapolis, 1922).

—— (ed.), *Governors Messages and Letters. Messages and Papers of Jonathan Jennings, Ratliff Boon, William Hendricks . . . 1816-1825* (*Indiana Historical Collections*, XII, Indianapolis, 1924).

——, *A History of Indiana.* 2 volumes (I, *From its Exploration to 1850*; II, *From 1850 to 1920*) [3d ed., Fort Wayne, 1924].

——, *Internal Improvements in Early Indiana* (*Indiana Historical Society Publications*, V, no. 2, Indianapolis, 1912).

——, "Organizing a State," in Lindley, Harlow (ed.), *Proceedings of the Tenth Annual Meeting of the Ohio Valley Historical Association held at Indianapolis, Indiana October 4 and 5, 1916 . . .*, 98-122 (*Indiana Historical Society Publications*, VI, no. 1 [Indianapolis, 1917]).

—— (ed.), *The Pioneers of Morgan County. Memoirs of Noah J. Major* (*Indiana Historical Society Publications*, V, no. 5, Indianapolis, 1915).

——, *see also* Monks, Leander J.

Ewbank, Louis B., "Blockhouse Stockades," in *Indiana History Bulletin*, III, extra no. 2, pp. 82-97 (March, 1926).

Ewbank, Louis B., and Riker, Dorothy L. (eds.), *The Laws of Indiana Territory, 1809-1816* (*Indiana Historical Collections*, XX, Indianapolis, 1934).

Farmer, Silas, *The History of Detroit and Michigan. . . .* 2 volumes (2d ed., Detroit, 1889).

Ferris, Ezra, *The Early Settlement of the Miami Country* (*Indiana Historical Society Publications*, I, no. 9, Indianapolis, 1897).

Fess, Simeon D., *The History of Political Theory and Party Organization in the United States* (Ginn and Company, 1910).

Finch, Fabius M., "Mr. Finch's Recollections," in *Indianapolis News*, March 19, 1896.

———, "Reminiscences of Judge Finch," reprinted from *Indianapolis Journal*, May 30, 1885, in *Indiana Magazine of History*, VII, 155-65 (December, 1911).

———, "The Ways of the Red Man," in *Indianapolis Journal*, October 30, 1887.

Finch, James G., "Early Days at Noblesville," in *Indianapolis Journal*, December 18, 1898.

———, "Settlement of Noblesville, Hamilton County," in *Indiana Magazine of History*, VI, 75-80 (June, 1910).

Fletcher, James C., "The Beginning of Indianapolis," in *Indianapolis News*, March 15, 1879.

———, "Early Days," in *Indianapolis News*, May 10, 17, 24, June 7, 14, 21, July 5, 12, 19, 26, August 2, 9, 16, 25, September 10, 19, 1879, May 11, 1881.

———, "Early Days in Indiana. The Life and Services of William Conner," in *Indianapolis News*, June 23, 1881.

———, "Early Indianapolis. The Fletcher Papers," in *Indiana Magazine of History*, II, 29-36, 73-80, 127-30, 187-90 (March-December, 1906).

———, "The Early Settlement of Indianapolis," in *Indianapolis News*, April 4, 1879.

———, "First Days," in *Indianapolis News*, April 12 and 26, 1879.

———, "First Things in Indianapolis," in *Indianapolis News*, April 19, 1879.

———, "Indianapolis. The First Survey and Settlement," in *Indianapolis News*, March 22, 1879.

———, "More First Days," in *Indianapolis News*, March 29, 1879.

———, "Old Events," in *Indianapolis News*, April 26, 1881.

———, "Some First Events," in *Indianapolis News*, March 10, 1879.

———, "Who Was He?" in *Indianapolis News*, April 13, 1881.

Ford, Henry A., "The Old Moravian Mission at Mt. Clemens," in *Michigan Pioneer and Historical Collections*, X, 107-15 (Lansing, 1888).

Ford, Paul Leicester (ed.), *see* Jefferson, Thomas.

Fordham, Elias Pym, *see* Ogg, Frederic Austin (ed.).

Forkner, John L., and Dyson, Byron H., *Historical Sketches and Reminiscences of Madison County, Indiana* . . . (Anderson, Ind., 1897).

Fox, Henry Clay (ed.), *Memoirs of Wayne County and the City of Richmond, Indiana* . . . . 2 volumes (Madison, Wis., 1912).

Franklin, W. Neil, "Pennsylvania-Virginia Rivalry for the Indian Trade of the Ohio Valley," in *Mississippi Valley Historical Review*, XX, 463-80 (March, 1934).

"The Games of Moccasin and Bullet," from the writings of Robert B. Duncan, in *Indiana Magazine of History*, I, 17-18 (1905).

Goebel, Dorothy Burne, *William Henry Harrison. A Political Biography* (*Indiana Historical Collections*, XIV, Indianapolis, 1926).

Graydon, Katharine Merrill (ed.), *Catharine Merrill. Life and Letters* (Greenfield, Ind., 1934).

Griswold, Bert J. (ed.), *Fort Wayne, Gateway of the West, 1802-1813. Garrison Orderly Books. Indian Agency Account Book* (*Indiana Historical Collections*, XV, Indianapolis, 1927).

Haimbaugh, Frank D. (ed.), *History of Delaware County, Indiana.* 2 volumes (Indianapolis, 1924).

Haines, John F., *History of Hamilton County, Indiana. Her People, Industries and Institutions* (Indianapolis, 1915).

Hall, Baynard Rush, *see* Woodburn, James A.

Hall, James, *A Memoir of the Public Services of William Henry Harrison, of Ohio* (Philadelphia, 1836).

Hamilton, John Taylor, *A History of the Church known as the Moravian Church, or The Unitas fratrum, or The Unity of the Brethren, during the eighteenth and nineteenth centuries* (Moravian Historical Society, *Transactions*, VI, Bethlehem, Pa., 1900).

A Handbook for the Exhibition Buildings of Colonial Williamsburg Incorporated . . . (Williamsburg, Va., 1936).

Hanna, Charles A., *The Wilderness Trail or The Ventures and Adventures of the Pennsylvania Traders on the Allegheny Path* . . . . 2 volumes (New York and London, 1911).

Hanway, Amos. "Reminiscences of Amos Hanway," in *Indiana Magazine of History*, II, 39-40 (March, 1906).

Harrison, Alfred. "An Old Man's Career. Outline of the Busy and Successful Business Life of Mr. Alfred Harrison," in *Indianapolis Journal*, February 1, 1885, p. 7, col. 3.

Harrison, William Henry, *A Discourse on the Aborigines of the Ohio Valley* . . . (*Fergus' Historical Series*, no. 26, Chicago, 1883).

Heckewelder, John, *History, Manners, and Customs of the Indian Nations who once inhabited Pennsylvania and the Neighbouring States* (Historical Society of Pennsylvania, *Memoirs*, XII, Philadelphia, 1876).

———, "Narrative of John Heckewelder's Journey to the Wabash in 1792," in *Pennsylvania Magazine of History and Biography*, XI, 466-75, XII, 34-54, 165-85 (Philadelphia, 1887).

———, *A Narrative of the Mission of the United Brethren among the Delaware and Mohegan Indians, from* . . . *1740, to* . . . *1808* . . . (Philadelphia, 1820).

Heineman, John L., *The Indian Trail Down the White Water Valley. Some Primitive Indiana History of the Connersville Neighborhood* (3d ed., Indianapolis, 1925).

———, *Two Chapters from the History of Fayette County of 1917* (B. F. Bowen & Company, Indianapolis, 1917).

Helm, Thomas B., *History of Delaware County, Indiana, with Illustrations and Biographical Sketches of Some of its Prominent Men and Pioneers* (Chicago, 1881).

———, *History of Hamilton County, Indiana, with Illustrations and Bio-*

graphical Sketches of Some of its Prominent Men and Pioneers . . . (Chicago, 1880).

Henry, Roberta Bolling, see *The Maryland Calendar of Wills.*

Herschell, William, *see* Rabb, Kate Milner.

Hill, Norman Newell, Jr. (comp.), *History of Coshocton County, Ohio* . . . (A. A. Graham & Co., Newark, Ohio, 1881).

Hinsdale, Burke Aaron, *The Old Northwest with a View of the Thirteen Colonies as Constituted by the Royal Charters* (New York, 1888).

"Historic Spots in Indianapolis," in *Indiana Magazine of History,* III, 46-47 (March, 1907).

History of Dearborn and Ohio Counties, Indiana. From the Earliest Settlement . . . (F. E. Weakley & Co., Chicago, 1885).

History of Fayette County, Indiana. Containing a History of the County; its Townships, Towns, Villages, Schools, Churches, Industries, etc. . . . (Warner, Beers & Co., Chicago, 1885).

History of Macomb County, Michigan, containing . . . *biographical sketches* . . . *the whole preceded by a history of Michigan* (M. A. Leeson & Co., Chicago, 1882).

A History of the National Guard of Indiana, From the beginning of the Militia System in 1787 to the present time . . . (Indianapolis, 1901).

Hodge, Frederick W. (ed.), *Handbook of American Indians North of Mexico.* 2 volumes (U. S. Bureau of American Ethnology, *Bulletin 30,* Washington, D. C., 1912).

Holloway, William Robeson, *Indiana. A Historical and Statistical Sketch of the Railroad City, a Chronicle of its Social, Municipal, Commercial and Manufacturing Progress, with Full Statistical Tables* (Indianapolis, 1870).

Homsher, George W., "Remains on White Water River, Indiana," in Smithsonian Institution, *Annual Report,* 1882, pp. 728-52 (Washington, 1884).

Howe, Daniel Wait, *Making a Capital in the Wilderness* (*Indiana Historical Society Publications,* IV, no. 4, Indianapolis, 1908).

An Illustrated Historical Atlas of Fayette Co. Indiana . . . (Chicago, 1875).

"Indian Torture Post in Delaware County," in *Indiana Magazine of History,* I, 176-79 (1905).

"Indian Towns of Marion County," in *Indiana Magazine of History,* I, 15-17 (1905).

The Indiana Gazetteer, or Topographical Dictionary of the State of Indiana (3d ed., E. Chamberlain, Indianapolis, 1850).

Indiana Territory. Laws. *See* Ewbank, Louis B., and Riker, Dorothy L.

"Indianapolis—the Past and Present," in *Indiana Democrat,* May 15, 1839.

Innis, Harold A., "Interrelations between the Fur Trade of Canada and the United States," in *Mississippi Valley Historical Review,* XX, 321-32 (December, 1933).

Jefferson, Thomas. Ford, Paul Leicester (ed.), *The Works of Thomas Jefferson.* 12 volumes (Federal ed., G. P. Putnam's Sons, New York and London, 1905).

——, *The Writings of Thomas Jefferson. Memorial Edition* . . . , Andrew A. Lipscomb, editor-in-chief, Albert Ellery Bergh, managing editor. 20 volumes (Washington, D. C., 1904).

Jemison, Mrs. Mary, *see* Seaver, James E.

Jenness, Diamond (ed.), *The American Aborigines. Their Origin and Antiquity* (University of Toronto Press, 1933).

Johnston, J. Stoddard (ed.), *First Explorations of Kentucky. Doctor Thomas Walker's Journal of an Exploration of Kentucky in 1750 . . . Also Colonel Christopher Gist's Journal of a Tour through Ohio and Kentucky in 1751* (*Filson Club Publications* No. 13, Louisville, 1898).

"A Joke in Pioneer Days," in *Indianapolis News*, February 14, 1902.

Jones, David, *A Journal of Two Visits Made to Some Nations of Indians on the West Side of the River Ohio, in the Year 1772 and 1773 . . . with a Biographical Notice of the Author, by Horatio Gates Jones* (New York, 1865).

"Journal of John G. Jungman," in Charles Cist, *The Cincinnati Miscellany, or Antiquities of the West . . .,* II (Cincinnati, November, 1845).

Kappler, Charles J. (ed.), *Indian Affairs. Laws and Treaties.* 2 volumes (Washington, 1904).

Kellogg, Louise Phelps (ed.), *Frontier Advance on the Upper Ohio, 1778-1779* (Wisconsin Historical *Collections*, XXIII, Madison, 1916).

———— (ed.), *Frontier Retreat on the Upper Ohio, 1779-1781* (Wisconsin Historical *Collections*, XXIV, Madison, 1917).

Kemper, General William Harrison (ed.), *A Twentieth Century History of Delaware County, Indiana* (Chicago, 1908).

Kettleborough, Charles, *Constitution Making in Indiana . . . .* 3 volumes (*Indiana Historical Collections*, I, II, and XVII, Indianapolis, 1916, 1930). See volume I.

King, Rufus, *Ohio. First Fruits of the Ordinance of 1787* (*American Commonwealths*, Cambridge, Mass., 1888).

Kohnova, Marie J., "The Moravians and their Missionaries, A Problem in Americanization," in *Mississippi Valley Historical Review*, XIX, 348-61 (December, 1932).

Krick, Thomas H., *see* Roberts, Charles Rhoads.

Lang, Frank H., *The Burning of William Crawford . . . June 11, 1782 . . .* (Upper Sandusky, Ohio, 1931).

Lasselle, Charles B., "The Old Indian Traders of Indiana," in *Indiana Magazine of History*, II, 5-13 (March, 1906).

Leeth, John, *see* Thwaites, Reuben Gold.

Lockridge, Ross F., "History on the Mississinewa," in *Indiana Magazine of History*, XXX, 29-56 (March, 1934).

Logan's Indianapolis Directory, embracing an Alphabetical List of Citizens Names . . . also, a . . . History of Indianapolis, from 1818 to 1868, by Ignatius Brown . . . (Indianapolis, 1868).

Loskiel, George Henry, *History of the Mission of the United Brethren among the Indians in North America*, translated by Christian I. La Trobe (London, 1794).

Loucks, Kenneth, "A Hoosier Hostelry a Hundred Years Ago," in *Indiana History Bulletin*, VIII, 308-15 (April, 1931).

——, "John Elder: Pioneer Builder," in *Indiana Magazine of History,* XXVI, 25-33 (March, 1930).

Luckenbach, Abraham, *see* Stocker, Harry Emilius (tr.).

McAfee, Robert B., *History of the Late War in the Western Country (Great American Historical Classics Series,* Bowling Green, Ohio, 1919).

McCoy, Isaac, *History of Baptist Indian Missions: Embracing Remarks on the Former and Present Condition of the Aboriginal Tribes . . .* (Washington, D. C., 1840).

McDonald, Daniel, *A History of Freemasonry in Indiana From 1806 to 1898* (Indianapolis, 1898).

McKee, Alexander. "Extract Taken from Alexander M'Kee, Esqr's, Journal of Transactions with the Indians at Pittsburg, &c., from the 1st May, to the 10th June, 1774," in [I. Daniel Rupp], *Early History of Western Pennsylvania, and of the West . . . Appendix . . .,* 203-13 (Harrisburg and Pittsburgh, 1846).

McLaughlin, Mabel Nisbet, "The Endicotts of Indiana," in *Indiana Magazine of History,* XXIX, 26-39 (March, 1933).

McMaster, John Bach, *A History of the People of the United States, from the Revolution to the Civil War.* 8 volumes (New York and London, 1883-1913).

McMurray, William J. (ed.), *History of Auglaize County, Ohio.* 2 volumes (Historical Publishing Company, Indianapolis, 1923).

"The Manners and Customs of the North-Western Indians," in *Fergus' Historical Series,* no. 26, pp. 79-96 (Chicago, 1883).

Marshall, John, *The Life of George Washington, Commander in Chief of the American Forces . . . and First President of the United States,* with an Introduction by Henry St. George Tucker. 2 volumes (Walton Book Co., New York, 1930).

The Maryland Calendar of Wills, compiled by Jane Baldwin and Roberta Bolling Henry. 8 volumes (Baltimore, 1904-1928).

Mason, Dr. Philip, *A Legacy to my Children, including Family History, Autobiography, and original essays* (Moore, Wilstach & Baldwin, Printers, Cincinnati, 1868).

Masters, Edgar Lee, *The Tale of Chicago* (New York, 1933).

Merrill, Catharine, *see* Graydon, Katharine Merrill.

Mitchener, Charles H. (ed.), *Ohio Annals. Historic Events in the Tuscarawas and Muskingum Valleys . . .* (Dayton, 1876).

Monks, Leander J., Esarey, Logan, and Shockley, Ernest B. (eds.), *Courts and Lawyers of Indiana.* 3 volumes (Indianapolis, 1916).

Montgomery, Thomas Lynch (ed.), *Report of the Commission to Locate the Site of the Frontier Forts of Pennsylvania.* 2 volumes (2d ed., Harrisburg, 1916).

Moores, Charles W., "Old Corydon," in *Indiana Magazine of History,* XIII, 20-41 (March, 1917).

Morse, Jedidiah, *A Report to the Secretary of War of the United States, on Indian Affairs, comprising a Narrative of a Tour Performed in the Summer of 1820 . . .* (New Haven, 1822).

Nolan, James Bennett, *Lafayette in America Day by Day* (Historical Documents, Institut Français de Washington, *Cahier VII*, Baltimore, 1934).

Nowland, John H. B., *Early Reminiscences of Indianapolis, with Short Biographical Sketches of its Early Citizens, and of a Few of the Prominent Business Men of the Present Day* (Indianapolis, 1870).

——, *Sketches of Prominent Citizens of 1876, with a Few of the Pioneers of the City and County Who Have Passed Away* (Indianapolis, 1877).

Ogg, Frederic Austin (ed.), *Personal Narrative of Travels in Virginia, Maryland, Pennsylvania, Ohio, Indiana, Kentucky; and of a Residence in the Illinois Territory: 1817-1818 by Elias Pym Fordham* . . . (Cleveland, 1906).

One Hundredth Anniversary, Warren Lodge No. 15, F. & A. M., Connersville, Indiana, 1822-1922 [Connersville, 1922].

Parker, S. W., "William Conner," in *Connersville Times*, August 29, 1855.

Parker, Warren, "Early History of Macomb County," in *Michigan Pioneer and Historical Collections*, XVIII, 485-502 (Lansing, 1892).

Parkman, Francis, *The Conspiracy of Pontiac and the Indian War after the Conquest of Canada*. 2 volumes (Boston, 1924).

——, *La Salle and the Discovery of the Great West (France and England in North America*, pt. 3, Boston, 1895).

Pirtle, Alfred, *The Battle of Tippecanoe (Filson Club Publications* No. 15, Louisville, 1900).

Power, Richard Lyle, "Wet Lands and the Hoosier Stereotype," in *Mississippi Valley Historical Review*, XXII, 33-48 (June, 1935).

Pratt, Julius W., "Fur Trade Strategy and the American Left Flank in the War of 1812," in *American Historical Review*, XL, 246-73 (January, 1935).

Proceedings of the Indiana Historical Society, 1830-1886 (Indiana Historical Society Publications, I, no. 1, Indianapolis, 1897).

Quaife, Milo M. (ed.), *Fort Wayne in 1790 (Indiana Historical Society Publications*, VII, no. 7, Greenfield, Ind., 1921).

—— (ed.), *The John Askin Papers, 1747-1820*. 2 volumes (Detroit, 1928, 1931).

Rabb, Kate Milner, and Herschell, William (eds.), *An Account of Indianapolis and Marion County*. 2 volumes (Dayton, Ohio, 1924).

Rave, Herman, "An Indiana Pioneer." Newspaper clipping in Finch Scrapbook, Indiana State Library.

Reifel, August J., *History of Franklin County, Indiana. Her People, Industries and Institutions* . . . (Indianapolis, 1915).

Rice, William H., *David Zeisberger and His Brown Brethren* (Bethlehem, Pa., 1897).

Richardson, John. *Richardson's War of 1812; with Notes and a Life of the Author by Alexander Clark Casselman* (Historical Publishing Co., Toronto, 1902).

Ridley, William, "The Old Capitol Building at Corydon—As Changed," in *Year Book of the Society of Indiana Pioneers, 1923-1924* (n. p., n. d.).

Riker, Dorothy L., *see* Ewbank, Louis B.

Roberts, Charles Rhoads, Stoudt, John Baer, Krick, Thomas H., Dietrich,

William J., *History of Lehigh County Pennsylvania and a Genealogical and Biographical Record of its Families.* 3 volumes (Allentown, Pa., 1914).

Roosevelt, Theodore, *The Winning of the West.* 4 volumes (New York and London, 1889-1896).

Ross, Robert B., and Catlin, George B., *Landmarks of Detroit. A History of the City* (rev. ed., Detroit, 1898).

Royce, Charles C. (comp.), "Indian Land Cessions in the United States," with an Introduction by Cyrus Thomas, in U. S. Bureau of American Ethnology, *Annual Report,* 1896-1897, pt. 2 (Washington, 1899).

Rupp, Isaac Daniel, *see* McKee, Alexander.

Rusk, Ralph Leslie, *The Literature of the Middle Western Frontier.* 2 volumes (New York, 1925).

Seaver, James E., *A Narrative of the Life of Mrs. Mary Jemison. Who was taken by the Indians, in the year 1755* . . . (Random House, New York, 1929).

Shaw, Archibald (ed.), *History of Dearborn County, Indiana. Her People, Industries and Institutions* . . . (Indianapolis, 1915).

Shetrone, Henry Clyde, *The Mound-Builders. A Reconstruction of the Life of a Prehistoric American Race, through Exploration and Interpretation of their Earth Mounds, their Burials, and their Cultural Remains* (New York and London, 1930).

Shirts, Augustus Finch, *A History of the Formation, Settlement and Development of Hamilton County, Indiana, from the Year 1818 to the Close of the Civil War* (n. p., 1901).

——, " 'Horse Shoe Prairie' Settlers," in *Indianapolis News,* April 2, 1896.

Shockley, Ernest V., *see* Monks, Leander J.

Sipe, C. Hale, *Fort Ligonier and Its Times* . . . *Based Primarily on the Pennsylvania Archives and Colonial Records* (Harrisburg, Pa., 1932).

——, *The Indian Wars of Pennsylvania. An account of the Indian Events, in Pennsylvania, of the French and Indian War, Pontiac's War, Lord Dunmore's War, The Revolutionary War and the Indian Uprising from 1789 to 1795* (Harrisburg, Pa., 1929).

Smith, Laura A., "McCormick Cabin's Story," in *Indianapolis Star,* June 28, 1925, pt. 5, p. 1, cols. 6 and 7.

——, "Native Hoosiers Urged to Keep Pioneer Relics," in *Indianapolis Star,* January 10, 1926.

——, "William Conner's Station," in *Indianapolis Star,* January 17, 1926.

Smith, Oliver H., *Early Indiana Trials: and Sketches* (Cincinnati, 1858).

Smith, William C., *Indiana Miscellany: Consisting of Sketches of Indian Life, the Early Settlement, Customs, and Hardships of the People* . . . (Cincinnati, 1867).

Smith, William L. G., *Fifty Years of Public Life. The Life and Times of Lewis Cass* (New York, 1856).

Spencer, Oliver M., *Indian Captivity: A True Narrative of the Capture of Rev. O. M. Spencer, by the Indians, in the neighbourhood of Cincinnati. Written by himself* (New York [1834]).

Stocker, Harry Emilius (tr.), "The Autobiography of Abraham Luckenbach," in Moravian Historical Society, *Transactions,* X, pts. 3 and
4, 361-408 (Bethlehem, Pa., 1917).

———, "A History of the Moravian Mission Among the Indians on the
White River in Indiana," in Moravian Historical Society, *Transactions,*
X, pts. 3 and 4 (Bethlehem, Pa., 1917).

Stoudt, John Baer, *see* Roberts, Charles Rhoads.

Sulgrove, Berry R., *History of Indianapolis and Marion County, Indiana*
(Philadelphia, 1884).

"Tecumseh and the Prophet," in *Indianapolis Press,* September 29, 1900.

Thomas, Cyrus, *see* Royce, Charles C.

Thompson, Charles N., "General La Fayette in Indiana," in *Indiana Magazine of History,* XXIV, 57-77 (June, 1928).

Thwaites, Reuben Gold (ed.), *Early Western Travels. 1748-1846. A
Series of Annotated Reprints of some of the best and rarest contemporary volumes of travel, descriptive of the Aborigines and Social
and Economic Conditions in the Middle and Far West, during the
Period of Early American Settlement* . . . . 32 volumes (Cleveland,
1904-7).

——— (ed.), *A Short Biography of John Leeth with an Account of his
Life among the Indians,* reprinted from original edition of 1831 with
introduction by Reuben Gold Thwaites (*Narratives of Captivities,*
Cleveland, 1904).

Thwaites, Reuben Gold, and Kellogg, Louise Phelps (eds.), *Documentary
History of Dunmore's War, 1774* (Wisconsin Historical Society, Madison, 1905).

——— (eds.), *The Revolution on the Upper Ohio, 1775-1777* . . . (Madison, 1908).

Tipton, John. "The Journal of John Tipton, Commissioner to locate Site
for State Capital—1820," in *Indiana Magazine of History,* I, 9-15, 74-79
(1905).

*A True History of the Massacre of Ninety-Six Christian Indians at
Gnadenhuetten, Ohio, March 8th, 1782,* reprinted in Burton Historical
Collection, *Manuscripts,* I, no. 7, pp. 275-86 (Detroit, April, 1918).

Utley, Henry M., and Cutcheon, Byron M., *Michigan As a Province,
Territory and State, the Twenty-Sixth Member of the Federal Union.*
4 volumes (Publishing Society of Michigan, 1906).

Volwiler, Albert Tangeman, *George Croghan and the Westward Movement,
1741-1782* (Cleveland, 1926).

Weesner, Clarkson W. (ed.), *History of Wabash County Indiana. A
Narrative Account of Its Historical Progress, Its People, and Its
Principal Interests.* 2 volumes (Chicago and New York, 1914).

Weinland, Joseph E., *The Romantic Story of Schoenbrunn the First Town
in Ohio* . . . (2d ed., Ohio State Archaeological and Historical Society,
n. p., 1929).

[Wharton, Samuel], *View of the title to Indiana,—a tract of country on
the river Ohio. Containing Indian conferences at Johnson-Hall, in*

May, 1765; the deed of the Six Nations to the proprietors of Indiana . . . (Philadelphia, 1776).

Wilcox, Frank N., *Ohio Indian Trails* (Cleveland, 1933).

"Wild Animals of Indiana," in *Indiana Magazine of History,* II, 13-16 (March, 1906).

"Wilderness of Indiana Conquered by Pioneers," in *Indianapolis News,* November 25, 1931.

Wilson, George R., *Early Indiana Trails and Surveys* (*Indiana Historical Society Publications,* VI, no. 3, Indianapolis, 1919).

Winsor, Justin, *The Mississippi Basin. The Struggle in America between England and France. 1697-1763* (Boston and New York, 1895).

────── (ed.), *Narrative and Critical History of America.* 8 volumes (Boston and New York, 1889).

──────, *The Westward Movement* . . . (Boston and New York, 1897).

Woodburn, James Albert (ed.), *The New Purchase or, Seven and a Half Years in the Far West,* by Robert Carlton (Princeton University Press, 1916).

Woollen, William Wesley, *Biographical and Historical Sketches of Early Indiana* (Indianapolis, 1883).

Woollen, William Wesley, Howe, Daniel Wait, and Dunn, Jacob Piatt (eds.), *Executive Journal of Indiana Territory, 1800-1816* (*Indiana Historical Society Publications,* III, no. 3, Indianapolis, 1900).

Young, Andrew W., *History of Wayne County, Indiana* . . . (Cincinnati, 1872).

Zeisberger, David, *see* Bliss, Eugene F. (tr. and ed.).

NEWSPAPERS

Connersville Times (weekly), August 29, 1855. Connersville, Ind.

Indiana Democrat (weekly), 1830-1833, 1837, 1839. Indianapolis, Ind.

Indiana Journal (weekly), 1825-1827, 1829, 1831-1834, 1836, 1839, 1840. Indianapolis, Ind.

Indiana State Journal (weekly), 1847, 1849; (daily), 1851. Indianapolis, Ind.

Indianapolis Daily Journal, August 22, 1855. Indianapolis, Ind.

Indianapolis Gazette (daily), 1822-1827, 1829. Indianapolis, Ind.

Indianapolis Journal (daily), 1885, 1887, 1898. Indianapolis, Ind.

Indianapolis News (daily), 1879, 1881, 1896, 1902, 1906, 1931. Indianapolis, Ind.

Indianapolis Press (daily), September 29, 1900. Indianapolis, Ind.

Indianapolis Star (daily), 1920, 1925-1927. Indianapolis, Ind.

Liberty Hall and Cincinnati Mercury (weekly), July 23, 1808. Cincinnati, Ohio. In possession of Historical and Philosophical Society of Ohio, Cincinnati.

Rochester Republican, November 20, 1895. Rochester, Ind.

Western Censor, & Emigrants Guide (weekly), 1823-1824. Indianapolis, Ind.

Western Sun (weekly), 1817-1819, 1825. Vincennes, Ind.

Newspaper clippings in Finch Scrapbook, Indiana State Library.

MAP AND DRAWINGS

Guernsey, E. Y., *Indiana. Influence of the Indian* . . . (Department of Conservation, *Publication No. 122,* Indianapolis, 1933).

Photostatic copies of measured drawings of Old State Capitol, Corydon, made by Historic American Building Survey, in William Henry Smith Memorial Library, Indiana Historical Society, Indianapolis.

INDEX

INDEX

Adams, John Quincy, 83, 145, 146, 155.
Adams, Richard C., 124-25, 179.
Alexandria (Ind.), platted, 171.
Ambrozene, John, 233.
American Fur Company, 176, 242.
Ancrum, Maj. William, 35.
Anderson, William (Delaware), 109, 112, 238-39; father-in-law of William Conner, 51; at Fort Wayne Treaty (1809), 57; at council with Tecumseh, 66; at Treaty of Fort Meigs (1817), 96; grants permission for Whetzel's Trace, 97; at St. Mary's treaties (1818), 104-5, 106; embittered by treaties, 226; departure with Delawares, 123, 124; Indian name, 201.
Anderson's Town (Andersontown, Wapeminskink), 112, 196; description, 43, 201; execution of Christian Indians near, 45-46; sale of lots, 202; size, 203.
Arms and ammunition, sale to Indians, 5.
Armstrong, John, secretary of war, 214.
Asbury (De Pauw University), 172.
Ash, Abraham, interpreter, 57.
Askin, John, 35.
Association for the Improvement of Common Schools in Indiana, 161.
Audrick (Andrick), ——, 121, 131, 132.

Backhouse, James, 206.
Baird, Patrick, 92, 101.
Baker, John E., 235.
Ballot system, in general elections, 102.
Baptiste, Jean, 128.
Barnett, Abraham, 234.
Barnhill, John, 141.

Barnhill, Robert, 141.
Barron, Joseph, interpreter and scout, 56, 57, 59.
Bartholomew, Joseph, commissioner to locate capital, 117.
Bates, Hervey, 158, 233.
Baynton and Wharton, 188.
Baxter, Allen, 129.
Baxter family, 121, 123.
Beasly, Abraham, 237.
Beaver (Delaware), 186.
Beggs, James, nickname, 91; state legislator, 92, 96.
Bishop, Austin, 234.
Bishop and Stevens, 234, 235.
Black Hawk's War, 168-69.
Black Swamp, 74.
Blackford, Isaac, 91, 92.
Blackmore, William C., 136.
Blake, James, commissioner to lay out Indianapolis—Fort Wayne road, 151; witness, John Conner's will, 156; early Indianapolis resident, 235-36, 236.
Blasdel, Capt. Jacob, 217.
Blockhouses, Conner blockhouse, 85, 216; Dearborn County (including Ohio and Switzerland), 85, 217; Franklin County (including Fayette and Union), 85, 216-17; Wayne County, 85, 216.
Blue Jacket (Shawnee), 7.
Blythe, Benjamin I., clerk, commission to locate capital, 118; at William Conner's wedding, 127.
Bolton, Nathaniel, 133.
Boon, Ratliff, state legislator, 92, 101; on educational committee, 161.
Bouquet, Col. Henry, 5; defeats Indians at Bushy Run, 4; demands return of white captives, 5, 14, 186, 195.

with Delawares, 65, 72, 83, 110-12;
possible militia service, 85; land
purchases, Franklin Co., 86-87,
218; mills near Connersville, 87,
88, 100; plats Connersville, 87-88;
senator from Franklin Co. (1816-
17, 1817-18, 1818-19), 89-96, 99,
219; from Fayette and Union cos.
(1821-22), 101-2; sheriff, Fayette Co., 94, 100, 219; witness,
Jennings' inquiry, 99; business and
real estate interests, Connersville,
99-100, 143, 218; commissioner to
locate state capital, 100, 117, 118,
119; to locate Ripley county seat,
100; director, Connersville Library
Association, 100; builds house,
Connersville, 100-1; agent for
William's land claim, 109; buys
lands at Horseshoe Prairie, 131-
32; mills and carding machine,
Hamilton Co., 132, 160; county
board meetings held at house of,
136; Indianapolis store, 142-43,
148, 233; war record attacked,
144-45; representative, Hamilton
Co. district (1825), 144-45, 150-53;
doubts growth of Indianapolis,
149; opposed to slavery, 153; interpreter at Washington with Le
Gris and Tipton, 154-56; death,
156-57; portrait, 157; Masonic interests, 158, 240; will, provisions
of, 159; personality and appearance, 44-45, 113, 157, 159, 239.
Conner, John, son of John Conner
and Delaware wife, 87, 124, 125,
218.
Conner, John, Delaware interpreter
in Texas, 125.
Conner, John Fayette, son of William and Elizabeth Conner, 160,
177.
Conner, Lavina (Winship), 133;
marriage, 50, 87.
Conner, Lavina, infant daughter of
John and Lavina Conner, 133.
Conner, Lavina, daughter of William

and Elizabeth Conner, 133, 160,
176, 177.
Conner, Margaret (Boyer), 8; birth
and captivity, 10-11, 185, 186;
name, 184-85; marriage, 11-12,
13; first-born pledged to Shawnee,
12, 14; at Connerstown (Ohio), 12-
13; interested in Moravian mission,
14; at Snakestown (Ohio), 14;
freed by treaty of Camp Charlotte,
14-15; at Pittsburgh, 15; joins
Schoenbrunn community, 15, 16-
17; friendship with Mrs. Jungman, 18; flees to Lichtenau, 19-
20; joins Moravian church, 21;
captured with missionaries, 24-26;
journey to Captives' Town, 26-27,
191; removal from Upper Sandusky Old Town to Lower Sandusky, 30-31; at Lower Sandusky,
32; removal to Detroit, 33-34; at
New Gnadenhütten, 34-35; last
years, 35-36, 193; Schoenbrunn
cabin restored, 187.
Conner, Margaret Crans, daughter
of William and Elizabeth Conner,
177.
Conner, Nancy, daughter of William Conner and Mekinges, 109,
124, 125.
Conner, Richard, of Maryland, 9.
Conner, Richard, 8; birth, 9, 184;
removes to Ohio country, 9-10;
marriage, 11-12, 13; first-born
pledged to Shawnee, 12, 14; at
Connerstown (Ohio), 12-13; visited by Rev. David Jones, 12-13;
and by David Zeisberger, 13-14;
at Snakestown, with Shawnee, 14,
186; at Pittsburgh, 15; redeems
son from Shawnee, 16, 17-18;
joins Schoenbrunn community, 15,
16-17; joins Moravian church, 19;
flees to Lichtenau, 19-20; carries
information to Brodhead, 23; captured with missionaries, 24-26;
journey to Captives' Town, 26-27,
191; pro-American sympathies,

William Conner
A Brief Afterword

William Conner was not Daniel Boone, though he was among the very first settlers in a new land. He was not George Washington, though he was looked upon as a leader. He was not even a William Henry Harrison, even though he helped carve the state of Indiana out of the forests. There was a William Conner in every state, every area, and very probably, in nearly every county in the Midwest. Although some aspects of his life were relatively unique, such as his immersion in the "Red and White worlds," they were not in themselves extraordinary. It should be noted that were it not for the efforts of Charles N. Thompson with this book, and Eli Lilly's role as preserver of the Conner home and story, William Conner would have been little more than a footnote in a local history.

This is not to say that Conner's life was unimportant, that it is without interest beyond the relatively narrow confines of central Indiana's history; it is more a comment on the vagaries of the study of history itself. William Conner left precious few documents from his own hand to explain himself. We have only a few letters, some deeds, and some business records to flesh out the story of one man in his time.

However, the true importance of William Conner's life goes beyond the mere recitation of the facts of his biography. It lies with our ability to see much of the ebb and flow of the first one hundred years of American history through his life and those of his forebears and descendents. By tracing the lives of William Conner, his parents, and his siblings in this book, and learning more of his Delaware Indian family, one can see much of the United States' early history unfold. In the lives of these people, the reader may view the larger stories of Native-American/White interaction, the creation of middle America and insistent movement westward onto new frontiers—no matter who had to be pushed out, or how. Thus, the most important part of the Conner story may not be what it tells us of them, but what it shows us of the bigger American story. This is particularly true of William Conner.

Conner's life, in many ways, was a balancing act, a tripping dance with equilibrium. The most obvious manifestation of this was his place between the Native American and Euro-American worlds. As it was with his parents, so was it with William and his family. Like his father, Richard Conner, William occupied an often wobbly perch between "White and Red" societies. He spoke the words of both, lived and dressed as both did. This legacy was passed on to his first, Delaware (Lenape) Indian, family.

His Delaware wife, Mekinges, and their children were carried along on America's westering tide as both "victims" and facilitators of that movement. His family was forced from its home by a treaty their father helped negotiate. Some family members survived two more removals and ended their lives in what is now Oklahoma.

Unlike most other Americans, their move westward was not voluntary. They, like other Native Americans, suffered mightily at the hands of an American society that saw them as little more than uncivilized peoples to be ignored, isolated, and forgotten. At least two of his sons, Captain John Conner and James Conner were noted scouts and guides who helped lead explorations that opened the west to American settlement. Both also became principal chiefs of the Delaware and played significant roles in the history of the Delaware nation. But both were also leaders who acquiesced in the Delawares' loss of tribal identity when they agreed to making that tribe part of the Cherokee nation. It was to take the Delaware more than a century to force the government to again recognize them as a separate tribe.

One of the most disturbing aspects of William Conner's life to the modern reader and museum visitor—and one that needs further amplification fifty years after the original publication of *Sons of the Wilderness*—is his "abandonment" of his first family. It would perhaps be less shocking had Conner not been such an active participant in the process leading to their removal. William Conner's role as interpreter and liaison during the Treaty of St. Mary's process was a continuation of his "government service" over the decade. At the back of his mind, he must have known that his participation would lead to a drastic, almost organic altering, of his life and that of his family. His world was changing too.

Conner worked in the background as something of a "fixer," helping the government assess what would be needed to get the Delaware to accept the treaty. Even before open negotiations began, he and the government sought "to prepare the minds of the Delaware for removal." As early as 1816, the government promised him the appointment as the Delawares' Indian Agent after their removal west of the Mississippi. This indicates that Conner initially intended to go west with his family. At some point between then and 1820 he changed his mind. In that change lies the tale of an important and controversial part of his life.

Conner was faced with three main choices after the treaty was signed: He could go with his family, as his partner William Marshall did, keep his family in Indiana (likely facing the scorn of newcomers as the man with the "half-breed" family), or stay in Indiana to start a new life while his family was pushed west to a perilous future. We know the choice he made. To modern eyes, it is the most disturbing part of the William Conner story.

That choice launched Conner into a new phase of his life. From 1820 on he can be viewed as the embodiment of yet another quintessential American character, the entrepreneur. With the removal of his Delaware family, William Conner stepped off the narrow path between two worlds and plunged fully into "new world" coming toward him on a wave of settlement. He became a facilitator of central Indiana's development, an entrepreneur involved in town-founding, railroad development, and various business interests. For the most part, he was successful, weathering the many economic upheavals of his time to live a comfortable life. In short, he became the flesh and bone personification of yet another cherished American "hero," the self-made man.

If the lives of his Delaware family can be said to mirror the tumultuous history of Native Americans, then those of his second family became a reflection of the larger American culture. The children of William Conner and his second wife, Elizabeth Chapman Conner, became farmers, businessmen, lawyers, and politicians. Some stayed near the land where they were born, while others ventured back East to New York or followed America west to new opportunities.

So, as you read this story of the Conner brothers, you were also glimpsing the story of early America. The Conner family led very American lives.

Timothy Crumrin
Historian, Conner Prairie
January 2000

Exterior and interior views of the William Conner house as it looks in the
year 2000.